The Travelers' Guide to

LATIN AMERICAN

CUSTOMS and MANNERS

Also by the Authors

European Customs and Manners

The Travelers' Guide to African Customs and Manners

The Travelers' Guide to Asian Customs and Manners

The Travelers' Guide to Middle Eastern and North African Customs and Manners

The Travelers' Guide to

LATIN AMERICAN

CUSTOMS and MANNERS

ELIZABETH DEVINE
and
NANCY L. BRAGANTI

ST. MARTIN'S GRIFFIN ❧ NEW YORK

Maps by Vantage Art Inc.
Illustrations by Raquel Jaramillo

www.stmartins.com

ISBN 0-312-26401-1

First Revised Edition: November 2000

10 9 8 7 6 5 4 3 2 1

To the memory of Jerry
and to Cheryl and to Frank,
with love and gratitude for the great times and the many laughs
E.D.

To my husband, Fausto, and my daughter, Tanya,
with love and appreciation,
and with love to Tova and Sam,
the next generation of travelers
N.L.B.

ACKNOWLEDGMENTS

✳ We wish to thank the following people for their help in this book, and we wish to thank those who assisted but who preferred to remain anonymous. Erica Adams, Marta Alemán, Antonio Ayala, Marcel Baković, David Ball, José J. Banús, Alice Barron, Sally Barron, Matthew Berman, Claudia Bishop, Beverly Brenner, John Burns, Denia Butler, Noela Cabrera, Ellen Caldwell, Susy Cárdenas, Roberto Carvalho, Daniel Costello, Juan Crespo, Evelyne DeLori, Jodi Deluty, Brita Dempsey, Olga Dentler, Rodrigo Dias, Claudia Diegos, Richard Diegos, Annette Dumbach, Silvia Faiguenbaum, Kate Fallon, Bernardo Fernandes, Joan Fontanilla, Alegría Freedman, Joan Freeman, Betsy Gannon, Jennifer George, Alicia Gray, Skye and Ricardo Glade, Antonio Gómez, Peter Greiff, Maria Guccione, Roger Haddad, Ellie Harrison, Claudio Heckmann, Rose Hendrick, Sandra Herrera, Sara Hoffmann, Bonnie Howard, Donald Howard, Teresa Huyck, Vera Iskandarian, Misko Ivčevič, Clarine Johnson, Susana A. Johnston, Elsa Khwaja, Sylvia Kywi, Hedy Laskie, Mario León, Sarah Lincoln-Harrison, Emma LoGuzzo, Carmen López-Blumenkron, Terry McCoy, Richard Mackler, Tina Mahler, Francesco Marchetti, Patricia Márquez, Ernesto Martelo, Carlos Mendoza, Richard Miller, Martha Montero, Denise Moretto, Maria G. Nanni, Donna Neff, Karen Nurick, Dr. Raquel Ojeda, Wendy Osterling, Monica Otálora, Julio Raúl Pabón, Margaret Pereira, Maria Pérez-Bisbal, Carroll Perry, Cary Perry, María Beatriz Plaza, Massimo Porciano, Lanie Pryor, Mark Quail, Irene Quinn, Alex and Beatriz Quiroga, Caitlin Randall, Jonathan Randolph, Diana Reynolds, Vladimir Reznikov, José Ricardo-Gil, Alan Robinson, Barbara and Roman Romero, Terry Ruthrauff, James Samiljan, Dr. Guillermo Sánchez, Lionilda Santos, Elizabeth Schuster, Sylvia Seidenman, Anne Skalicky, Jan Smith, D. V. Springgate, Leah Steimel, Pasquale Tató, Jennifer Valko, Maria Van Dusen, Lucía Velásquez, Dr. Juan Carlos Vera, Felicidade Vieira, Alejandro Mora Viera, Lesley Vossen, Ulrike Welsch, Adam Wynne, Nora Fonseca Zabriskie.

CONTENTS

The Travelers' Guide to

LATIN AMERICAN

CUSTOMS and MANNERS

INTRODUCTION

From the sublime writing of Nobel laureates Gabriel García Márquez and Octavio Paz to the athletic feats of soccer star Pele to the sultry tango, Latin America has given the world many riches. However, many people who wish to explore the glorious cultures of Latin America worry that they will inadvertently embarrass themselves or—probably worse—embarrass others.

When traveling to another culture, we often feel like round pegs trying to jam ourselves into square holes (or vice versa). If we leave the protective umbrella of the escorted tour, we worry that we won't know how to deal with people and won't correctly interpret their behavior.

For the increasing number of people traveling to Latin America, we offer a guide to help you feel confident that you're doing the right thing, whether as a businessperson or as a visitor.

For easy reference, we have divided each chapter into a series of topics:

Greetings: To make a good impression, it's often important to know how you will be greeted and to react properly. In many parts of Latin America, greetings are rather effusive. People sometimes shake hands and sometimes kiss or embrace. In some places single women will be kissed three times on the cheek—twice in greeting and once as a wish for marriage.

Remember that most people use the family names of both parents in their surname, the father's first. José Díaz Rodríguez, for example, can be referred to or addressed formally as "Señor Díaz Rodríguez" or, more commonly, simply as "Señor Díaz."

Don (when addressing a man) and *doña* (when addressing a woman) are untranslatable titles of respect, once confined to nobility but now commonly used. Use them with the first name, although the last name may be added. *Don* is used to address any man, but *doña* is used only for an unmarried woman. The titles are used to show both closeness and respect to people of higher rank for whom *señor* or *señora* would be too formal.

Conversation: A few things to keep in mind. People from English-speaking countries often believe in being open, frank, and direct. Latin Americans take pride in being tactful and diplomatic. In both speech and writing they may be indirect, elaborate, and complimentary. Follow suit to avoid giving offense.

Try to learn before you go. A visit to any country is richer when you know something about it in advance, but to make a good impression in business or to strike up an acquaintance, it's essential to know something about the other person's world. Learn about soccer, a sport that is an obsession in most of Latin America. (In some sections of the U.S., your best sources will be kids in grammar school and high school who have taken up soccer enthusiastically.) It would be helpful to learn something about bullfighting, especially if you're visiting Mexico, Peru, Venezuela, or Colombia, where it is regarded as an art.

Remember that few people can resist the flattery of being asked for their opinion about sights to see, things to do, and places to eat. (We have one friend who, at the drop of a question, prepares a five-page mini-guide to her area.)

While people will usually enjoy discussing their country, resist the temptation to offer comparisons to your own country's wealth, employment rate, housing, traffic, roads, and so forth.

Also note that, while people of course have a national identity, there is also a strong identification with Latin America, rather than with Spain. And note that Latin Americans think of themselves as Americans (*americanos*)—inhabitants of the Americas—and might resent people from the U.S. using that term solely for themselves.

Finally, don't be insulted if someone refers to you as a *gringo*. The word doesn't necessarily have negative connotations. For instance, in Peru it refers to a blond, fair-skinned person.

Telephones: Expect to find a wide range in the efficiency of telephone service.

We've tried to take some of the mystery out of dealing with public telephones in the places where they can be found and to suggest alternatives where they can't.

Telephone directories list people *first* by their (paternal) last name. Many people may have the same last name, so it's important to know the *second* (maternal) last name—e.g., Ricardo Diego Hernandez—Diego is the father's family name and Hernandez is the mother's family name. Since there will no doubt be many people named Diego in the telephone directory, it's important to know the Hernandez part of the name.

If you're planning to make long-distance or overseas calls and would like to make them from your hotel (rather than from the telephone company office), be sure first to inquire whether the hotel imposes a surcharge and, if so, how much.

In some cases, it's much cheaper to call into the country from abroad than to call out of the country, and you might want to arrange to have business associates or family and friends phone you at prearranged times.

In Public: Some public manners and gestures don't travel. You may offend when you least intend to. For example, in conversation Latin Americans naturally tend to stand very close. Don't back away, or you might be considered snobbish and aloof. In some countries, you'll see men walking down the street arm in arm. The gesture has no sexual meaning.

Be careful about talking with your hands. Gestures mean different things in different countries. An illustration: the cheerful "okay" sign with thumb and index finger of the right hand in a circle is obscene in most Latin American countries.

Once again, in the desire not to offend, in some countries in Latin America, people will often tell you what they think you want to hear rather than the truth. If you ask someone, "Is the post office down that street?" he or she is likely to say "Yes," whether it is or not. Similarly, if you invite people to dinner, they may accept, whether or not they have any intention of coming. After enough time in Latin America, you'll develop a sixth sense about whether people mean what they say.

When you're taking an elevator in a hotel or public building, look for the following symbols:

0 = basement
B or PB (*planta baja or piso bajo* = ground floor
1 = second floor
2 = third floor, etc.

Remember that life in Latin America centers on the family and extended family. You'll find children at social occasions everywhere. One of the great occasions in a family's life is a girl's fifteenth birthday. You may be lucky enough to be invited to a mass and great ball held in honor of the young woman, marking her entrance into the adult world.

Women especially should be sensitive to the local standards of behavior. If you are in one place—even a large city—for a long time, you will come under scrutiny. This holds true particularly in more conservative or traditional areas. If you engage in behavior that could be construed as disreputable—e.g., going out alone or associating with married men—you'll be the subject of gossip and your company avoided. If you're staying with a family, your behavior will reflect on them.

One way for a woman to avoid having a purse with a long strap snatched is to wear the purse with the strap around the neck and the purse in front (much as one would wear a medallion).

A few words about the less fortunate: In most of Latin America, there are no extensive welfare programs such as those found in the U.S. and Europe, so even local people usually give to beggars. And at the many markets, if you buy from women vendors, you can be sure that the money will be used for their children. If you wish, buy a meal for a child or for children.

Dress: One of the easiest ways to offend is to dress inappropriately. North Americans are pretty much used to wearing whatever they want, but dress that is too casual, or in the case of women too revealing, is very offensive in some areas of Latin America. When selecting your traveling wardrobe, remember that you rarely err by being on the conservative side.

Before packing, be sure to check on the altitude of the areas you'll be visiting. You'll need warm clothing for the many places at high altitudes.

If your shoe size is a large one, be sure to bring an extra pair, as it will be difficult for you to find shoes in your size.

Meals: First, we'll tell you at what times people eat and what foods are usually served. For quick reference, in most Latin American countries, breakfast is *el desayuno* (el deh-sah-**yoo**-noh), lunch is *el almuerzo* (el ahl-**mwehr**-soh), and dinner is *la cena* (lah-**seh**-nah) or *la comida* (lah koh-**mee**-dah). This is an area of some regional variation. For instance, in Mexico breakfast is *el desayuno* or *el almuerzo*, lunch is *la comida*, and supper is *la cena*. In many places you'll find that the main meal is at noon, followed by a siesta. At high altitudes, it's a good idea to have your heaviest meal at noon, because it will be easier on your digestive system. Also, avoid alcoholic beverages at high altitudes.

Next we take up the meal itself—where you'll probably sit, how the meal will be served, and how long you should stay after dinner at a person's home. And we also identify in this section table manners generally observed by people of each country. We should note here, though, that there is a great deal of variety in this area. Depending on the context of the meal or of the people involved, you can see everything from formal table manners in a pure, upper-class European fashion, to eating without silverware, with the ubiquitous *tortilla* taking its place (it's the spoon you can eat!). In general, though, in more formal settings, Latin Americans eat in the continental style, with the knife in the right hand and the fork in the left, using the knife to push food onto the fork. Also, the custom of keeping the left hand on the lap is not observed; keep both hands above the table.

Then we cover one of the major reasons many people travel—the wonderful variety of the world's cuisines. Latin America is especially rich in diverse cuisines, both from the many ethnic groups that have immigrated to Latin America, and from the ancient cultures native to the American continent. We also cover the different kinds of eating establishments available and the kinds of fare you'll likely find there. A word of caution: street bars in Latin America can tend to be rather sleazy. The local women usually do not go to these bars. The traveler, man or woman, would probably do well not to do so either.

We can't emphasize too strongly the importance of being *very* cautious in matters of food and drink. If you have even the slightest doubt about an item, don't eat or drink it. In most places, you must avoid raw vegetables, unpeeled fruit, and raw shellfish. Drink only bottled water, and don't drink fruit juices made with tap water. Don't use ice cubes made from tap water. Always ask for drinks *sin hielo* (seen yeh-loh), "without ice."

Hotels: While we don't recommend specific hotels, we try to describe different types of hotels available. Some countries offer interesting and agreeable alternatives to luxury hotels.

A caution about using water in bathrooms, both in hotels and in private homes: *C* stands for *caliente*, meaning hot, *not* cold. (In Brazil, *Q* stands for hot.) Pay close attention to the instructions for operating showers both in homes and in hotels. Turning on the water and electric heating unit in the wrong order can lead to disaster. Sometimes, you may not find soap in your room. If you call the bellboy, he will bring some, but you'll be charged for it. It's best to have a bar or two in your luggage.

Many travelers like to use one hotel as their base and fan out for one- or two-day trips. Most hotels, even small ones, have a luggage storage area that you can use if you've been a guest. Don't leave your luggage unless you're sure that the area is locked, and be sure to label the luggage carefully.

Tipping: Who *isn't* mystified by tipping? We've given advice on the amount to give people you're accustomed to tipping (porters, taxi drivers, etc.) and others you may not be accustomed to tipping, such as gas station attendants and ushers. Keep a supply of dollars for tipping. People every-where appreciate being tipped in dollars. In many countries the rate of inflation is so high that it renders precise amounts obsolete in a matter of days. So we often provide amounts in U.S. equivalents.

Private Homes: Especially once you begin to establish a friendship with people, they are likely to invite you to their homes. Nothing gives a better insight into a culture than such a visit. On the other hand, it can turn into an awkward situation if you are not—in general—aware of what is expected of you or of what you might expect from your hosts. In order, the items in a street address are: street name, street number, floor number, and apartment door number.

We've given advice on how to behave when staying with a family. Most of us aren't used to having servants to perform such chores as laundry, but many Latin American families, even in the middle class, do. Although it may be difficult for people raised in egalitarian societies, be sure to respect the boundary between servants and employers. Don't become too friendly with the maids and don't ask the maid directly to perform a chore, because you may appear to be undermining the authority of the woman of the house.

Note that some families are more traditional than others; try to fit in with the customs of the family with whom you're staying. For example, traditional families expect everyone to eat together and be on time for meals. Remember, too, that the kitchen is the woman of the house's do-main. Never go in unless you're invited. Men should be especially careful not to offer to help clear the table or to do a task in the kitchen. Less traditional homes are more flexible about such matters.

If you're staying with a family for a few days and buy some food, be sure to share it with the family. Don't put it in the refrigerator and say, "This is mine."

To endear yourself as a guest, observe these rules when using the bath-room: 1) Hang your towels in the patio area rather than in the bathroom. Keep your toilet articles in your room. 2) Be sure to leave the bathroom floor dry after you've taken your shower or bath. 3) Women should never throw sanitary napkins or tampons down the toilet. Wrap them and put them in a wastebasket.

Again, single women especially should keep in mind that your behavior will be fairly closely observed by the community. Your actions will reflect on the family you're staying with. You should be considerate of your hosts, particularly in the more conservative or traditional homes.

In this section, there's also advice about good gifts to bring. Electronic items are often a good choice. For young people, illustrated T-shirts and CDs are popular.

Business: In this section we start off by providing basic data about hours for businesses, government offices, banks, and shops, and the national currency. Then we provide information about business practices. Succeeding in business can be really trying if you don't know a few of the ground rules. Most important, if you're not willing to put the time into establishing a personal relationship before getting down to business, don't even consider doing business in Latin America. You'll have to spend a long time talking about yourself, your family, your background, and so on. Personal friendship and the accompanying feeling of trust is the strongest possible underpinning for business success.

You'll make a good impression if you study the politics, culture, and economy of the country so that you can participate in a conversation on those subjects.

Remember that you don't just get in touch with someone and plan to do business. Contacts are essential. We've tried to suggest some avenues for gaining contacts if you don't have any. If you're a member of an international organization (e.g., Rotary Club International or Lion's Club International) you may find business contacts through them. When you arrive at your destination, arrange to attend a meeting. (One businessman, whose flight home from Caracas was canceled and who faced being stranded for days, was given a seat on the next plane, thanks to the influence of a man he had met at a Rotary Club meeting and who happened to be at the airport also.)

In searching for contacts through an embassy, you needn't confine yourself to your own. Seek out the commercial division of the British, Canadian, U.S., and French embassies. Try to arrange an invitation to one of their cocktail parties. Such parties are an excellent way to obtain information from government officials—information for which, otherwise, you'll spend hours waiting in offices to see people.

If you receive a letter in Spanish, be sure to answer in Spanish.

Try to develop as large a network of contacts as possible. There are many subtle political changes occurring with great frequency in Latin American countries, and contacts can often help you understand what is going on.

Be sure that you always deal with the very top people in a company, since they are the ones who make the decisions.

Even if you have established a personal relationship with people at a company, always have a lawyer and an accountant in the country where you'll be doing business. Major law firms in your country will probably be able to recommend a lawyer. Send copies of any agreements to her or him. In Latin America, a major difference in this area is the existence of the *notario*. Although the name translates as "notary," the *notario*'s is a full-fledged profession which requires four years of college work, and which ranks barely below that of lawyer. In fact, a *notario* is authorized to handle many matters that in the U.S. could only be handled by a lawyer.

Keep in mind that top-level officers usually speak English, so you won't need an interpreter when dealing with them. In fact, the management of a Latin American company might well be reluctant to do business in the presence of an outside party. The company will usually have a bilingual lawyer or *notario* available to do any necessary interpreting.

A few other cultural differences that are pertinent to business affairs: (1) The metric system reigns in Latin America, and should be used in any size and weight specifications. (2) Latin Americans write dates in the European style—first the day, then the month, and then the year, so 2/4/99 is April 2, 1999. (We had a person refuse to honor a travelers' check which was dated U.S. style.) (3) In some countries, when people write out amounts of money, periods distinguish thousands and commas denote fractions. Example: C$5.000,50 is 5,000 Chilean *pesos* and 50 cents. (4) The hours of the day are often written out on the basis of the full 24 hours of the day, not on that of the two 12-hour periods. In this system—familiar to many of us as "military time"—for example, 2:00 A.M. is 0200, and 2:00 P.M. is 1400. You'll find this usage especially prevalent in the case of train and plane schedules. (4) The number 7 is written with a line through it: 7, and the number 1 is written with a lead line: /.

There are some abbreviations to know: S.A. = incorporated, Cía. = company, A.C. = a nonprofit organization, EE.UU. = United States, ENTEL = National Telecommunications Enterprise, F.F.C.C. = railroads.

You'll need only an adapter to use your laptop, since most laptops operate on 110 and 220 volts.

Remember that a Latin American's sense of priorities may be different. If someone has an appointment with you, and a friend drops in, he or she will never say to the friend, "I'm sorry. I can't see you now. I have an appointment." Friends always come first, even if they stay three hours.

Small tips for business meetings: (1) In most countries, people are less than compulsive about getting to a meeting precisely on time. (2) Always exchange business cards immediately when you meet someone, and keep the cards.

When phoning people in Latin America from abroad, always call person-to-person. You'll waste less time, especially if secretaries don't speak your language. You should note that many businesses in Latin America, especially those involved in international commerce, make regular use of E-mail and fax.

Etiquette for business gifts is a little different in Latin America: (1) Don't bring business gifts until a friendly relationship has been established. (2) If you're planning several trips to the country, it's appropriate to ask colleagues what sort of gift they would like from abroad. (3) Don't give gifts in a business environment—wait until the setting is social.

For women traveling on business, see also the advice, "Some Special Words for Women," later.

Holidays and Special Occasions: If you're on a pleasure trip, you may want to plan it around a holiday, but if you're on a business trip, you may want to avoid holidays. Be sure to have an adequate supply of local currency before a holiday begins, because you probably won't be able to find many places to change travelers' checks.

Be sensitive to the many religious festivals in Latin American countries. Don't drive through parades or photograph festivals without permission of the participants.

One special religious festival you'll notice is celebrated widely in Latin America is the Feast of the Epiphany, on January 6. This is called *el Día de los Reyes Magos* (the Feast of the Magi) and commemorates the visit of the Magi bearing gifts for the infant Jesus. In many places, children receive gifts on this day rather than on Christmas.

Transportation: We've covered both public transportation and driving. In the same country, you may find modern subways and first class, four-lane roads, together with the most primitive transportation. In cities, the best advice is to take taxis. Though the ones around hotels are generally the most expensive, they're also usually the most reliable. And, in many cases, the drivers know some English. When dealing with train and bus schedules, remember that these are usually posted in military time.

In some places, it's possible, and convenient, to rent a car. (Remember that gas is sold by the liter in most countries of Latin America.) But, unless you have experience driving through herds of cattle, it's often best to stay off the rural roads of Latin America. (Cars hitting cows are a major type of auto accident in Mexico.) In many cases, you'll find flying to be the best way to get from one city to another.

If you decide to rent a car and plan to use a credit card, check before you leave your country to learn the limit of the liability the card will pay for automobile damage. You may end up wanting to add additional liability insurance when you rent the car.

Legal Matters, Safety, and Health: "Legal" raises the issue of bribery, a matter that will touch both the businessperson and the tourist. It is common knowledge that bribery is part of the way of life in much of Latin America. But, what would be considered bribery by others, in Latin America is often thought of as little more than a tip. As we tip the maître d' to get a better table or to be seated sooner, people in some Latin American countries employ the *mordida* to expedite matters. Unless you are using money to persuade a policeman to ignore a traffic offense, you're not trying to get a person to do something illegal; you just want to speed up a legal process. In business, you might want to get a proposal or permit from the bottom of the pile to the top, and the $25 to $50 you pay a bureaucrat may be well worth it.

Bring with you some passport-size photos in case you lose your passport or decide to visit another Latin American country and need a visa. It's also a good idea to make a photocopy of your passport, and keep it—with some extra money—in a location separate from your actual passport and your money supply.

Be aware that, while many drugs available only by prescription in North America are available over-the-counter in many Latin American countries, the name and the dosage may be different.

If you are considering taking fruits and vegetables into a Latin American country, check with its consulate beforehand. Most countries have restrictions on bringing in produce.

To make sure you're not venturing into an unsafe environment, if you're planning a trip from the U.S., call the Citizens' Emergency Center Division of the State Department to find out about any particular trouble spot in Latin America. The phone number is (202) 647–5225, and they're available from 8:15 A.M. to 5:00 P.M. Monday through Friday; and from 9:00 A.M. to 3:00 P.M. on Saturday, Eastern Standard Time. In Great Britain, call the Consular Advice to the Public, a division of the Foreign Office at (01) 270–4129. Canadians should phone the Consular Operations Division of the Department of External Affairs at (613) 992–3705.

You should always, of course, be alert to possible threats to your safety. Wherever you are, ask friends, business colleagues, or hotel porters to advise you which areas of the city should be avoided.

To have a healthy trip, in the U.S., call the Centers for Disease Control in Atlanta, Georgia—(404) 639–3311—to learn about required immunizations and about any special health problems.

Canadians should write or call for the brochure "Travel and Health," which gives information about health precautions when traveling outside Canada. Address: Health and Welfare Canada, 5th Floor, Brooke Claxton Building, Tunney's Pasture, Ottawa K1A OK9. Phone: (613) 957–2991.

British travelers should ask their travel agents about health conditions, since the agents are updated frequently by the Department of Health and Social Security.

British travelers should call the Hospital for Tropical Diseases Clinic, Mortimer Market Centre, Capper Street, London, WC1. It's open Monday through Friday, 9:00 A.M. to 5:00 P.M. The phone number is (0171) 530-3454. Request a copy of *Health Advice for Travelers*. You can also obtain this booklet at many chemists and in the surgeries of some GPs.

Australians should contact the Travellers' Medical and Vaccination Centre, 7/428 George Street, Sydney. The phone number is (029) 221-7133.

Keep in mind that you may have to pay an airport tax when leaving a country, and you must pay it in local currency, not in travelers' checks.

Be sure to bring a more than adequate supply of any prescription drugs you may be taking. Since drugs have different names, and dosages may be different, ask your physician to provide you the generic names of all prescription drugs you are taking, plus prescriptions for them. Pack your medication in your carry-on bag.

If you wear glasses, bring an extra pair as well as a copy of your prescription.

In addition to any medications you may be taking, bring an antidiarrhea medication and a broad-spectrum antibiotic.

Also consider bringing: aspirin or your favorite headache/fever remedy, an antacid, a laxative, a motion-sickness remedy, insect repellant, lotion for insect bites, sunscreen, a cream to relieve sunburn, an antibiotic ointment, Band-Aids, cough medicine, a remedy for muscle pains, salt pills to combat heat exhaustion, ear plugs, an eye mask, condoms, and a thermometer. Women may wish to include remedies for menstrual cramps and vaginal yeast infections. Women should also note that supplies of tampons are available in major cities. Bring a supply of sanitizer gel for times when no soap and water are available for washing. You rub it on your hands, and you don't need to rinse it off. There are many brands.

Key Words and Phrases: At the end of the book, we've added lists of useful words and phrases in Spanish and Portuguese. Learning the basic courtesies, numbers, and words for common items or places will be a real help.

Some General Advice

Learn before you go. To appreciate the wondrous and mysterious cultures of the Aztec, the Inca, and the Maya, read about the pre-Columbian cultures. Here are some suggestions: Michael D. Coe, *The Maya: Ancient People and Places* (1999, $18.95) and *Mexico* (1994, $16.95)—both published in New York by Thames and Hudson; John Hemming, *The Conquest of the Incas* (Orlando, Florida: Harcourt, 1973, $22.00); William H. Prescott, *The Conquest of Mexico and Peru* (New York: Irvington, $22.95).

Don't judge. Being different is neither better nor worse. Resist the impulse to compare to the way things are done in your country. Your country may be more efficient, but to Latin Americans efficiency is not a god. It is more important to enjoy life than to worry about whether papers have been processed or tickets issued quickly.

Some Special Words for Women

If you're traveling alone—whether for business or pleasure—you might consider wearing a wedding ring. And if someone asks you where your husband is, say that he'll be joining you soon.

In general, as long as you're in the business section of a city, you won't encounter much more harassment from men than you'd encounter in any busy city in the U.S. or Europe. But, especially if you stray from this territory, you might find the sexual signals to be rather overt and annoying.

A good refuge from unwanted advances can be other women, and children. On a bus or train, sit next to an older woman, who will likely be protective of you. Be friendly to women in small villages. They may be helpful if you have trouble. When one woman traveler's bus was canceled in a small village, a woman she had met at the bus stop took her home and put her up. If you're staying with a family, you might invite a child with you on sightseeing excursions.

Also, dress on the conservative side. And, don't forget that it is not customary for a woman to enter street bars. If you want a drink, the best choice is sitting at a table in a hotel bar.

The road for a foreign businesswoman in Latin America will not be an easy one. You must be *extremely* professional, but should never come across as "superwoman." Avoid saying "I," but say instead, "We at our company." Be firm in refusing any personal approach; don't give ambiguous signals merely because a businessman made the approach. Be careful about giving gifts to colleagues and customers, as they may be interpreted as an overture. Stay at a hotel from one of the American chains or at one of the top-of-the-line local hotels. To ensure a good table in a restaurant, if you're dining alone, make a reservation for two. It might be convenient to hire a car and driver for the duration of your stay rather than relying on taxis.

Remember that businesspeople will form an opinion of you in the first ten minutes, judging you on the way that you present yourself.

If a Latin American businessman invites you for a drink, dancing, or a meal in a restaurant and you wish to accept, ask him whether his wife or other members of the firm will come along. This will let him know that you do not consider his invitation to be an approach.

And, finally, there's the issue of time—and the different ways Latin Americans perceive it. Nowhere does the visitor feel more like Mark

Twain's round peg trying to stuff itself into a square hole (or the other way around) than in coping with the Latin view of time.

When we were being interviewed on a radio call-in show about our book on European customs and manners, a woman called to say that even though Brazil wasn't in Europe, she had to ask us a question. "I went to visit cousins in Rio," she said. "I was staying at a hotel, but I was spending a good deal of time with them. We would make arrangements for them to pick me up at noon for lunch. I would be in the hotel lobby at noon, and they might arrive at one-thirty—with no apology. The second time this happened, I said perhaps we should adjust our time of meeting. They said there was no need to, that they would come at noon. And they came at two o'clock. What should I have done to make them be on time?"

We gave the only possible answer: Nothing. Frustrating and aggravating though it may feel, a visitor is not going to single-handedly change basic cultural traits (nor should he or she automatically presume that his or her way is better). Remember, you're the visitor.

ARGENTINA

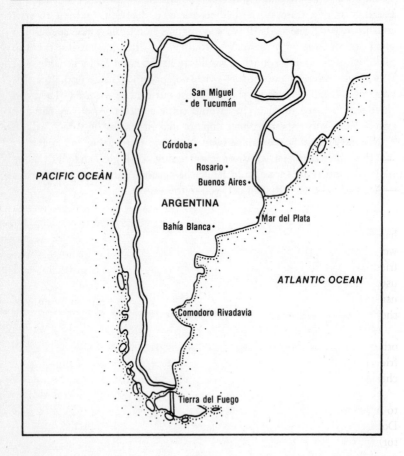

Interested in a country in which Paris and Texas live side by side? Head for Argentina, where Buenos Aires has earned the title "Paris of the Americas." In fact, you'll find that fashion, architecture, cultural life, and manners in Buenos Aires are very close to those in Europe. Argentina's enormous immigrant population, largely from Italy and Spain, explains the Old World flavor.

Some visitors, however, have likened Argentina to Texas—citing the long stretches of grassy pampas, the large ranches (an average of 25,000 acres), and the huge steaks common in Argentina's restaurants.

Visit Argentina, and decide for yourself whether the Old or New World dominates.

GREETINGS

• When introduced, men shake hands with other men. If men and women are introduced by a woman friend, they sometimes kiss, but usually they shake hands. Women usually kiss other women when they're introduced.

• Close male friends hug one another in greeting. Women who are friends kiss one another on one cheek.

• Use titles. They are important to Argentines. Some common titles: Doctor (for Ph.D. and medical doctor); architect; engineer; lawyer; professor. (See "Key Words and Phrases" at the end of the book for Spanish equivalents.) Use the title with the last name.

• At large parties, introduce yourself. At small parties you will be introduced by the host or hostess. At either type of party, shake hands and say good-bye to each person when you leave.

CONVERSATION

• If possible, bone up on soccer. Men love to discuss sports—especially soccer. Women enjoy discussing the latest trends in fashion and plastic surgery.

• Note that people enjoy talking about the theater, current plays, and movies—as well as the latest gossip about Hollywood. In Buenos Aires, people enjoy discussing the tango.

• Ask people to recommend sights and restaurants to visit.

• With businesspeople, feel free to discuss unemployment rates as well as current government decrees and how they are affecting prices.

• When doing business, don't ask at your first meeting if the other person is married or has children.

• Women should expect personal questions, i.e., "Do you have children?" "If not, why not?" People often make critical comments about physical appearance in front of others, e.g., "Are you going to lose weight?" Don't take it too seriously; it's friendly banter, an Argentine trademark.

• Compliment people about their home and children.

• Never discuss politics or government when first meeting someone. (Especially avoid mentioning the Perón years.) People tend to become very aggressive when discussing politics, since passions run high about Argentina's recent past. After you know people a while, they will ask your opinion of Argentine politics. Read up on the country's most recent history before going to Argentina.

• Keep in mind that Argentines pride themselves on their European heritage (Italian, British, Spanish, German). In general, there is a tendency to look down on indigenous people. Don't ask anyone if he or she is of indigenous descent.

• Steer clear of discussions about religion.

TELEPHONES

• Look for public phones on the street, inside cafes, pizzerias, and bars. A few will accept coins of 25 *centavos*, 50 *centavos*, or 1 *peso*. A screen on the telephone runs continuously to show how much money (and therefore time) you have left. During the day, you will get less time for your money than at night.

• Note that some telephones take phone cards, which can be purchased at kiosks, magazine stores, or at the telephone company.

• Remember that in the north of Argentina, the telephone company is Telecom. In the south, it's Telefónica de Argentina. The two companies' phone cards are interchangeable.

• Don't accept telephone cards without a sealed wrapper with an unbroken seal.

• Be aware that in 1998/1999 all phone numbers were changed. The added number depends on the region. Check with telephone operators for the correct number.

• Realize that you can't make collect calls to phone numbers within Argentina.

• For good fax and telephone service in major cities, seek out the *Centros de Llamadas*.

• To make long-distance calls in a small town, go to the telephone office.

• When people answer the phone, expect them to say, "*Hola!*"

• Emergency numbers: Police and general emergencies—107; Fire—100; Ambulance—342-4001 or 342-4004.

IN PUBLIC

• Some gestures to note: (1) Shaking the right hand with the index finger hitting the thumb and middle finger means "a lot, a great deal," or "hurry up"; (2) Brushing the top of the hand from under the chin out means "I don't know" or "I don't care"; (3) Extending the fingers of the right hand and twisting it—thumb up, thumb down, thumb up, thumb down—means something is "so-so." (4) Rotating the forefinger in front of the ear signals that you have a phone call.

• Stifle any urge to yawn in public, because people think it rude.

• If you're smoking, always offer cigarettes to the people in your group. Nonsmoking sections anywhere are very limited, and you will find people smoking almost everywhere.

• When you ask Argentines for directions on the street, they will give you very detailed instructions, even if they have no idea where your destination is. It's a matter of pride for Argentines to act as if they know the correct response.

• Note that people love to be photographed but poor people may ask to be paid.

• Bargain in artisan markets and in the Andean northwest, but, in general, bargaining is not a way of life as it is in other Latin American countries.

• For a public bathroom, feel free to use the ones in restaurants (even if you're not a patron). Even in remote areas, most gas stations usually have decent bathrooms. As a precaution, bring your own tissues.

DRESS

• If you're going to visit Argentina during its winter (June to August), remember that both men and women need warm clothes and topcoats. Central heating is not customary in either public buildings or homes. Homes often have only electric heaters, so you'll need to dress warmly if visiting or staying with a family.

• For business during the summer months (December to March), men should wear lightweight dark suits and women may wear lightweight suits or dresses, and heels.

• Casual wear for men is a sweater, shirt, and pants or just shirt and pants. For women casual wear is a top with very chic pants or a skirt.

• Men who wear earrings should think twice about wearing them in the Argentine provinces. They will be the objects of negative comments and outright hostility.

• Both men and women may wear Bermuda shorts on the street, but not short-shorts. Argentines find it very odd when people wear kneesocks with Bermuda shorts.

• Note that Argentines often wear very skimpy bikini bathing suits, but they never go topless.

• When invited to a meal in a home, men should wear jackets and ties and women a skirt and blouse or dress. To an *asado* (an outdoor barbecue), men and women should wear nice but casual clothes.

• When dining in a formal restaurant, men should wear a jacket with a tie or ascot, and women should wear a dress or skirt.

• Formal wear for men is a tuxedo and for women, mid-calf dresses. Formal wear is for gala functions, such as an opera, a theater or nightclub opening, or a political inauguration.

• Argentines are quite conscious of dress, and are said to evaluate people's attire starting with the shoes.

MEALS

Hours and Foods

Breakfast: Between 7:00 and 9:00 A.M. and on weekends sometimes 10:00 A.M. The food will be a *media-luna* (a sort of croissant) or *pan de leche* (a muffin with cream on top). Beverages: coffee with milk, tea with milk, or *mate* (Argentina's national drink—see "Beverages").

Lunch: Usually served about 1:00 P.M. The meal may begin with *picadas*—appetizers such as sausage, cheese, peanuts, salami, olives—served in the living room with drinks or at the dining table. Next will be soup, *empanadas* or *matambre* (see "Specialties"), or an antipasto of cold meats and cheeses. Then there'll be a main course such as *milanesa de carne* or *milanesa de pollo* with french fries and a salad or a pasta dish such as ravioli or cannelloni. A typical dessert is *flan con dulce de leche*. The meal ends with coffee, espresso style.

From 4:00 to 6:00 P.M. is tea time, *la hora del té* (also called *la hora de la leche*—"the milk hour"—for children). Adults have cakes, cookies, tea or coffee with milk, or *mate*. Children have toast with butter, jelly, or honey, and milk or chocolate milk.

Dinner: Served about 9:00 P.M. (later on weekends). Dinner may be a complete meal similar to lunch, e.g., steak and salad or a dish in the *milanesa* style with fruit, dessert, and coffee.

Beverages: *Mate*, a very popular drink, is a type of tea drunk from a gourd and sipped through a silver straw. It is made from the young leaves of an evergreen tree of the holly family. The dry tea is called *yerba mate*. The drink is usually passed from one person to another. *Mate* is served only in homes, not in restaurants. *Mate* is served in a variety of ways: with sugar, anise seeds, orange peel, or milk. People often drink it instead of coffee; it contains considerable caffeine.

• Common drinks before dinner are vermouth, either plain or with soda, *Gancia* (a type of sweet vermouth), or wine. The most popular after-dinner drink is Scotch.

• In summer, people drink a white wine *sangria* called *clericó*.

• The usual drinks with meals are wine and mineral water.

Table Manners

• If you're invited to dinner in a city, expect drinks in the living room before dinner, but in a rural area guests usually go directly to the meal, and no drinks are served before.

• Should you be the guest of honor, expect to sit at the head of the table.

• Note that some families serve family style, while in others a maid serves each person individually.

• If you wish to cut meat as Argentines do, hold it with your fork, and cut the meat through the prongs of the fork.

• Because the major food is grilled meat, bring along floss (to use in private) if you don't want to keep putting your fingers or toothpicks in your mouth.

• Resist any urge to belch. People from the lowest to the highest classes regard the gesture as extremely rude and crass.

• Don't pour wine by grasping the neck of the bottle with your hand and rotating the hand backwards so that the palm turns upward. Always pour with your right hand, palm facing down, never your left.

• To indicate that you have finished eating, cross your knife and fork (prongs down) on the plate.

• Anticipate spending a long time at a meal. People enjoy spending time over coffee and conversation after a meal.

• After dinner, adjourn with others to the living room for coffee and liqueurs, a custom especially observed in winter.

Eating Out

• Remember that Argentine cuisine is mainly Italian or Spanish. Buenos Aires, however, has a huge immigrant population, so, in addition to Creole and Italian restaurants, you'll find many German and French restaurants and Jewish delicatessens. You'll also find Chinese restaurants, Middle Eastern restaurants, and North American fast-food restaurants. Certain areas of Buenos Aires have Japanese and Indian restaurants.

• *Picadas* specialize in hundreds of appetizers—seafood, beans, beef dishes, cheese dishes, nuts. Alcoholic and nonalcoholic beverages are available.

• In *churrasquerías*, where you have all the meat you can eat for one price, waiters circulate with skewers, and you tell them when you want what they're serving. With Argentines, innards (kidney, brain, intestines, sweetbreads, etc.) are most popular, but they will understand if you are not used to them.

• For bread and pastries to take home, seek a *panaderías*.

• *Rotiserías* are like delicatessens. They offer chicken cooked on a rotisserie, cheese, *empanadas* (turnovers), *tartas* (pies with vegetables such as spinach), and alcoholic beverages. *Rotiserías* don't permit you to eat there. Everything is for take-out.

• *Whiskerías* are informal cocktail lounges that serve all kinds of alcoholic beverages, but sandwiches are the only food.

• To assuage your sweet tooth, try *confiterías*. Other places for sweets are *heladerías* (ice-cream shops).

• There are very few vegetarian restaurants, since Argentines are such great consumers of meat.

• Don't join strangers at their table.

• In Buenos Aires, expect to find steak houses, *confiterías*, and hotel restaurants open all day long. If you want to have an early dinner, go to one of them. Outside Buenos Aires, you won't be able to have dinner until 8:30 or 9:00 P.M., when restaurants open. However, most restaurants stay open until 2:00 A.M.

• Be aware that food such as steak is usually served already salted. If you're on a low-sodium diet, tell the waiter, *"No use sal, por favor"* (Noh ooh-seh sahl, pohr fah-vorr).

• Note that in ordering meat, *cruda* means very rare. To request your meat medium, say *"un poquito cruda."*

• Order only locally made alcoholic beverages, or you'll pay a fortune because of taxes and import fees. Always say *"nacional"* (nah-syoh-**nahl**) following the generic name, e.g., *"whiskey nacional."*

• Note that Argentina produces many wines. As a rule, the inexpensive red wines are better than the inexpensive white wines. You will usually get good value by ordering the house wine (*vino de la casa*).

• Don't summon the waiter by making a "kissing" noise, as you'll hear some people do. It's rude. To call the waiter, say "mozo" (moh-soh).

• Remember that who pays depends on the circumstances. When couples are dining together, each couple usually pays for its own meal. An older person may pay for a group of younger people.

Specialities

• Since Argentina is such a meat-loving country, you'll find many meat specialties: *churrasco* is grilled steak; *bife de lomo* is filet mignon; *asado* is barbecued meat served with french fries—no sauce, just a lot of salt; *parrillada* is a mixed grill of short ribs, tripe, sausages, sweetbreads, and blood sausages; *carbonada* is a stew of beef, corn, squash, and peaches, baked in a pumpkin shell; *milanesa de carne* is thinly sliced beef, covered with bread crumbs and eggs and then deep fried.

• For appetizers you may be offered *matambre* (which means "hunger killer")—an hors d'oeuvre of marinated flank steak stuffed with either spinach, hearts of palm, ham, and/or boiled eggs, then baked; or an *empanada de carne*, a turnover, either oven-baked or fried, filled with ground beef, olives, onions, eggs, and red peppers; *empanada de queso y jamón* (cheese and ham), *de verdura* (spinach); and *de humita* (corn).

• A special sauce used when barbecuing any kind of meat is *chimichurri*, made of finely chopped onions, tomatoes, garlic, and parsley, and oil and vinegar.

• A few fish specialties: *salmón*—sea salmon; *dorado*, a local freshwater fish; *corvina*—white sea bass; *calamares*—squid.

• A popular chicken dish is *milanesa de pollo*, which is the same thing as *milanesa de carne*, but made with chicken cutlets.

• Favorite desserts: *dulce de leche*—milk simmered with sugar, vanilla and, sometimes, chocolate, served on *flan*, pastry, toast, or in cakes; *dulce de membrillo*—a thick quince preserve cut into slices and served with cheese; *dulce de batata*—sweet potato preserve cut into thick slices; *flan*—crème caramel (custard).

• A very popular sweet is *alfajores*. They are a mix between a biscuit and a cake, layered like a sandwich, with *dulce de leche* in the middle. Sold at kiosks and supermarkets, they are very popular as both a snack and a dessert.

HOTELS

• Be aware that some second-class hotels, many of which have English names, have the same service and comfort as first-class hotels. They may not be as modern inside, but they are very comfortable and less expensive than first-class hotels.

• Note that most hotels in large cities are air-conditioned.

• Be aware that orders for room service often take a long time to arrive.

• Think twice before having your hotel do your laundry. Such service is *very* expensive.

TIPPING

• Give hotel porters the equivalent of $1.00 (U.S.) for all your bags.

• Note that only taxi drivers near hotels expect tips. Tip the driver 15 percent of the fare.

• Tip gas station attendants only if they wash your windshield. Give them the equivalent of $1.00 (U.S.).

• Give porters at the airport the equivalent of $1.00 (U.S). per bag.

PRIVATE HOMES

• Don't feel obliged to call in advance before visiting, unless you're coming a long distance. Don't visit at lunch time, and outside of Buenos Aires, don't call or visit during the siesta (1:00 to 3:00 P.M.).

• If you're invited to a home for dinner at 9:00 P.M., arrive at 9:30 or 10:00, unless the host has specified "American time."

• When visiting a family, don't just enter a room and sit down on your own. You may be taking the chair of an important family member. Wait until your hostess asks you to sit down and motions you to a chair.

• Keep in mind that Argentina has a larger middle class than other Latin American countries, so many people don't have live-in maids, although they may have women who come a few times a week to clean and do the laundry. If you're staying with a family, it's best to keep your room neat, make your bed, and do your own laundry.

• Note that most families don't have cooks. Usually the hostess does all the cooking, but she doesn't expect help with it.

• When taking a bath, ask your hostess about heating the water, since it may need to be heated for 30 minutes. Take your shower or run your bath as soon as the water is ready, since the hot water doesn't last very long.

• Insist on paying for all long-distance phone calls you make from a private home.

• If you go out with the family you're visiting, offer to pay for your share of expenses such as restaurant meals and public transportation.

• Remember that families tend to adapt to a guest, rather than hoping the guest will adapt to them. They will be concerned about you and probably won't let you go sightseeing on your own.

Gifts: If you know that a family will be entertaining you, send or bring flowers or imported candy. You may also send flowers after the visit.

• If you know someone likes Scotch, note that the most popular brand is Chivas Regal, with Johnnie Walker second. Other popular liquors are champagne and wine. However, don't bring California wines from the U.S. Argentines don't like them.

• If you are invited to dinner by people you know well, bring pastries, called *masas*, which are sold by the kilo, or a plant.

• Avoid bringing personal items, such as ties and shirts.

• If you know a woman very well, bring her (from abroad) a scarf, or the latest perfume. Bring clothing or toys to children you know. Men enjoy aftershave, Cross or Parker pens.

BUSINESS

Hours

Business: Monday through Friday, 9:00 A.M. to 7:00 P.M. Outside Buenos Aires, businesses are open from 8:00 A.M. to noon and 4:00 to 8:00 P.M. In the summer, afternoon hours are 3:00 to 7:00 P.M.

Government Offices: Some offices are open Monday through Friday, 9:00 A.M. to 1:00 P.M. Others are open Monday through Friday, 1:00 to 5:00 P.M. Call to find out the correct hours for the offices you wish to visit.

Banks: Monday through Friday, 10:00 A.M. to 4:00 P.M.

Shops: Monday through Friday, 9:00 A.M. to 6:00 P.M., and Saturday, 9:00 A.M. to 1:00 P.M.

Currency

• Note that in 1992, the official currency changed from the *austral* to the *peso*. One *peso* equals one hundred *centavos*.

• Coins: 5, 10, 25, and 50 *centavos* and 1 *peso*.

• Notes: 2, 5, 10, 20, 50, and 100 *pesos*.

• Realize that because coins are practically worthless, most people don't give change but round the price of an item up to the next highest *peso*. In a store, the clerk may throw in a piece of candy to make up for the lack of change. This "rounding-up" tactic is not an attempt to cheat foreigners.

• For the best exchange rate, go to a bank. You can also exchange money in hotels and at travel agencies. It's difficult to cash travelers' checks in a small town. If you are able to cash them, there will be a loss on the exchange. The better strategy is to use credit cards.

• Bring your credit cards. Most places in major cities and provincial capitals accept American Express, Diners Club, Visa, and Master-Card.

Business Practices

• Plan to make several trips to accomplish your goal. If your business style is fast paced, you will have to adjust because there is no way to push people to go faster. At every step you'll find red tape and bureaucracy. Businesspeople have to obtain the consent of many others for approval of a project.

• Expect to find a business community that is, in general, gracious, sophisticated, and efficient. The business climate shows the influence of immigration from Italy, Spain, Germany, and Britain.

• Realize that it's indispensable to have contacts (e.g., to help arrange appointments) in the government if you're planning to do business with the government (contacts are less important for a nongovernment business deal). If you don't have a contact, get in touch with your embassy in Argentina.

• Be aware that even though you have an appointment, many people don't keep them; the higher the person is in an organization the more likely he is to neglect an appointment or to keep you waiting a long time.

• Bring business cards and documents you'll be using translated into Spanish.

• If you need to send a fax or want E-mail or Internet service, seek out one of the telephone offices called Telefónica.

• To find a good, reliable interpreter, contact the commercial attaché at your embassy. Hotel translation services may not be adequate.

• Be prepared for the work day to extend until 10:00 P.M. Don't be surprised if someone suggest an 8:00 P.M. business meeting.

• Remember that people don't like to do business on the phone. Argentines prefer personal interactions.

• Be prepared for local businesspeople to arrive five to ten minutes late; foreign businesspeople should be on time.

• Expect executives in most large businesses to speak English. Try to speak a few words of Spanish. It will make a most favorable impression.

• Even if you won't finish your cup, you might accept the offer of coffee, which is always served during business meetings. Coffee is served with sugar on the side, but *not* with milk.

• Remember that meetings always begin gradually with discussions of extraneous topics, and they conclude in the same way. Never grab your briefcase and dash out without making small talk at the end of the meeting. Allow the chief Argentine in the group to decide when the meeting should conclude. Leave only then.

• Realize that Argentines are very efficient businesspeople who use computers and other advanced technology. The only technological problem you'll encounter in doing business is the telephone system.

• Be aware that people are meticulous about details, especially when attorneys are involved in negotiations and contracts. It is difficult for people to sign anything without first dealing with a massive amount of bureaucratic red tape.

• Women should not experience special problems doing business in Argentina, as long as you are professional in manner and dress.

• Be careful not to appear to be threatening or confrontational. Unless you're tactful, you'll be regarded as abrasive and won't accomplish your goals.

Business Entertaining: Keep in mind that business lunches are not popular because people usually return home for lunch.

• Note that Argentines will rarely invite you to their homes, which they regard as places for relatives and extremely close friends. They will entertain you in a restaurant.

• Remember that Argentines don't like to talk business during a meal, whether lunch or dinner. They prefer to socialize. The more cosmopolitan businesspeople will agree to a business lunch, if a foreigner insists on one, but they won't enjoy it.

• If you're being entertained, don't order imported drinks, which are very expensive in comparison to local drinks.

• Whether you are guest or host, expect a dinner in a restaurant to be scheduled for about 10:00 P.M.

• If you're entertaining a business colleague in Buenos Aires, suggest a restaurant in one of the areas popular among businesspeople—Recoleta or Puerto Mavero.

• In an invitation to dinner at a restaurant, include your Argentine colleague's wife.

HOLIDAYS AND SPECIAL OCCASIONS

The following are national holidays when you will find banks, businesses, and most shops closed. Check with the tourist office to learn if there are local festivals or holidays which will mean that offices, banks, and stores will be closed in that area.

Holidays: New Year's Day (Jan. 1); Maundy Thursday (Thursday before Easter—only some offices are closed); Good Friday; Labor Day (May 1); Anniversary of the 1810 Revolution (May 25); Malvinas Day (June 10); Flag Day (June 20); Independence Day (July 9);

Anniversary of the Death of José de San Martín (Aug. 17); Columbus Day (Oct. 12); Christmas (Dec. 25).

• Except in parts of the north, don't expect Carnival to be celebrated in Argentina as extravagantly as it is in Brazil.

• Note that many people traditionally celebrate January 6 (Epiphany). The holiday is really for children; they put their shoes outside the bedroom door so that the Three Kings can fill the shoes with gifts.

• Don't look for bus service on December 25 or 31.

• Don't expect banking services to be available on December 31.

• Realize that banks and public offices close on Holy Thursday and on December 8, the Immaculate Conception.

• Try not to walk in Buenos Aires around Christmas and New Year's. Firecrackers are set off in the streets and thrown from high-rise apartments. The use of the firecrackers is poorly regulated, and they are very dangerous.

TRANSPORTATION

Public Transportation

• To take a bus in Buenos Aires, look for the list of streets on the route at the bus stop. Each bus has its number and its destination marked on the front. Pay when you get on; you don't need exact change. Keep your ticket in case an inspector gets on to check. Local buses are usually uncomfortably crowded.

• Note that *colectivos* are buses found in cities and owned by the driver. Each route has a number and a color. Ask at your hotel for the appropriate *colectivo* for your destination.

• Realize that service from black taxis with yellow roofs is available 24 hours a day.

• For transportation in Buenos Aires, consider the subway, which is excellent. Entrances are marked "*Subte.*" Buy tokens at the entrance. The fare is one token (called a *ficha*) for all destinations. Subways are closed between 1:00 and 4:00 A.M. If you speak or read Spanish, obtain a copy of *Lumi*, a detailed guide to the entire transportation system in

Buenos Aires. Purchase one at a kiosk or at a subway station.

• Expect many long-distance buses to have reclining seats.

• Realize that for the most part trains are not in good condition. However, the train from Buenos Aires to Mar de Plata is luxurious. During the 6-to-7-hour ride, you will have heat or air-conditioning. There will also be heat and air-conditioning on a first-class sleeper, but not in ordinary first class; however, it will have comfortable seats. Avoid second class; you'll find it uncomfortable.

• Be aware that there are four classes on trains—not necessarily on every route. (1) The most expensive and most comfortable for long trips is the *coche cama* (sleeper compartment); (2) the *Pullman* has reclining seats and air-conditioning; (3) the *Primera* (first class) has air-conditioning but smaller reclining seats; (4) the *turista* (second class) has hard bench seats.

• For travel during holidays such as Christmas and Independence Day (July 9), make reservations well in advance, because there is a great demand for train travel during those times.

• Take taxis, which are inexpensive, rather than renting a car. Parking in cities is a problem.

Driving

• Don't drive unless you're a very confident, aggressive driver.

• Realize that it is almost impossible to find a parking place in Buenos Aires. Rather than driving, use taxis, or hire a car and driver—especially for business.

• Remember that if a car has seat belts, they must be worn.

• Check which is the *best* road to take to your destination. If you stop at a gas station and ask, "Is this the road to _____?," people may say "Yes," when indeed there may be a better, shorter way.

• Be alert for mountain roads with hairpin curves. Be sure to blow your horn as you're turning at the curves.

LEGAL MATTERS, SAFETY, AND HEALTH

• If your passport, credit cards, and money are stolen, go to your hotel. They will pay your taxi fare and will help you make calls canceling your credit cards.

• The police don't list details of your missing property. Go to them simply to obtain a receipt for your insurance company. Regard your property as permanently lost.

• If you have been robbed or attacked, call 370-5911. The Federal Police at that number speak both English and Spanish.

• If you are a pedestrian, be very cautious. Automobiles have the right of way, and, even at crosswalks, some drivers don't stop.

• Realize that Argentina is one of the safest countries in Latin America. However, there is a trick sometimes played in major cities. You will be sprayed with mustard or some other substance. The person cleans you off while taking your wallet. If you are sprayed, just keep walking.

• Usually, unaccompanied women do not go out after dark, especially in small towns. Try to stay in a good hotel in the town's center.

• Women should be prepared for men to stare at them in restaurants. They may send the waiter to your table with a drink or food. If you want no further contact with the person, a gracious but cool response should be sufficient.

• Women should realize that traveling in Argentina is safer than in any other Latin American country. However, be prepared for unwelcome physical contact on crowded public transportation. Also, expect crude comments from men as you are walking. Just ignore them.

• In Buenos Aires, it is fairly safe to drink tap water and eat raw vegetables. Outside the city, observe the usual precautions—drink only bottled water, don't eat raw vegetables or fruit you can't peel. Don't drink anything with ice cubes made from tap water.

• For information on drugs and hygiene supplies, see "Legal Matters, Safety, and Health" in the Introduction.

BELIZE

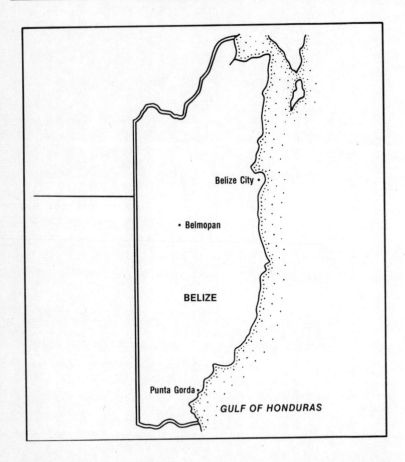

Belize City •

• Belmopan

BELIZE

Punta Gorda •

GULF OF HONDURAS

　　Belize's early settlers were pirates who found that its coral reef afforded excellent protection to their ships. Now the great reef (second in size only to Australia's Great Barrier Reef) welcomes scuba divers from all around the world who want to explore the multitude of sea life in the area.

　　Belize (formerly British Honduras) offers other opportunities for adventure, with 65 percent of its land area uninhabited jungle, where some 500 species of wildlife—including jaguars and other great cats—live. In fact, Belize boasts the world's only jaguar preserve.

But that's not all. Belize was once part of the Maya empire, and it contains ruins of that mysterious civilization, including the great ceremonial center at Xunantunich.

GREETINGS

Language: The official language of Belize is English. A creole dialect of English is widely spoken, and Spanish is common in the North.

• Note that men shake hands with men when they are introduced. Men and women sometimes shake hands, though women don't usually shake hands with other women.

• Close friends of both sexes hug one another in greeting.

• If you meet women from villages or older women, they will probably give you a one-armed hug and pat on the back.

• Remember that titles are very important (reflecting earlier British influence). Use "Doctor" for a Ph.D., a lawyer, or a medical doctor; and "Professor" where appropriate.

• With a group of ten or fewer, expect to be introduced to each person by your host. With more peo-

ple, you'll probably be presented to the group as a whole.

CONVERSATION

• Remember that people do not want just a quick "hello." They anticipate a real conversation.

• Bone up on Belize before you go there. People take great pride in their country, so it's good to compliment the village or town, or the country as a whole. Ask people about the interesting sights of their particular area. They will enjoy telling you about them.

• Avoid discussing politics, race, or religion.

• Expect people to talk about how they need the U.S. to help them and to ask what more America can do for them.

TELEPHONES

• Realize that Belize has a modern phone system with pay phones throughout the country. Rural areas have community telephones, which are often fixed cellular phones in someone's house. Pay the person who operates the phone.

• Note that there are two types of prepaid phone cards: the Telecard, which you can use at any touch-tone phone with the PIN number you get when you purchase the card, and the Payphone card, used at pay phones. Buy the cards at gas stations, hotels, shops, and Belize Telecommunications Limited (BTL) offices.

• Use fax machines at most businesses, hotels, and BTL offices. Belizeans use both E-mail and the Internet. You can go on-line in one of Belize City's BTL offices.

• Emergency numbers: Ambulance or Fire—90; Police—911.

IN PUBLIC

• When looking for a certain address, be prepared for people to give directions by describing how many blocks the place is from a well-known landmark. Many streets aren't named, and house numbers may be obscured.

• To be polite, ask permission before you photograph people. Some may request a fee.

• Don't photograph airports. Army troops often use them for maneuvers.

• Don't expect to find casinos. Gambling is illegal.

• Look for public bathrooms only in hotels and restaurants. In the countryside you won't find any.

• Expect to pay set prices in stores, but feel free to try bargaining with vendors and in markets.

DRESS

• For casual wear, jeans are acceptable for both men and women. In fact, you can wear anything comfortable as long as it isn't provocative.

• If you're planning a long trek through the jungle, be sure to bring hiking boots to protect yourself from insects and snakes.

• For business, suits and ties are appropriate for men, and dresses for women.

• For dressy occasions, men should wear a dark suit and women a dress. There's no need to bring a tuxedo.

• Women should avoid short-shorts or revealing dresses on the street and should never enter a church wearing shorts.

MEALS

Hours and Foods

Breakfast (called Tea): 6:30 or 7:00 A.M. People eat eggs or beans, tortillas made of corn flour among the Maya and wheat flour among the Creoles, and thin oatmeal made like a drink. Occasionally there is ham or sausage and sometimes fried jack (like fried dough). In the cities, people often eat bakery bread. Beverages are coffee or tea.

Lunch (referred to as dinner): 12:00 or 1:00 P.M. A typical meal is rice and beans (cooked together with coconut milk—the national dish) with chicken, meat, or fish. There may also be soup with tortillas. Accompanying the meal may be fried plaintains as well as a salad of shredded cabbage and carrot with vinegar dressing.

Dinner: 6:00, 7:00, or 8:00 P.M. Dinner at home is a lighter meal than lunch. There is usually rice and beans or soup and a little meat—usually leftovers from noon dinner—with coffee or tea as the beverage. (Dinner is also referred to as "drinking tea," e.g., "Come to our house to drink tea.")

• Since both the noon and the evening meal have the same name, ask what time you're expected if you're invited to dinner.

• Remember that there are two kinds of beer—lager (light) and stout (a little heavier). These beers have nothing in common with the British beers of the same name.

• Don't anticipate cocktails and appetizers before dinner, although they may be offered in the city. A popular drink before dinner is rum and Coke.

• Don't expect dessert or coffee after a meal.

• Common beverages with meals are soft drinks, juice, and water.

Table Manners

• If you are a guest, expect to be seated first. In the countryside or in a small village, the family may then eat in shifts, with guests eating first. In fact, the guest may be served alone, with the family eating later. A female guest may end up eating with the men, who are always served first—even in middle- and upper-class families.

• Tear up your tortilla and pick up food with pieces of it.

• Finish everything on your plate. *Always* accept any food and drink offered. To refuse such an offer is

impolite, especially in smaller towns.

• To indicate that you've finished, push your plate forward with the silverware on it.

Eating Out

• Look for the small cafes, which Belizeans frequent, to be open all day until 10:00 P.M.

• Be prepared for many restaurant, especially those in the cities, to be closed on Sunday.

• If you're backpacking through villages where there are no cafes or restaurants, go to a pub, a grocery store, or a church, and ask if there is a housewife who might be interested in preparing a meal for you for a fee. Agree on the price beforehand.

• In the north and west, expect restaurants to serve mainly local dishes—tortillas, black beans, and charcoal-grilled beef.

• Expect to find many Chinese restaurants in Belize.

• Note that it's rare for menus to be posted in restaurant windows.

• Note that Belizeans don't have a tradition of dining out, so restaurant meals may not be very creative.

• In small restaurants, don't expect a wide variety of dishes.

• Don't join strangers at their table, but at very informal restaurants people do sometimes join one another.

• If you see *gibnut* on the menu of a local restaurant, be aware that the reference is to a rabbitlike rodent.

• Realize that seafood—shrimp and lobster—and fish are abundant and fresh. However, if you're inland, fish is not recommended.

• Note that fish is usually served whole with the head on.

• Strict vegetarians will have a hard time, since rice and beans are always prepared with lard.

• When ordering beer, remember that imported beer costs twice as much as beer produced in Belize.

• To call the waiter, say "Miss" or "Mister," while raising your hand. Never shout loudly.

• If you suggest a meal in a restaurant, pay for the meal. Women don't pay for men, however. If a group informally decides to go out to lunch, each one pays individually.

Specialties

• Try some of Belize's creole dishes: conch fritters; white rice and kidney beans cooked together or separately—one of Belize's staple dishes; stewed turtle (first fried) with tomatoes, onions, sweet peppers, and seasonings; Johnnycakes— flour, shortening, and coconut cream, first mixed and then baked; dumplings—same ingredients as Johnnycake but boiled and served as a side dish in a "boil up."

• At least twice a month, families have a "boil up": there will be yams, plaintains, cabbage, pickled pig tails, boiled conch, and steamed fish, all served on a single plate and covered with a sauce made of fried onions, tomatoes, and coconut oil.

• Other creole specialties: cow-foot soup with potatoes or yams; conch soup made with okra; creole bread, which is round and made with flour, yeast, and coconut milk; stewed chicken with tomatoes, onions, and sweet peppers; fried fish; iguana—served only in homes, not in restaurants, it tastes like chicken.

• Creole desserts: bread pudding, sweet potato pudding, lemon meringue pie, rice pudding, coconut tarts and pies.

• Belize also offers: *Tamales*— chicken or pork rolled in cornmeal dough and wrapped in banana leaves or aluminum foil. Don't eat the wrapping! *Empanadas*—ground corn, seasoned, flattened, and filled with fish or refried beans and then shaped into half moons. They're served with a sauce made of boiled chopped onions and vinegar. *Gornachas*—fried tortillas spread with refried beans, onions, and Edam cheese. *Relleno*—a thick soup made of boiled chicken, seasonings, onion, tomatoes, and sweet pepper.

HOTELS

• Realize that you will find a wide range of accommodations in Belize—budget rooms, charming guesthouses, simple cabins, luxury hotels, and houseboats. In Maya guesthouses, there are usually outhouses, no indoor plumbing.

• In isolated areas, don't be surprised to find that there are no telephones, electricity, or hot water in rooms.

• Be aware that most budget hotels accept only cash.

• Expect credit cards and travelers' checks to be accepted at most hotels.

• If you're visiting one of the cays (pronounced keys)—small islands—bring a flashlight. The hotel's generator may not run all night.

• Remember that you can make collect or credit card calls overseas from a large hotel, but if you stay at a small hotel or you want to pay for the call you have to go to the local office of the Belize Telecommunications Authority.

TIPPING

• Note that local people don't tip for certain services, but in tourist areas, service people expect tips from foreigners.

• Remember that most restaurants and hotels include a service charge in the bill. Check to see if a service charge has been added. If not, give the waiter 10 to 15 percent. Be sure to hand the tip to the server. Don't leave it on the table.

• Give a doorman or porter $1 or $2 Belizean for carrying bags.

• Don't tip a taxi driver unless he carries your baggage. In that case, give him $1 or $2 Belizean.

• Give drivers who serve as guides or fishing guides $2 or $3 Belizean per each member of the group.

PRIVATE HOMES

• Feel free to visit friends in the evening or almost any time on the weekend. Dropping in isn't regarded as impolite. People don't usually call in advance, since few people have phones. If you know that your friend has a phone, call before visiting.

• After dinner in a home, leave about 30 minutes to an hour after the meal, if conversation is the only after-dinner activity. If your hosts expect you to stay longer, they will suggest games, a video, or looking at photographs.

• In a home, pay for any long-distance calls that you make, but it isn't necessary to pay for local calls.

• If you're staying with a family, feel free to take a daily bath or shower.

• During an extended stay with a family, offer to help with food shopping, household chores, and cooking. Most families will welcome such help, but some upper-class families won't accept help from guests.

• Expect your host family to want to do everything to please you, in-

cluding taking you on sightseeing or shopping expeditions.

Gifts: When invited to a meal, bring wine or a dessert. Your hosts won't expect such a gift, but they will welcome it.

• Good gifts from abroad: crystal vases, French perfumes and cosmetics, pocket calculators, blank VCR videocassettes, videotapes of American films, cassettes or CDs of American music, Scotch or a liqueur.

BUSINESS

Hours

Businesses: Monday through Friday, 8:00 A.M. to noon and 1:00 to 5:00 P.M.

Government Offices: Monday through Friday, 8:00 A.M. to 5:00 P.M.

Banks: Monday through Thursday, 8:00 A.M. to 1:00 P.M. and Friday 8:00 A.M. to 1:00 P.M. and 3:00 to 6:00 P.M. Hours vary in small towns.

Shops: Monday through Friday, 8:00 A.M. to noon and 1:00 to 5:00 P.M.

• Note that some shops and businesses work a half-day on Wednesday and Saturday.

Currency

• Remember that the Belizean dollar (abbreviated B$) is divided into 100 cents. Coins are 1, 5, 10, 25, and 50 cents, and 1 dollar. Notes are 1, 5, 10, 20, and 100 dollars.

• Note that a 25-cent coin is often referred to as a "shilling."

• Be aware that U.S. currency is accepted in many places. The U.S. quarter, dime, and nickel are often used as coins. Prices are sometimes quoted in U.S. dollars and sometimes in Belizean dollars.

• Be prepared to pay in Belizean currency on the street, on boats, in cafes, and in other small establishments.

• Keep in mind that hotels and shops that accept your American Express, Visa, or MasterCard may add a surcharge to your bill to cover what they must pay the credit card company. In more remote areas you may not be able to use credit cards.

• Remember that Barclays Bank has the only ATMs which accept foreign-issued cards.

Business Practices

• If you plan to use any sort of electrical equipment—e.g., a laptop—bring an adapter. The electrical current is 220 volts, and some outlets take plugs with two round prongs.

• To ensure success doing business in Belize, have a contact in the country. If you don't have one, the Belize Chamber of Commerce can be helpful in obtaining one.

• Make appointments from abroad at least one week in advance.

• Be sure to be on time. Punctuality is standard in the Belizean business world, but not in other areas.

• Realize that time estimates are not usually reliable. People may offer a variety of excuses for not completing work on time.

• Remember that business decisions are made by a few top people in any company.

• Keep in mind that you need include only people with whom you're negotiating when entertaining business associates.

HOLIDAYS AND SPECIAL OCCASIONS

Expect business, government offices, banks, and many shops to be closed on the following national holidays. Check with the tourist office to learn if local areas will be having celebrations or festivals during your visit. Everything in the area may be closed at such times.

Holidays: New Year's Day (Jan. 1); Baron Bliss Day (March 9—celebrating an Englishman who fell in love with Belize and left an enormous amount of money to the country); Good Friday; Holy Saturday; Easter Sunday; Easter Monday; the Queen's Birthday (April 21); Labor Day (May 1); Commonwealth Day (May 24); National Day (Sept. 10); Independence Day (Sept. 21); Columbus Day (Oct. 12); Garinagus Settlement Day, commemorating the arrival of the Garinagus (black Caribs) in Belize in 1823 (November 19); Christmas (Dec. 25); Boxing Day (Dec. 26).

TRANSPORTATION

Public Transportation

• Check with the Tourist Board for schedules of long-distance buses. Realize that everywhere there's a road, there's a bus. Several private companies compete for passengers. On some buses there is music. Some longer-distance buses offer movies. Standing is not allowed, but some drivers stuff three people in one seat. Buses make frequent stops; you will be dropped wherever you want.

• To ensure a seat on a long-distance bus, buy a ticket in advance. You can pay on the bus, but you won't be guaranteed a seat. Fares vary according to your destination. The conductors or drivers will make change, so you don't need to have the exact fare.

• To go from town to town, consider flying as an alternative to buses. Scheduled flights in small planes are the most convenient way to get around. Fares are reasonable—and you'll be able to take in some scenery because the planes fly low.

• Be aware that there are no subways or trains in Belize.

• Keep in mind that taxi fares are fixed by the government. Check with the tourist board for rates, and then make sure the driver agrees to accept the rate before you set off. You can call for a taxi or hail one on the street. Taxis have green license plates.

Driving

• To rent a car, bring an International Driver's License. If you're driving only in a city, a car should be fine. If you're going to drive in the countryside, rent a Jeep, Land Rover, or other four-wheel-drive vehicle. Be sure to check that the vehicle is in good shape. You will be asked to leave an imprint of your credit card, travelers' checks, or a cash deposit. Most companies require that you be at least 25 years old.

• Note that car rentals are expensive—as is gasoline—but finding both is simple.

• Expect gasoline to be sold in American gallons.

• In Belize City, always leave your car in a guarded parking area.

• Note that many roads—especially the Southern Highway—are unpaved and become muddy during the rainy season (from June to mid-November) and are extremely dusty during the dry season (December to May). Many are filled with potholes.

• Be aware that there are no traffic lights in Belize. There are speed-limit signs on the roads, and the police enforce these limits—but not frequently.

• Keep in mind that there are no "on the spot" fines, and Belizean police are not easily bribed.

• Remember that Belizean laws on drinking and driving are not very strict; however, if you're caught there are penalties.

LEGAL MATTERS, SAFETY, AND HEALTH

• When you arrive, declare the amount of currency you're bringing into the country.

• If you get involved with the police, expect a great deal of time to be spent before any decision on the matter of your involvement is reached. The police expend much time on paperwork and procedures.

• Look for the specially trained tourist police. They wear green T-shirts and baseball caps.

• Realize that it's illegal to remove or export coral, to take orchids from a forest preserve, to remove archeological artifacts, or to spearfish while scuba diving.

• Beware of accepting the services of those who claim to be guides or who offer to help you find a hotel. For an official guide, ask at the Belize Tourist Office or at better hotels.

• Don't carry valuables around; it's better to keep them in your hotel's safe.

• Don't go out alone after dark in Belize City. Women should not go out alone at any time in Belize City. Neither men nor women should walk in towns or cities late at night.

• Women traveling alone should feel free to take taxis; taxi drivers are reliable.

• Women alone will not usually be harassed. However, men frequently whistle at women and make suggestive comments, especially in small villages. Local women are not offended, because they regard these actions as compliments. Foreign women should just ignore the men and continue walking.

• Women should not hitchhike; it can be dangerous.

• If you're going to be hiking for an extended period, make an appointment with a doctor beforehand. Usually, these doctors are acquainted with the pitfalls in the areas you'll be in and can advise you about precautions to take. If you have a medical problem when you're in the wilderness, you will have a doctor you know. (Many were trained in the U.S. and speak English.)

• For advice on medicine and hygiene products, see "Legal Matters, Safety, and Health" in the Introduction.

BOLIVIA

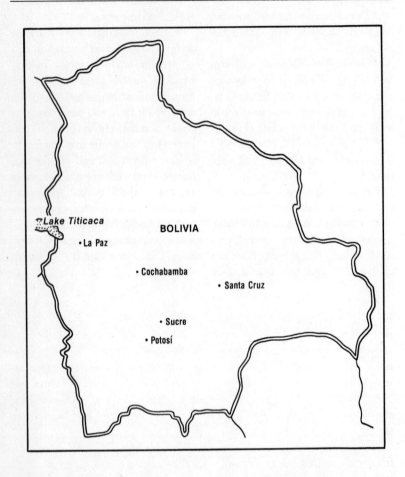

Bolivia has the distinction of having the world's highest capital, La Paz (almost 12,000 feet), and the world's highest navigable body of fresh water, Lake Titicaca (12,500 feet). The country also boasts the world's highest airport, the world's highest golf course, and the world's highest ski slope. In fact, it's nicknamed "the rooftop of the world."

Unfortunately, although rich in natural resources, Bolivia has the lowest per capita income in South America, as well as a high percentage of illiteracy.

The warmth Bolivians feel for North Americans is illustrated in an anecdote recounted by traveler Amy Miller in *The Boston Globe*. She and a companion waited interminably in the countryside for a bus to Cochabamba. They asked two young Bolivian men if they were waiting in the right place. After assuring them that they were, the two young men went into a nearby cafe. Miller recalls, "They came back with two hot dinners wrapped in foil and handed one of them to us. No words, just a simple sign of caring."

GREETINGS

Language: The first official language of Bolivia is Spanish. Second is Quechua, the language of the indigenous people. Other languages of the indigenous people are Aymara and Guaraní.

• When first introduced, people shake hands, with members of both sexes.

• Note that women who are good friends kiss on both cheeks in greeting, and close male friends give each other a hug (*un abrazo*) and shake hands. Even if good friends meet several times a day, they greet one another each time.

• Be aware that in the countryside people shake hands, tap each other's left shoulders, and then shake hands again. Both men and women greet each other this way, and men greet women this way as well.

• Always use the expressions for "good morning," and "good evening" (see "Key Words and Phrases: Spanish" at the back of the book) with older people and people you don't know well. Use *"Hola"* (Hi) with young people.

• Use titles. They are important to Bolivians. Some common titles: *Doctor* (used for Ph.D.'s and lawyers, as well as for medical doctors); *Arquitecto* (architect); *Ingeniero* (engineer); *Abogado* (lawyer); *Licenciado* (a college graduate).

• At large parties, expect to introduce yourself. At a traditional party hosted by an older person, you may be introduced by your host to each guest.

CONVERSATION

• Learn something about Bolivian culture. People will be impressed if you know about the country and its background.

• Other good topics for conversation are families, soccer, and food.

• Avoid political discussions—international, national, or local.

• Don't praise Chile while in Bolivia. The two countries have been engaged in border disputes since 1880. Bolivia lost its access to the ocean, making it one of South America's two landlocked countries.

TELEPHONES

• Expect to find pay phones in most cities. Purchase a card to use them at ENTEL, the long-distance company. The cards come in denominations of 5, 10, and 20 *bolivianos* and higher. It's best not to buy cards in denominations higher than 20 *bolivanos*, because the cards sometimes break, and you cannot get a refund. Use your phone card from a public phone, a hotel phone, or in a private home. For local calls, time is unlimited.

• For another option, make calls at ENTEL offices. Get in line, wait for a phone, and pay at the end of your call. In small towns and small cities, you will probably have to wait a long time.

• Expect people to say "Alo" when they answer the phone.

• For emergencies of all kinds, call 110.

IN PUBLIC

• Never whisper to anyone when you're in a group. You would cause suspicion and hurt feelings.

• Expect to see women walking arm-in-arm and teenage girls holding hands with one another.

• Note that if someone pats you on the shoulder, it's a sign of friendship.

• Always make eye contact with the person to whom you are talking. Not to do so is insulting.

• Be aware that middle- and upper-class Bolivians identify with their Spanish heritage rather than with the heritage of the indigenous people. It's considered very insulting to refer to someone as an indigenous person. People with slightly dark skin but who are not indigenous will always volunteer, "I'm not indigenous."

• Do not refer to indigenous people as *indios* but as *campesinos* (peasants).

• If you're with a group and encounter a black, don't be surprised if a friend pinches you and says, *"Negro, negro, buena suerte"* ("A black person. Good luck!"). There are very few blacks in Bolivia and seeing one is so rare it's considered good luck.

• Be aware that Friday nights in cities are called *viernes de soltero* (bachelor Friday). Men go out drinking with male friends. Women NEVER accompany them.

• Note that holding up the fist with the thumb between the index and the middle finger is an obscene gesture.

• If you're at a market and the vendor holds out his right hand with fingers separated and flips the hand—alternating thumb up and thumb down—he means "there isn't any."

• In dealing with customs officers, policemen, and government employees, the offer of a bribe is fairly standard practice. Since government salaries are very low, accepting bribes is the only way for many of them to live. Ask, "How can I help you?" or "Does this cost something? I don't want you to incur any expenses." If stopped for a traffic violation, ask, "Will $5.00 [equivalent] be sufficient?"

• Don't bargain in grocery stores or stores with fixed prices. In open markets, people love to bargain. Before you engage in bargaining, try to become informed as to what the going price of an item really should be. Ask local people or at your hotel what the price should be.

• Ask people for permission to take their picture before you take your camera out.

• Remember that indigenous women don't like to be photographed, because they think that a camera will capture their souls; they will usually run away. Indigenous men usually don't mind, but they will sometimes ask for payment. During a big festival or parade, however, people don't mind your taking their picture.

• Public bathrooms: In cities, you'll find public bathrooms in some restaurants and hotels, and city-maintained public bathrooms, called *baños públicos*. In the countryside, the only public bathrooms are in restaurants and hotels. Buses usually stop at a place with a bathroom and food, but, in villages, you'll have to use the fields, as local people do. Women may want to be prepared by wearing a long skirt. Be sure to bring toilet tissue with you. In general, the only clean bathrooms are in five-star hotels.

DRESS

• Be prepared for the different climates in various parts of Bolivia. La Paz is cold year-round because of the altitude. Santa Cruz is warm year-round, Cochabamba is spring-like except during the rainy season, from December through February or March.

• Remember that even the poorest people make great efforts to look their best, wearing clothes that are always ironed and very clean. People will be offended if you appear in dirty, wrinkled clothing. If you need to iron something, just ask. Everyone owns an iron.

• For casual wear, both men and women can wear jeans but should not wear shorts. Women may, however, wear shorts while sightseeing in warmer areas such as Santa Cruz, but they may not be allowed into churches and official buildings.

• Men's business dress in La Paz is a three-piece dark suit; in Santa Cruz, a lightweight suit or a *guay-abera* (a dressy shirt worn over pants); in Cochabamba, a two-piece dark suit.

• For business, women may wear a suit, a dress, or skirt and blouse, and should be sure to wear stockings.

• Women should wear bras and should not wear miniskirts or revealing dresses. Men will make comments to women in revealing clothing.

• When invited to a meal in a home for the first time, men should wear a dark suit and tie and women a dress or a skirt and blouse or sweater.

• Formal wear, suitable for diplomatic functions or lavish private parties, is a dark suit for men and a cocktail dress for women. Tuxedos aren't worn.

• Don't wear clothing that is appropriate to the indigenous people, because indigenous people may believe that you're making fun of them, and middle- and upper-class people will think you very strange.

• Women should not wear men's clothing, e.g., a man's hat or poncho.

• Recall that people think foreign women wearing pants are bizarre.

• Bolivians regard beards or long hair on males as unprofessional.

• Note that indigenous women wear bowler hats. If a foreign man should wear one, he makes himself ridiculous.

MEALS

Hours and Foods

Breakfast: About 8:00 A.M. Bread, butter, and jam are accompanied by hot milk with a little coffee added (Bolivian coffee is very strong).

Lunch: Noon to 2:00 P.M. The day's main meal is usually a hearty one. A typical lunch will offer soup, followed by a main course (e.g., rice topped with fried eggs and a small piece of steak, or fried beef served with rice and potatoes), fruit, and then coffee. Water is the usual beverage with meals; on special occasions beer or wine is served. Also popular is a drink similar to "Kool-Aid"—a powdered substance mixed with water and soda water.

Tea: Around 4:00 P.M., women invite other women for tea, coffee, soft drinks, cakes, pastries, cookies, and bread with *dulce de leche* (a sweet made with condensed milk). This light meal is usually served in the dining room.

• Note that many families don't

have dinner but repeat the 4:00 tea about 9:00 P.M.

Dinner: In La Paz people may start dining as early as 7:30 P.M. or as late as 9:30 P.M. In Cochabamba people begin eating sometime between 6:30 and 8:00 P.M. Formal dinners usually begin around 9:00 P.M.

• A formal dinner will have several courses: *entrada*, an appetizer (e.g., lettuce, ham, hard-boiled eggs, and tuna); soup; a main course of meat, rice, and potatoes; fruit; and cake or pudding on special occasions. People drink water with the meal, except on special occasions, when they will have beer or wine. Coffee (with sugar, but never milk or cream) is served afterward.

Beverages: When invited to a meal, you'll usually be offered wine or beer before dinner. Unless it's a special party, there won't be hors d'oeuvres. Another popular pre-dinner drink is *pisco* (a colorless grape brandy) and orange juice.

• In villages, you'll be offered *chicha*, an alcoholic beverage made from corn. It's less strong than wine, but foreigners often find it difficult to digest. Drink slowly, because your host will refill your glass as soon as it is empty.

• Be aware that, in rural areas, *campesinos* often drink excessively. They spill a bit of *chicha* on the ground as an offering to *Pachamama* (Mother Earth). The only way to politely avoid drinking heavily and becoming completely intoxicated is to say that you can't drink at all. (Invent a health problem.)

• *Chufle*, another popular drink, is a mixture of soda, *singani* (distilled liquor made from grapes), and lemon juice.

Table Manners

• When invited to dinner, always arrive 15 to 30 minutes late. It's rude to be on time because your host and hostess may not be ready.

• If you are a special guest, expect to be served first. Usually the father of the family is the first served. Food is often placed on individual plates in the kitchen and then brought to the table.

• In middle- and upper-class families, if there are children in the group, expect them to eat earlier than the adults or separately in the kitchen while the adults are eating.

• Note that the table will be set with fork at the left, knife at the right, and soup and dessert spoons above the dinner plate. There will always be cloth napkins, although if you're staying with a family, your napkin may not be changed every day.

• Never eat with your hands—not even chicken—unless your host does.

• Always use your fruit knife and fork to eat fruit—even bananas.

• Always keep your hands over the table. Don't put your hands in your lap.

• Be careful of red and green peppers in food. One type, called *locoto*, is extremely hot.

• Don't pay a compliment about a dish unless you really like it, because then you'll surely be given a second helping of it. However, be sure to compliment the food at the end of the meal.

• Wait until second helpings are offered. Don't ask for them.

• Never say "Yes" the first time you're offered more food. Wait until your hostess insists.

• To be polite eat some of each food, and clean your plate.

• Be aware that it's *very* insulting to pour wine or any other beverage with your left hand. And note that pouring a drink backward into a glass, rather than forward, indicates that you hate the person you're serving. Such a gesture could lead to a fight.

• After a meal in a home, stay about 30 minutes and then leave.

Eating Out

• *Confiterías* are coffee shops serving light meals, alcoholic beverages, and soft drinks.

• Don't eat in markets. They may not be very clean.

• Women should not go to bars unaccompanied.

• Note that most restaurants serve two meals—lunch from 11:30 A.M. to 2:00 P.M. and dinner from 6:00 to 9:00 P.M.

• Look for a fixed-price menu at both lunch and dinner. It is usually much less expensive than ordering à la carte.

• Realize that some restaurants offer only one dish at lunchtime. If you start going through the menu, and the waiter keeps repeating that the restaurant doesn't have the dish, just ask what they *do* have.

• Be aware that many of the dishes in the Altiplano are very pungent because hot red pepper is one of the main ingredients.

• Look for two hot sauces, *llajua* (**yah**-huah) and *halpahuayca* (ahl-pah-**wy**-kah), on restaurant tables.

• Expect steaks to be tougher and drier than the average.

Specialties

• Try *sopa de maní*—roasted peanut soup. In fact, most soups in Bolivia are excellent, both filling and nutritious.

• Some meat dishes to sample: *empanada salteña*—meat turnovers; *salteñas*—small pies stuffed with meat or chicken, potatoes, hard-boiled eggs, and olives—sometimes hot; *pique a lo macho*—bits of fried beef, French fries, pieces of hot dogs, raw onions, and tomatoes, all mixed in one dish; *silpancho*—very thin breaded steak served with rice, French fries, fried egg, and tomato; *picante de lengua*—a spicy tongue dish.

• If you're near Lake Titicaca, try *trucha*, trout, fried in oil.

• *Picante de pollo* is a spicy chicken dish.

• One variety of potato is *chuño*—freeze-dried potatoes.

• A specialty in the La Paz area is *fricassé*—pork cooked in a hot sauce with potatoes and white corn.

• In Santa Cruz, try *sonso*—baked yucca and cheese.

HOTELS

• Expect to find a choice of first-class and deluxe hotels in major cities. They provide central heating, air-conditioning, room service, restaurants, and (often) pools.

• Before registering, check your room to make sure that the heater and/or air-conditioning work (depending on the area of the country) and that all the bathroom facilities function. If you find problems, ask for another room.

• If you're staying at a cheaper hotel in one of the country's cold areas, be sure to ask if there is heating. Some cheaper hotels don't have it. Another problem with cheaper hotels is that they don't always supply towels, soap, and toilet paper—

and in the higher regions they may not provide blankets.

• Realize that cheaper hotels have curfews. Be sure to know and adhere to the time; otherwise, you may be locked out.

• **Do not** flush toilet tissue down the toilet, or the toilet will become blocked. Even in the best hotels, use the basket next to the toilet to dispose of tissues.

• Expect a constant supply of hot water, even in inexpensive hotels. The water is heated as it passes through hot coils. To take a shower, turn on the water; then turn on the electricity by turning the switch outside the shower stall. Be sure you turn the water on first; otherwise the coils could get burned out. Don't touch the switch if you're wet or standing in water. Be sure to dry yourself thoroughly before turning off the water.

TIPPING

• Don't tip taxi drivers (the drivers own their taxis) except for a very long journey. In that case, give them the equivalent of U.S. $2.00.

• Give porters at airports the equivalent of 50 cents per bag.

• If you agree to let a boy watch your parked car to prevent the theft of your hubcaps or windshield wipers, tip him 25 to 50 cents.

• Give a gas station attendant who fills the tank and washes the windshield 25 cents.

• It's not necessary to tip at restaurants. Service is included in your bill.

PRIVATE HOMES

• Remember that lunchtime is very important to Bolivian families. If you're staying with a family and plan to lunch with them, be prompt.

• Expect the family's maid to make your bed, but offer to do your own laundry. Ask your hostess where you should do it or pay the maid to do it. Ask your hostess how much to give her. However, be sure to wash your own underwear.

• Use a shower in a home as you would in a hotel. (See "Hotels" for instructions.)

• If you're staying with a family, expect the evening's main entertainment to be watching a soap opera on TV, beginning at 8:00 or 9:00 and lasting for an hour.

Gifts: If invited to a meal, realize that a gift isn't expected. You may bring a bottle of wine or *pisco*, however, or flowers, such as roses. Don't give yellow flowers, which signify contempt, or purple flowers, which are associated with funerals.

• Don't give electronic gadgets. They are now very inexpensive at Bolivian street markets.

• Good gifts are name-brand leather briefcases, leather chess sets, beautiful backgammon sets, and sheets and towels. Women enjoy receiving kitchen gadgets.

• Bolivians appreciate anything—e.g., T-shirts or beach towels—with U.S.A. written on it. Children enjoy receiving key chains with logos on them.

• Don't expect your gift to be opened in your presence.

• Realize that people are most appreciative of any gift. The fact that you've thought to bring them something is much more important than the actual gift.

BUSINESS

Hours

Businesses: Monday through Friday, 9:00 A.M. to noon and 2:00 to 6:00 P.M.; and Saturday, 9:00 A.M. to noon.

Government Offices: Monday to Friday, 9:00 A.M. to noon and 2:00 to 6:30 P.M.; and Saturday, 9:00 A.M. to noon.

Banks: Monday through Friday, 9:00 A.M. to noon and 2:00 to 4:30 P.M. Unlike other businesses, banks are closed Saturday.

Shops: Monday through Friday, 9:00 A.M. to noon and 2:00 to 6:00 P.M. Some shops are open on Saturday morning.

Currency

• Coins are 2, 5, 10, 20, and 50 *centavos* and 1 and 2 *bolivianos*.

• Notes are 2, 5, 10, 50, 100, and 200 *bolivianos*.

• Realize that making change can become a full-time occupation.

Since people can't make change early in the morning, you won't be able to buy anything. Many merchants refuse to make change. One traveler said, "A 200-*bolivano* bill can be used as a napkin, since no one will be able to make change for it."

Business Practices

• Make appointments from abroad two to three weeks in advance.

• Don't rely on telephone calls to speed up your business. Face-to-face meetings are very important to Bolivians.

• Realize that Bolivians write very flowery and formal letters. Try to emulate that style in your correspondence.

• Since there are so many local festivals, when businesses will be closed, obtain a calendar from the Bolivian Tourist Office to make it easier to schedule your business trip.

• Realize that several trips may be necessary to accomplish your goal unless your company has a representative in Bolivia.

• Note that the best months for business trips are April, May, September, and October. People usually vacation sometime in the months of January through March. Avoid business trips during Carnival, which begins the Saturday before Ash Wednesday. Also avoid the first week in August, during which the country celebrates its independence.

• To arrange business contacts, use the Chamber of Commerce in major cities, and the commercial section of your embassy. If you speak Spanish reasonably well, go to Bolivia's Ministry of Commerce or its Ministry of Finance.

• Arrive in advance of your appointments, so that you can rest the first day. It often takes a day or two to get used to the altitude. Eat lightly, and don't drink alcoholic beverages or smoke for your first few days in the country.

• If you need an interpreter in La Paz or Cochabamba, call the language school *Centro Boliviano Americano.*

• Note that there are many places to send and receive E-mail in major cities. ENTEL also provides access to E-mail.

• Send and receive faxes from post offices, ENTEL offices, and even some shops. Fax machines are sometimes turned off, so you'll have to call to confirm that your fax has been received.

• Bring copies of proposals with you. They can be copied in Bolivia, but it may take as much as a week.

• Realize that Bolivians aren't very strict about punctuality, and delays are tolerated. As a rule, however, foreigners should be on time.

• Since foreign names are often difficult for Bolivians to remember, always present a business card. Have your card printed in Spanish, a process which takes only two days in Bolivia.

• Have sales literature available in both English and Spanish.

• Distribute copies of your proposals to a few people at the top of the organization.

• Enhance your proposals with charts and visuals. Both will impress.

• Make your sales approach understated and low-key, so that Bolivian businesspeople don't feel any pressure.

• Be aware that Bolivian women are going into business in increasing numbers, so a foreign businesswoman in Bolivia will cause no surprise.

• Expect tea to be served in offices every day at precisely 4:00 P.M.

• You will present an impressive image by staying in the best hotels and eating in the best restaurants.

• Expect business entertaining at lunch or dinner to be in restaurants, rather than in homes. If the meal is strictly business, lunch is the more popular meal. Wives are not usually included in business meals.

• When entertaining, include only those with whom you are negotiating.

• Note that the most popular restaurants for entertaining Bolivians are those where native food is served.

HOLIDAYS AND SPECIAL OCCASIONS

• Following are national holidays on which you can expect to find banks, businesses, and many shops closed. Check with the tourist office to learn about local holidays during which banks, etcetera, may be closed in a specific area.

Holidays: New Year's Day (Jan. 1); Monday before Ash Wednesday, Shrove Tuesday, and Ash Wednesday; Good Friday; Holy Saturday; Corpus Christi (the Thursday after the eighth Sunday after Easter); Labor Day (May 1); Independence Day (Aug. 6); Columbus Day (Oct. 12); All Souls' Day (Nov. 2); Christmas (Dec. 25).

• Be alert during Carnival, when people throw water-filled balloons at everyone in sight. In some cities, people put paint or shoe polish inside balloons. They may also use spray cans of foam. If you go out during Carnival, don't take anything of value, and protect your clothing by wearing a poncho.

• An important local holiday is

the January 24–31 Alasitas Fair in La Paz. It's held in honor of Ekeko, the pre-Columbian god of prosperity and good fortune. Traditionally, Ekekos made of gold, silver, tin, clay, or rock are kept in the homes of indigenous people. Miniature objects are sold at the fair; whatever you purchase in miniature, you'll obtain in real life.

TRANSPORTATION

Public Transportation

• When taking a bus in a city, pay the fare when you get on. Be careful of your wallet, since there are pickpockets who slash bags. Keep your wallet in your front pocket, and wear your backpack on your chest.

• Consider taking a *colectivo* or microbus. *Colectivos* are like taxis and run along certain routes. The fare is based on the distance traveled. They take no more than five people. The microbuses, small versions of regular buses, go on different routes. There's one fare, whatever the distance, and they're often as packed as a New York sub-

way car. Minivans, called *trufi*, which carry 14 to 20 people are used primarily by students and business-people. Again, beware of pickpockets in crowded situations.

• For inter-city buses, buy tickets in advance, and bring food and drink along if the trip is a long one.

• Consider taking one of the long-distance buses, called *buscama*. Although they are double the cost of a regular long-distance bus, they have reclining seats, footrests, movies, and bathrooms.

• Note that trains, improved in the last several years, run only between large cities. The best and fastest service is the *ferrobus*—two comfortable first-class carriages. Regular trains have Pullman class and second class. Pullman has compartments with two beds for night and comfortable upholstered seats for daytime travel. It also has dining cars and cafeterias. Seats in second class are not so comfortable. Some trains don't offer both Pullman and second class. Be prepared for trains to be cold at night.

• If you wish, reserve your train accommodations in advance at the train station. Advance booking is necessary only during the Christmas season, since there isn't much demand for train service during other times of the year.

• Prepare for long train delays due to heavy rains during the rainy season (December through February/March).

• Consider planes for transportation between cities. They aren't expensive and they are much more comfortable than a long train ride. However, planes are frequently delayed due to weather.

• Be aware that taxis don't have meters. Find out from your hotel or from an acquaintance what the approximate fare to your destination should be, and arrange the fare with the driver before you start the trip.

• Note that many taxis take several passengers to different destinations. If you want to have a taxi to yourself, arrange it through the hotel concierge.

Driving

• Don't drive between cities; roads are not usually paved outside major cities. Driving within cities isn't a big problem. There are no parking meters, but children will volunteer to "watch your car." Give them the equivalent of 25 to 50 cents when you return to the car.

• Don't forget that drinking and driving is a problem in Bolivia, so be careful both as driver and pedestrian.

• At intersections, expect to hear people honk horns or put on their high beams for right of way.

• Keep in mind that, though there are no laws regarding drinking and driving, if you're involved in an accident and are drunk, you can easily be sent to jail. An arrest may cost a great deal in bribes, but bribing may not work with a judge.

LEGAL MATTERS, SAFETY, AND HEALTH

• Remember that chewing and making tea of coca leaves is legal, but cocaine is not. Drug laws in Bolivia are very harsh. Before trial, there's a long waiting time in prison, and then, if you're found guilty, there could be a long prison sentence.

• Women should not walk alone at night or take taxis after dark. Bolivian women don't do anything alone. They are always in groups.

• Don't worry about violent crime. There isn't any in Bolivia. However, people will try various ruses to get your money. For example, someone drops money on the ground. You pick it up, and another person says, "Split it with me." You open your wallet to make change, and the person grabs your wallet.

• Don't drink the tap water. Use mineral water instead.

• Don't eat raw vegetables or fruits that cannot be peeled.

• If you visit La Paz, take precautions because of the 12,000-foot altitude. Rest for a few days, avoid alcoholic beverages, and eat lightly. Remember that, at high altitudes, every single alcoholic drink is the equivalent of two. Drink plenty of water.

• Bring suntan lotion if you visit La Paz; even in the winter (June–Sept.), you can get sunburned.

• For information about medicines and hygiene products, see "Legal Matters, Safety, and Health" in the Introduction.

BRAZIL

In movies, people seem to go to Rio the way the rest of us go to the corner drugstore. Fred Astaire and Ginger Rogers went *Flying Down to Rio.* Jane Powell led Ann Southern, Scotty Beckett, and many others on a merry chase in *Nancy Goes to Rio.* And when his love affair went sour, Michael Caine had to *Blame It on Rio.*

One taste of Rio—the bronzed bodies on Copacabana Beach or the colorful frenzy of Carnival—and you'll understand the reasons for all the fascination.

Brazil itself is conscious of its place in film. One of Rio's tourist attractions is the Carmen Miranda Museum, a tribute to the film star of the forties, who introduced the fruit-salad headdress to the world.

Of course, there is more in Brazil than just Rio. There's the economic boomtown of São Paulo, the rain forest of the Amazon, and the amazing Iguaçu Falls, where the water falls over 2½ miles.

If you venture into the wild and unspoiled center of the country, you may identify with naturalist Alfred Wallace's 1848 experience: "We received a fresh inmate into our verandah in the person of a fine young boa constrictor." Its breath, he wrote, sounded "like high-pressure steam escaping from a Great Western locomotive." Wallace's reaction? He bought the boa.

GREETINGS

Language: The official language of Brazil is Portuguese, *not* Spanish.

• Note that when first introduced to a person of either sex, men and women shake hands. When two men are introduced, they shake hands for quite a long time. When two men know each other well, they shake hands and slap each other on the back, shoulder, or stomach. Most women kiss each other on each cheek for "hello" and "good-bye." (The gesture is really two pecks in the air.) Married women kiss twice—on alternate cheeks. If one or both women is single, they kiss a third time to wish marriage for the single.

• When kissing while greeting someone, go to their *right* cheek with your *left* cheek. Kiss once, and then go to the other cheek if you're good friends. To wish good luck, give a third kiss on the first cheek.

• Prepare for first names to be used in introductions. To show respect to elders, strangers, or politicians, use *senhor* plus the first name for a man and *dona* plus the first name for a woman. Doctors, professors, and priests usually go by their title plus their first name (e.g., *Doutor Antonio*). (In fact, if you're looking for someone's name in a list or file, remember that they are usually alphabetized by first name.) Remember that people with university degrees as well as lawyers and M.D.'s are addressed as *Doutor*.

• In business, address men as *Senhor* plus his family name and a woman as *Senhora* plus her family name.

• At a party—in fact, any time you meet a group of people—shake hands hello and good-bye with each person. If you don't, people will be insulted.

CONVERSATION

• Good topics of conversation: with men, soccer, politics, and places to visit; with women, family and children.

• Other good subjects are Brazilian dances and the positive aspects of Brazil's industry.

• Don't be surprised if Brazilians are *extremely* candid about personal characteristics, even negative ones—e.g., "You're really fat." Try not to interpret such comments as personal insults; they aren't intended to be.

• Don't ask about a couple's marital status, unless a Brazilian mentions it first.

• Don't refer to Brazilians as Hispanics. They're not. Although they certainly identify with the rest of Latin America, they're proud of their unique place as Portuguese-speakers, and of their culture. They are generally more informal, fun loving, and less reserved. It sounds like a stereotype, but sometimes it seems as if Brazilians are always ready to have a party.

• Expect people to stand very close to you when they talk to you. Try not to back away, because such action may be interpreted as aloofness. Keep constant eye contact during a conversation. Brazilians also touch frequently while conversing—a sign of friendship.

• Don't be surprised (or offended) at constant interruptions during casual conversation. Brazilians regard them as a sign of enthusiasm.

• Delicate subjects are the political situations in Brazil and Argentina, AIDS, and Brazil's role in destroying the rain forest.

TELEPHONES

• Note that public phones are called *orelhões* (big ears). From green public phones, make calls with either coins or phone cards. Buy the cards at newspaper stands.

• In an emergency, ask someone on the street for a phone card. Most people carry a supply.

• To make a local call from a public phone, pick up the receiver and listen for a dial tone. (Be aware that many public telephones don't work. If one doesn't, try another.) Insert several coins or a phone card into the slot, wait for another dial tone, and then dial. To prevent being cut off during a long call, deposit several coins or a more expensive phone card; what you don't use will be returned. If you don't deposit enough coins or a phone card with enough time, you'll hear a beep after three minutes. Again, to avoid being cut off, deposit more coins or a more expensive card.

• To make a long-distance call outside your hotel, go to an office of EMBRATEL—the name of Brazil's telephone company. You may also hear people refer to the *cia telefónica*, a popular nickname for the telephone company. The cashier in the telephone office will give you a key. Go into the phone booth, and insert the key into a slot underneath the phone. Make your call. Return the key, and pay the cashier when you're finished.

• When you place a call to Brazilians, expect them to answer by asking, *"Quem fala?"* (keym fah-lah), which means "Who is speaking?" Respond with your name.

• Emergency phone numbers differ from place to place. You'll find them listed in the phone book under *Bombeiros or Policia Civil*. In Rio, the emergency numbers are: Police—190; Ambulance—193; Fire—193.

IN PUBLIC

• Don't be surprised when people bump into you in crowded places and don't apologize.

• In lines at banks or stores, be prepared fro people to stand much closer to you than people do in the U.S. or northern Europe.

• If you see someone you know across the street, don't shout at her or him.

• Don't eat while walking on the street.

• Never chew gum in a social or business situation, even though you will see a great many Brazilians chewing gum on the street. They don't, however, disapprove of littering—throwing paper cups, napkins, or cigarette butts on the ground. Fortunately, city streets are cleaned daily.

• Note that Brazilians do not usually send greeting cards or flowers. They regard such gestures as too impersonal, a way of avoiding personal contact.

• Some gestures to recognize: (1) To add emphasis to a statement, Brazilians snap the fingers while whipping the hand. (2) The ends of the fingers brushed under the chin means "I don't know." (3) You may see older people taking the earlobe between the thumb and forefinger to express appreciation for food. (4) Patting people on the shoulder, either men or women, is a sign of friendship. (5) Shaking the hands with the index finger hitting the thumb and middle finger means "a lot, a great deal." (6) Clenching one fist with the thumb between the index and middle fingers says "Good luck." You'll see Brazilians wearing amulets showing this gesture. (7) The American "O.K." gesture (thumb and finger forming a circle) is an obscene gesture in Brazil.

• To attract someone's attention in a store or restaurant, copy the Brazilian habit of snapping fingers, hissing, or saying "shhh."

• If you go to an outdoor market, anticipate a crowd of teenage boys at the entrance who will pester you to let them carry your parcels or perform other services. If you let one of them perform some chores, give him the equivalent of a dime. If you don't want their services, be very firm in refusing.

• Try bargaining in markets, but be aware that you get the best bargains only if you speak Portuguese. In stores where prices are marked, you can ask for a discount if you buy in quantity, e.g., four tapes instead of one.

• Don't expect to encounter begging, but people may try to sell you pencils, emery boards, or other small items. If you simply refuse, they won't bother you.

• Keep any photographic equipment in a simple bag so as not to invite theft.

• You have to leave your camera at the entrance to churches or museums. There will be someone to watch over it.

• Ask people before you take their photograph. Most people will be friendly and receptive.

• Don't photograph religious ceremonies. Be especially careful of *macumba* (known in different regions also as *candomblé or xangô*), a kind of voodoo practiced in Brazil. If you're curious about these ceremonies, ask at your hotel about a group going to one. It's safe to go with a group, but it's not a good idea to go alone.

• To find a public bathroom—a scarce commodity—go to a hotel or a restaurant. You'll find public toilets at every airport, train, and bus station. Usually, there's an entrance fee. Restrooms are labeled *mulher* (woman) or *senhor* (man). You can't flush used toilet paper, since there isn't enough water pressure. You'll find a basket for the used paper.

DRESS

• Try not to dress so that you will easily be identified as a foreigner—and thus invite robbery. Avoid sneakers, sandals with socks—and a large camera. For casual wear, men should wear shoes (not sneakers) and slacks, Bermuda shorts, or clean, pressed jeans. Women can wear pants, skirts, dressy jeans, or Bermuda shorts.

• Note that jeans are universal informal wear for adults as well as young people.

• Never wear an outfit of green and yellow—the colors of the Brazilian flag. People will laugh at you.

• Women should dress modestly unless they want to attract attention. They should not wear short-shorts, except along the beach. Women wear dressy short skirts or Bermuda shorts with a dressy T-shirt or shirt to work or shopping or to the movies.

• In Rio, men must wear trousers in cinemas and restaurants. However, unless the event is for business or one with some formality, jackets are not required in restaurants.

• When invited to a home to a meal, men should wear suits and women should wear dresses or skirts and dressy blouses.

• Restaurants rarely require jackets and ties. However, men should wear a jacket, and women a wrap—because air-conditioning may make one necessary.

• Note that executive men wear two-piece suits, while office workers wear regular suits. Men should always wear long-sleeved shirts.

• Businesswomen from abroad should dress elegantly in suits, dresses, or skirts and blouses. Short-sleeved blouses and jackets are acceptable. Be sure that your nails are manicured.

• If an event requires formal wear—tuxedos for men, cocktail dresses for women—the invitation will tell you.

• Both sexes should wear clothing of natural—not synthetic—fabrics because natural fabrics are much cooler.

MEALS

Hours and Foods

• First, a caution. Don't drink tap water or fruit juices to which unboiled tap water has been added. Don't use ice cubes made from tap water. Don't eat any raw vegetables or unpeeled fruit. Don't eat raw shellfish. And don't eat food bought from street vendors.

Breakfast: Between 7:00 and 9:00 A.M. The usual meal is juice (sometimes drinks made in a blender with fruits, milk, and ice—called *vitamina*), plain fruit juices, bread and butter, sometimes fruit, and coffee with milk, called *café com leite*.

Lunch: Noon until about 2:00. Usually the day's main meal, it frequently features soup as a first course, followed by a main course of meat (steak or chicken) or fish with rice and beans—possibly with a plate of salad on the side, then fruit or fruit salad, and finally coffee.

• At 4:00 or 5:00 P.M., Brazilians pause for an afternoon snack (*lanche*) of cookies, cake, and a beverage.

• Also at 4:00 or 5:00 P.M., many women give parties to which other women come for about an hour and a half before going home to dinner with their husbands. These teas play a very important role in the social lives of middle- and upper-class women.

Dinner: From about 7:00 until 9:00 P.M. Usually, it's a light meal. Dinner parties, however, don't begin until 9:30 or 10:00 P.M. with drinks and hors d'oeuvres before dinner. The meal itself may appear about midnight. People may stay until 2:00 A.M., even on a weeknight; sometimes people stay up talking until 6:00 or 7:00 A.M. Never rush to leave right after the meal.

• Expect Brazilian food to be very flavorful due to the use of a variety of condiments. The African influence dominates in Bahia, in the east of Brazil, and the food is very spicy.

• In Bahia, you'll find a hot sauce, called *pimenta malagueta* (pee-**mehn**-tah mah-lah-**geh**-tah), on the table along with salt and pepper. Be careful. It's *very* hot. The sauce is made from the *malagueta* pepper, which is not a chile pepper, but rather resembles black pepper. It's also common in the north and northeast.

• Throughout Brazil, look for another shaker on the table, with toasted *mandioca* (cassava) meal, which Brazilians sprinkle over many dishes. It tastes somewhat like cream of wheat. Because they use so much *mandioca*, most Brazilians don't eat bread as much as North Americans and Europeans do. The most common bread is *pão francês*, similar to French bread.

• Brazilians usually serve fruit as a separate course after all lunches and dinners. It's usually peeled and sliced, and eaten with a knife and fork.

• Cheese may be served with the dessert course, e.g., guava paste and cheese or coconut pudding with a wedge of cheese.

Beverages: Beer is usually considered a man's drink; women drink wine, liqueurs, or hard liquor. To order draft beer, ask for *chopp* (**shaw-pih**).

• With meals, people drink water, carbonated beverages, fruit punches, or beer.

• A very popular drink is *cachaça*, sugarcane brandy. Mixed with lemon and sugar, it's called *caipirinha* and is similar to a margarita.

• The most popular soft drink after Coca-Cola is *guaraná*, made from the berry of a plant in the Amazon. Those who have drunk it report that it tastes like lipstick.

• After-dinner coffee—the very strong *cafezinho*—is always served in a demitasse, with lots of sugar. It's quite strong, and most Brazilians drink only one cup, but feel free to drink more.

Table Manners

• Realize that it's far more common for Brazilians to entertain you in a restaurant rather than at home.

• If you're the guest of honor, expect to be seated at the head of the table. The host and hostess usually sit at one side of the table.

• At the table, expect to see forks to the left of the plate and the knife to the right. Spoons will either be on the left nearest to the plate or above the plate.

• Remember that formal meals are always served in sequence, course following course. Informal meals are usually—but not always—served that way.

• When not using your knife, place the tip of it on your plate with the handle resting on the table.

• Don't use the side of the fork to cut—even the softest foods. Always cut with your knife.

• Don't use your hands to eat anything. It's considered both bad manners and unhygienic. Any food eaten with the hands is wrapped in a napkin so that the fingers don't touch it.

• Should you be dining with a wealthy family, expect a servant to prepare the meal; he or she will then proceed around the table, serving each person in turn. After dinner, coffee will be served in the living room.

• Help yourself as the platters of food are passed around.

• If sandwiches are served on a

plate, eat them with a knife and fork. Brazilians usually serve sandwiches as appetizers or at teas.

• To indicate that you have finished eating, place your utensils horizontally across your plate. Don't overlap the knife and fork.

• Don't smoke during a meal. Many Brazilians smoke (you'll see very few *"Proibido Fumar"*—"No Smoking"—signs in the country), but they usually don't light up until coffee is served at the end of the meal.

• Never drink directly out of a bottle or can. Even in the most humble establishments, Brazilians drink from glasses.

• Be aware that any time people are eating and a friend or visitor arrives, they feel obligated to share their food. If you are the visitor, always decline, since there may not be enough food.

Eating Out

• *Rodízios* are restaurants where you eat all the meat you want for a set price. Waiters bring around spits of barbecued meat and carve it onto your plate. They will also bring a selection of side dishes throughout the meal.

• In the southeast, for meats grilled on charcoal, look for *churrasquerías*.

• *Barzinhos* are street-corner bars that offer food and alcoholic drinks. Some have tables, but others are just stands. The quality of food varies greatly, but you can usually judge the place by the appearance of its exterior. Women should never go into one of these bars unescorted.

• *Vitaminas* serve fresh fruit drinks made in blenders.

• *Padarias* (bakeries) are a good choice for light snacks: *empanadas*— a small pie filled with meat, palm heart, or shrimp; *pastel*—a fried savory pastry; *coxinha*—spiced chicken rolled in manioc dough and fried.

• A *lanchonete* is a cross between a bar and a cafe. It offers snacks, coffee, soft drinks, and sometimes light meals. At both *padarias* and *lanchonetes*, it is customary to pay first, obtain a receipt, and then order.

• Expect São Paulo to have the widest range of ethnic restaurants— e.g., Japanese, Arab, Portuguese, and Italian.

• Check to see if the menu is posted in the window or outside the restaurant. Some places follow this European practice.

• Be aware that many restaurants don't open until 8:00 or 9:00 P.M. for dinner. They often stay open all night, however.

• In a casual restaurant, seat yourself. In elegant restaurants, wait to be seated.

• Realize that, while smoking is prohibited in most restaurants, the ban is not always observed. Ask for a nonsmoking section, if you see people in the restaurant smoking.

• Don't be surprised if the waiter appears, shortly after you sit down, with little appetizers, such as olives, carrots, etc. There is a cover charge for these goodies. If you don't want the hors d'oeuvres, ask the waiter to take away all or part. The charge is usually modest.

• Be aware that many dishes are priced for two people. You have to pay, even if you want just one portion.

• At a buffet-style restaurant, be prepared for food to be priced by the kilo. Serve yourself from the buffet, and then pay for the weight on your plate. The practice is called *comida por kilo.*

• To summon the waiter, say *"Garçom"* You can also glance at him and beckon with your index finger. You will hear people calling "Psst," but don't do it—it's rude. Never snap your fingers to get the waiter's attention. That's the way Brazilians call a dog or cat.

• Expect the waiter to serve you from platters.

• If you don't want sugar in your coffee, be sure to tell the waiter that when you order it. Say, *"No azucar"* (ah-**soo**-kahr).

• In fast-food places, pay when you order or as soon as your food is served. In more formal restaurants, ask for your check. The waiter won't bring it until you ask for it.

• Don't ask for separate checks, and remember that your check won't be itemized.

• If the service charge is not included, don't leave the tip on the table. Hand it to the waiter, or give a large bill to pay for the check and leave before receiving the change.

• Note that 18 is the age limit for

buying and drinking alcohol, but the limit is not observed.

• If your conscience is bothered by the street children, give them some of your leftover food in a napkin. It may be a problem if there's not much food and there are many children in a group.

Specialties

• *Feijoada* is a typical Brazilian dish: black beans, rice, dried beef, smoked bacon, *mandioca* meal, and slices of pork sausage and orange. Most restaurants offer it on Wednesdays and Saturdays.

• Try *frango com arroz*—chicken and rice with peas, olives, and hard-boiled eggs—also called *risoto de frango;* and *churrasco gáucho*—barbecued pork, steak, and sausages served with peppers, onions, and *mandioca* meal.

• Observe the yellow-orange color of much Brazilian food. It's the result of *dendê* oil, a palm oil which is used a great deal in typical Bahian food. You'll also find the *malagueta* pepper, a very hot type of ginger, used frequently in Bahia.

• Fish and seafood lovers, sample *bacalhau*—dried, salted cod, served grilled or in a sauce; *moqueca*—shellfish fried with onions, tomatoes, and coconut milk; *acarajé*—a dumpling appetizer made of dried shrimp, onions, and mashed beans dropped by spoonful into hot oil; *vatapá*—a stew with fish and dried shrimp in a sauce made of onions, tomatoes, coconut milk, peanuts, cashew nuts, coriander, ginger, and *dendê* oil. Popular in Bahia are *peixe em moqueca*—fish cooked in banana leaves; and *caruru*—shrimp, okra, and coconut cooked with hot pepper and ginger.

• A popular side dish is *farofa*, made with *mandioca* meal with eggs and seasoning, and fried in butter. Sometimes it contains cheese, bacon, vegetables, and olives. *Farofa* can also be used as stuffing for poultry.

• A popular meat dish is *picadinho com quiabo*—chopped meat with okra.

• Note that Brazilians don't care much for vegetables. Japanese immigrants, however, have increased vegetable and fruit production, especially in the region of São Paulo. A favorite way of eating vegetables is to make them into croquettes, adding meat or shrimp, e.g., *chuchu com camarão*—chayote (a green, pear-shaped, squash-like vegetable) with shrimp.

• In the north, expect *cuscuz* to be a dessert made of tapioca, fresh grated coconut, coconut milk, water, sugar, and salt. In São Paulo in the south, *cuscuz* is made with cornmeal to which vegetables, meat, or fish are added.

• Be prepared for Brazilian desserts to be very sweet. *Doce de leite,* which looks like fudge or caramel, is made of slowly simmered milk and sugar. *Goiaba* is guava paste.

HOTELS

• Note that hotels are rated from one to five stars, although that doesn't mean that hotels without a star are not good. A *quarto* is a room without a bathroom; an *apartamento* is a room with a shower; an *apartamento de luxo* is a room with a small refrigerator with drinks. The latter two categories usually are equipped with telephones, air-conditioning, and TV. Small family-run hotels are called *pensôes*. The quality varies a great deal.

• Make reservations well ahead if you want to stay in a middle-range to exclusive hotel in July or December through February, especially in Rio.

• To reserve a room in one of the best hotels during Carnival, book a year in advance.

• Be aware that motels are reputedly for lovers and often are rented for just a few hours at a time.

• Ask whether the price of your room includes a buffet breakfast. Many hotels offer this bonus.

• Realize that hotels offering discounts during the low season may accept only cash, not credit cards.

• Always ask for a discount before taking a hotel room. There are often discounts for paying cash or for staying longer than a few days. Make sure that the desk clerk writes the discount down immediately to avoid misunderstanding when you leave.

• Even at the best hotels, check the room before accepting it to make sure that air-conditioning, toilet, shower, etc., function. You might also want to check the view (are you facing a stone wall?) and look around to see if the area is likely to be noisy.

• To see how people in the country live, plan a stay on a farm, or *fazenda* (your travel agent can make the arrangements). The family will probably have one or two rooms for paying guests; you'll share the bathroom with the family.

TIPPING

• Note that restaurants add a 10 percent service charge. Give the waiter an extra 5 percent.

• After taking a taxi, round the fare up to the nearest *real*.

• Tip porters the equivalent of U.S. 50 cents per bag.

• For small services, give doormen, ushers, and washroom attendants the equivalent of U.S. 25 to 50 cents.

• Tip chambermaids the equivalent of $1.00 per week.

PRIVATE HOMES

• Respect the strong Brazilian sense of privacy about the home and the family. Don't expect to be invited to someone's home, even if you know them very well. They aren't being unfriendly or cold. They, however, find the North American notion of needing time alone to be bizarre. To them, being alone indicates sadness. In Brazil, extended families usually share one roof, and all branches of a family gather to spend Sunday afternoon and evening together.

• Never drop in without calling first. People will feel obliged to entertain you, even if they have something important to do.

• Remember that most people take a siesta between 1:00 and 3:00

P.M. Don't phone or drop in on people during those hours.

• Realize that you're more likely to be invited to a party at a private club than to one in a home. Should you be invited to a home, always arrive between 15 and 30 minutes late.

• If you're invited to a small party and must leave early, inform your host or hostess when you arrive.

• Be aware that Brazilians almost always accept when invited to do something. People often make promises—to avoid offending by refusal—and then forget them. Be sure to formalize the invitation with a follow-up telephone call. (Brazilians, in general, tend to be evasive if they don't wish to accept an invitation, because they don't want to hurt anyone's feelings.)

• In a country area where the door of a house is hidden behind a wall, clap your hands to get your host's attention. Don't shout or scream. If no one appears, go to the door and knock on it.

• If you pay an afternoon visit, leave by 5:00 P.M. so that the family can prepare dinner.

• Expect to find servants in most middle-class homes. Never offer to help servants. If there aren't any, however, offer to help clear the table.

• If you stay with a family a few days, ask if you may tip the servants and, if so, how much you should give each one.

• Expect hot water only in the

homes of the rich and of many middle-class families in the south. The water tends to be tepid rather than cold. Most families take four or five showers a day because of the heat and find it strange if foreigners don't do the same.

• Keep in mind that Q on the water faucet stands for hot and F for cold. Because of the great variety of hot- and cold-water controls, be sure to ask your hostess how they work.

• A woman staying with a family that has male servants should be careful to be formal with them, or her behavior might be misinterpreted.

Gifts: When invited to dinner, bring a basket of strawberries, candy, or a bottle of champagne.

• Don't give purple flowers; they're associated with death.

• Good gifts: CD players with headphones (classical music for adults and the latest pop for teenagers); a Walkman; software for computers; T-shirts and watches for children and servants.

• Note that working-class people enjoy Christmas decorations of all types from abroad—ornaments for the tree, Santa Claus figures, and any decorative items for the holiday.

BUSINESS

Hours

Businesses: Monday through Friday, 8:00 A.M. to 12:00 noon, and 2:00 to 6:00 P.M.

Government Offices: Monday through Friday, 9:00 A.M. to 5:00 P.M.

Banks: Monday through Friday, 10:00 A.M. to 4:30 P.M. They usually stop changing money at 2:00 or 3:00 P.M.

Shops: Times vary from city to city. In Rio, Monday through Friday, 9:00 A.M. to 6:30 P.M. (closed for lunch from noon until 2:00 P.M.); and Saturday, 9:00 A.M. to 1:00 P.M. Shopping malls are open 10:00 A.M. to 10:00 P.M. during the week, and until 6:00 P.M. on Saturday and Sunday.

Currency

• Remember that the monetary unit is the *real*; the plural is *reais*. 1 *real* = 100 *centavos*.

• Coins: 1, 5, 10, 20, 25, and 50 *centavos* and 1 *real*. Coins look very similar, so check carefully.

• Notes: 1 *real* (green); 5 *reais* (blue/purple); 10 *reais* (red); 50 *reais* (brown); and 100 *reais* (blue).

• When you change money, ask for a supply of small bills (less than the equivalent of U.S. $10). There is a shortage of small change all over Brazil, especially in the northeast. Change is often not available at kiosks, restaurants, on buses, or in taxis. People who don't have change will often offer you candy.

• Be sure to keep receipts when you exchange your currency for Brazilian currency. You will need the receipts when you leave the country and want to change the Brazilian currency back to your currency.

Business Practices

• Plan to do business in Brazil only if you're interested in a long-term commitment to working in the country. Those are the terms on which Brazil welcomes foreign investment.

• Write to the Brazilian Trade Bureau in your country. They offer free publications on doing business in Brazil, including opportunities in and restrictions on foreign investment. The American Chamber of Commerce in Brazil is very active and offers a wide array of personal and business services.

• Avoid business trips to Brazil from mid-December to the end of February, when most people are on summer vacation, and in July, a school holiday month.

• If you're planning to bring anything electronic with you—e.g., a laptop—bring a converter, since electrical current is not standard.

• Note that fax services are available in main post offices in major cities, at telephone offices, and in private offices.

• Investigate Brazil's import controls; they are dedicated to making it easy to export from Brazil and difficult to import into the country.

• Be aware that there is often great distrust of a foreigner who wants to buy a share of a company.

• If you are planning to set up a new enterprise in Brazil, realize that while unskilled labor is plentiful, skilled labor may be difficult to find.

• Keep in mind that you'll have to deal with at least one of Brazil's regulatory agencies, and that these agencies have broad discretionary powers to control manufacturers' selling prices.

• Cultivate patience. Brazilians find some North American attitudes to business offensive, e.g., getting straight to the point and aggressive confrontations. You may feel frustrated with the inefficiency and the bureaucracy, but don't let it show.

• Be prepared for several trips to Brazil, especially if you're involved in negotiations. (Brazilians love to bargain, so the negotiating process can be drawn out.) If you're involved in a project that involves building, expect a protracted period

while you're getting permits from many different agencies or authorities.

• Realize that it's *very* important to have a contact in the country. The Chamber of Commerce and the Brazilian Trade Department can help. If possible, bring the business card of a mutual acquaintance with a note from her or him introducing you.

• Hire a *despachante*, an expediter who will help you deal with the various bureaucracies.

• Enlist the help of secretaries at firms you'll be visiting to help you find an interpreter.

• Stay in the best hotels to enhance your image. It's not, however, necessary to eat at the best restaurants, except when you're entertaining Brazilian colleagues; then you should be sure to go to the best places.

• From abroad, make appointments two weeks in advance.

• Try to schedule one morning and one afternoon appointment, so you won't be running frantically from place to place—especially since the Brazilians have a very flexible sense of time. The best times for appointments are between 10:00 and 11:30 A.M. and 3:00 and 5:00 P.M. In big cities, lunch lasts for just one hour. In smaller cities and towns, lunch may last up to three hours.

• Expect Brazilians to use first names very quickly. Wait until they use your first name before addressing them by theirs.

• Before getting down to business, engage in preliminary conversation about interests or hobbies. Don't discuss family or salary unless a Brazilian brings them up.

• Be sure to bring business cards to exchange at your first meeting. Have them printed in Portuguese and English, which can be done in a stationery shop in Brazil in about 24 hours.

• Don't lower your estimate of someone who's sharing an office. Only the most senior businesspeople have private offices.

• Expect to be offered coffee when visiting businesses. You should probably accept, even if you don't finish it. It will be served black and in small cups. Brazilians add a large amount of sugar.

• Have materials you plan to present translated into Portuguese. *Never* use materials in Spanish. Bring enough copies so that they can be distributed to the top people in management.

• Be prepared for Brazilians to be anywhere from 30 minutes to an hour and 15 minutes late for an appointment. If the meeting is very important, they may be only 15 minutes late. People tend to be more punctual in business centers such as Rio, São Paulo, Belo Horizonte, and Pôrto Alegre.

• Don't be surprised if people you're meeting with are often interrupted. Public officials especially deal with many issues and people simultaneously. One way to get around this is to invite your colleague to lunch.

• Expect Brazilian businesspeople to talk constantly; there's no such thing as a moment of thoughtful silence at a Brazilian business meeting.

• Anticipate a great deal of physical contact during a meeting—pushing, tugging, and so on.

• Don't telephone a business associate at home unless he suggests that you do so.

• Foreign businesswomen can have successful dealings with Brazilian businesspeople as long as they act in a professional manner and don't appear aggressive or confrontational.

• If you plan to entertain a client, ask the secretary of a top-level manager to recommend a restaurant. Secretaries will know the type of luxurious restaurant at which Brazilian businesspeople appreciate being entertained.

HOLIDAYS AND SPECIAL OCCASIONS

Expect businesses, banks, and many shops to be closed on the following holidays and on election days, which are considered holidays. Remember that there are many regional holidays; check with the Brazilian tourist office to find out about holidays celebrated only in certain regions. Remember that some shops and businesses close early the day before a holiday and that some holidays are celebrated on the nearest Monday so that people can have a long weekend.

Holidays: New Year's Day (Jan. 1); Epiphany (Jan. 6); Feast of Saint Sebastian (Jan. 20); Carnival (from the Saturday before Lent through Ash Wednesday); Easter; Labor Day (May 1); Ascension Day (40 days after Easter); June Festival (June 24–29); Feast of the Assumption (Aug. 15); Independence Day (Sept. 7); Our Lady of the Apparition (Oct. 12); All Saints' Day (Nov. 1); All Souls' Day (Nov. 2); Declaration of the Republic (Nov. 15); Flag Day (Nov. 19); Christmas (Dec. 25); New Year's Eve (Dec. 31).

• Carnival (*carnaval*) begins on the weekend preceding Ash Wednesday. Though you must book hotel rooms a year in advance, expect only minimal services during the festivities—rooms not cleaned, late breakfast, and so on. Carnival has three main aspects: costume balls, the street carnival held at the Sambódromo in both Rio and São Paulo, and *blocos* (street parades held by residents of city blocks). These are too violent. Tourists should not go.

• Carnival is especially famous for the balls, most of them given by semi-private organizations such as athletic and social clubs. Tourist agencies can arrange an invitation to a private club. The ultra-posh ball is the Municipal Ball, held on the final night of Carnival. The most spectacular event is probably the parade of the *samba* groups, *escolas de samba*, also on the final night. *Escolas de samba* (literally, "*samba* schools") are clubs or groups of dancers and musicians, usually organized by neighborhoods. Each year each *escola* has a special theme for the parade, and its members compose a special song and prepare elaborate costumes to go with the theme. The parade route is lined with judges, police, press, TV and movie crews and ordinary spectators. Each *escola* takes its place in the parade—playing music, chanting, dancing, and marching in a rapture of rhythm and melody. It may take an hour for a single *escola de samba* to pass in front of the judges. The *blocos* are local celebrations and usually not of interest to travelers.

• Try to go to Carnival with a group of people you know. It's not wise to go alone.

• More cautions for Carnival: Don't walk on dark streets or on the beach at night. Don't wear any jewelry, not even costume jewelry. Keep money in your underwear, or wear a money belt. Be wary of thieves and pickpockets.

• Don't attempt to drive in cities during Carnival. There are impromptu parades everywhere, and streets can be blocked for hours.

• On New Year's Eve, expect to see people dressed in white. It's a ritual to touch water at the stroke of midnight. The beaches are filled with people carrying lit candles. At midnight, they launch little rafts with offerings for the goddess of the sea.

TRANSPORTATION

Public Transportation

• At whichever airport you arrive, go to the taxi stand, state your destination, and buy a voucher. The voucher covers your fare, so you have no additional cost but the tip.

• Try to avoid buses in cities. If you don't speak Portuguese, you may not know when to get off. Other problems are the incredible overcrowding and the ever-present pickpockets and chain-snatchers.

• Realize that the bus systems are very complicated. Some require that you purchase electronic tickets beforehand. Some you enter by the front door, some by the rear. Stay away from them unless you're with people who know what they are doing.

• If you're seated on a bus, don't be surprised if standing passengers ask you to hold their bundles—or even their child.

• In all Brazilian cities, look for vans, usually called *perueiros*. They steal passengers from the buses.

• In Rio, São Paulo, Belo Horizonte, Pôrto Alegre, and Recife, consider taking the subway. Both systems are modern, safe and fast, although they go only to limited parts of the cities.

• Note that buses that run between cities are air-conditioned and have bathrooms. They have attendants who serve coffee, and they make stops for food.

• Ask your travel agent about the inexpensive travel pass valid for a few weeks' flying between cities within Brazil. You must buy this pass outside Brazil.

• Note that the trains between Rio and São Paulo are inexpensive and comfortable, and provide dining cars and food service in your compartment.

• Remember that taxis in Rio are more expensive between 10:00 P.M. and 7:00 A.M. Drivers also charge night rates for traveling up steep hills.

• If you're feeling adventurous, especially in the northeast, hire a motorcycle taxi. Just hop in the rear seat.

• Be sure that the taxi driver turns the meter on. Recently the government has been changing fares. If your charge is more than that shown on the meter, the driver must show you the latest charts indicating the increases. Taxis in small towns and rural areas do not have meters. Agree to the fare in advance.

• Note that you can save money by sharing a taxi with several friends. Drivers don't mind.

• If you leave the airport at Manaus to fly to another Brazilian city, remember that you'll have to go through customs. Manaus is a duty-free city.

Driving

• The best advice about driving in Brazil: don't. Take taxis in cities and planes for long-distance trips. Travelers have likened driving in Brazil to "jungle warfare." There are potholes everywhere and there is general disregard of traffic laws.

• Don't drive unless you have a knowledge of Portuguese. It's difficult to find your way, and you'll almost surely have to ask directions.

• If you decide to drive, bring an International Driver's License.

• Remember that front-seat passengers must wear seat belts. If you don't wear them and are stopped, there will be a stiff fine.

• Be aware that people ignore stoplights and stop signs—especially at night, when they're afraid of robbery.

• Remember that drivers—not pedestrians—have the right-of-way.

• Note that only parking lights are used at night in cities. Drivers honk when they see other drivers with their headlights on at night. People sometimes drive at night with no headlights on at all. Brazilians disregard one-way streets. Driving is not policed, and there are few traffic violations.

• Realize that roads between cities are narrow, in bad condition, and filled with truck traffic.

• Always slow down when you enter a town. You may encounter speed bumps.

• Remember that there are no laws regarding passing other cars.

• Expect to see children on every street corner serving as "parking attendants." They will guard your car while you're parked. Give them the equivalent of 25 cents. If they wash your car, give them the equivalent of $1. 00 (total). Adults control this informal parking security.

LEGAL MATTERS, SAFETY, AND HEALTH

• If the police stop you, and you speak English, you will usually be allowed to go. Police do, however, expect formality and deference. If, for any reason, you need to go to the police station, don't wear shorts or grubby clothes.

• Note that Brazil has no liquor laws. The only time liquor isn't sold is when the polls are open for an election.

• Never bring valuables to the beaches. There are signs at the beaches telling you never to leave your car unattended. You'll see little boys asking to guard your car for a small fee. Always hire one.

• In the cities—even if you're just out for a walk—leave jewelry, watches, and money in the hotel safe.

• Women walking alone can expect to hear remarks about them and to be the subject of obvious stares. At Carnival, whether you're alone or in a group, expect to be pinched and grabbed. If such behav-ior bothers you, the only way to avoid it is not to go out. Foreign women traveling alone are very intriguing to Brazilian men. Mainly, there will be staring and flirting. Never go with a man you don't know, and never go into the jungle with only a male guide.

• Drink only bottled water. Even the most remote towns sell mineral water—sparkling (*con gas*) or still (*sem gas*). Accept only bottled water that has a serrated seal, not a cork or top. With a seal, you can be sure that the bottle has not been filled with tap water. Don't have ice in your drinks. Milk sold in plastic bags must be boiled. Milk sold in cardboard cartons does not require refrigeration and is safe without boiling.

• For advice about medicine and hygiene products, see the "Legal Matters, Health, and Safety" section of the Introduction.

CHILE

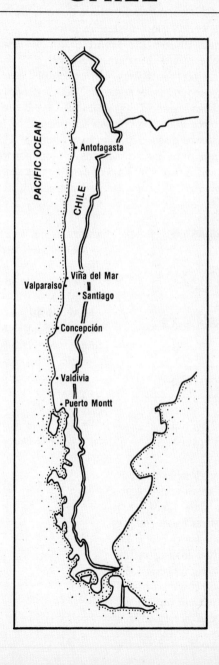

Stretching between the Andes and the Pacific Ocean, and with islands well into the Pacific, Chile offers the visitor destinations as varied as Santiago, with its laid-back urban scene, lakes in the South that rival the beauty of Alaska, the world's driest desert in the North, and Easter Island, one of the world's most mysterious places.

In Santiago, join Chileans in favorite pastimes—eating shellfish and enjoying the excellent wine the country produces.

Even though science, technology, and exploration have solved many of the mysteries of outer and inner space, no one has definitively cracked the riddle of Easter Island, some 2,300 miles off Chile's coast and the most isolated inhabited island on earth. It was "christened" by Jakob Roggeven, the Dutch admiral who discovered it on Easter Sunday, 1722. Visiting the volcanoes, the great stone statues, and the "factory" in which the statues were made, you will realize why Easter Island's enigmas provoke pilgrimages by anthropologists, archeologists, and adventurous travelers.

GREETINGS

Language: The official language of Chile is Spanish.

• Expect men to shake hands with other men when they are introduced. After they know each other well, they shake hands and pat one another on the back.

• Remember that kissing in the air, right cheek to right cheek is the standard greeting between men and women and women and women, especially at a social occasion. If a woman is not sure whether a man intends to greet her with a kiss, she should offer her hand to be shaken. She will usually end up with a kiss as well.

• At a small party, greet each person individually. At a large party, simply say "Hello" to the group as a whole. When saying good-bye at a social gathering, the standard practice is to kiss everyone at the party.

• Note that the only title regularly used is *Doctor*—for a medical doctor.

CONVERSATION

• As a conversation opener, ask about families, children, and the like. However, don't ask people their occupation. Wait for them to volunteer that information.

• Ask advice about what to see and do, where to eat, and so forth. Chileans enjoy helping others enjoy their country.

• Before visiting Chile, learn about the country's background. Chileans really appreciate foreigners having some knowledge of the country. Businesspeople should make a special point of learning about Chile's economy. Chileans enjoy discussing their exports, of which they're very proud. Chileans are very proud of the country's reputation as the "Tiger of South America," earned because of the unparalleled growth of their economy in the 90s.

• Try not to be offended by negative comments about personal appearance. Chileans may comment on your weight, or they may say that they don't like your haircut. Rather than respond, just ignore the comments.

• Keep in mind that many Chilean businesspeople have traveled abroad. If you have traveled, bring up the places you've visited. It's a good way to establish rapport.

• Avoid any references to politics, especially issues relating to human rights.

TELEPHONES

• Look for telephone booths on main streets in cities. A call from a pay phone requires a $1.00 coin or a phone card. When the time is up, you'll hear a buzzing. Deposit more money or a phone card with more time available or the call will be cut off.

• Buy phone cards at the airport or at street-corner kiosks. However, be aware that there are several different phone companies in Chile (CTS, Teléfonica, Manquehue, and Entel, to name a few), and their phone cards are not interchangeable.

• If you can't find a phone booth and you're making a local call, ask to use the telephone in a bar. If you don't want to do that (or the bartender says "no"), go to a Compañía de Teléfonos, where you can make local calls.

• To make a long-distance call, go to a telephone office. Phone cards can also be used to make long-distance or international calls, but the rates are much higher than those at a phone-company office. There are several long-distance carriers, and their rates are all different. One is Bell South; its operator can be reached by dialing 181–182 from any local Santiago phone.

• Note that most long-distance operators are bilingual.

• Realize that when Chileans answer the phone, they say "Alo" or "Hola" (Hello).

• In an emergency, call the police at 133. They will direct your call to another department, such as the fire department or the ambulance service, if necessary.

IN PUBLIC

• Be careful to avoid any behavior that could be interpreted as aggressive. Chileans, who emphasize respecting people and never hurting anyone, regard aggressive actions as very rude.

• Some gestures to note: (1) Palm up with fingers separated means stupid. (2) Clenched right first slapping the open palm of the left hand is obscene. (3) A driver sticking his hand out the window and holding it as though he's holding an apple is also making an obscene gesture. (4) Right fist raised to the level of the head is a Communist sign (*not* recommended).

• Don't be surprised if there's a long wait to change money in banks. People pay their bills there.

• To mail a package to an address outside Chile, bring string and wrapping paper to the post office. Don't wrap the package first, since the clerk must check to see what's in it. After the clerk has checked the contents, you wrap the package and the clerk puts sealing wax on it. To avoid the long wait that this process entails, ask for a courier at your hotel and pay for him to take care of the mailing.

• Never photograph strikes or street demonstrations. The most likely dates for such events are May 1 and September 11.

• Don't try to bargain, even at markets or with street vendors. If you buy a great deal in one store, you may ask for a discount—but expect it to be minimal. Every time you buy something, ask for a receipt. The shop owner may say, "I'll give you a discount and *no* receipt." He then won't have to report the sale for taxes; however, both the shop owner and the customer would be fined for such a transaction. You have to choose whether or not to break the law.

• Look for public bathrooms in hotels and restaurants, at train and bus stations, and at airports. Always bring your own tissues, since there may not be toilet paper in public bathrooms. If there is a wastebasket next to the toilet, put the used paper in it. If there is no wastebasket, flush the paper down the toilet.

DRESS

• When planning your wardrobe, remember that Chile has extremes of heat and cold, depending on the altitude. Temperatures vary tremendously during the day year-round, as the sun is so very strong. It is not unusual for it to be 50°F (10°C) at 7:00 A.M. and 86°F (30°C) at 3:00 P.M. in the same city. As soon as the sun goes down, rapid cooling takes over.

• For business and social occasions men should wear a conservative suit of good quality. Never wear a sports jacket. Don't wear anything in the lapel. Women should wear a suit and heels for business.

• Note that men put their jackets

on every time they leave the office—even for lunch.

• On weekends, expect to see Chilean men and women wearing good jeans for shopping, errands, and the like; they don't, however, wear shorts.

• If invited to dinner, men should wear a suit and tie and women a dress.

• For elegant restaurants, men must wear a tie, and women should wear a dress.

• Note that formal dress is rarely worn, even for weddings. If an occasion is formal, the invitation will so state. Men should wear a dark suit and women an elegant black cocktail dress.

MEALS

Hours and Food

Breakfast: Between 7:00 and 9:00 A.M. It's usually a light meal—instant coffee or tea with milk, and toast. Some people have larger breakfasts, e.g., ham and eggs. It's not unusual for Chileans to eat breakfast in bed.

Lunch: 1:30 P.M. until about 3:30 P.M. Expect several courses: the meal opens with soup or an avocado half or *empanadas* (turnovers filled with meat, cheese, or seafood); the main course may be steak, seafood (clams, mussels, oysters, or abalone), or a meat dish such as *cazuela* (chicken, corn, and squash cooked together); lentils and mashed potatoes are popular side dishes; fruit or ice cream for dessert.

• At 5:00 or 6:00 P.M. comes a snack called *once*, featuring cheese, toast, cookies, and tea or coffee.

Dinner: Usually at 9:00 P.M. The meal will be similar to lunch. After dinner, you'll be offered a demitasse of instant coffee and a selection of herbed teas (mint, anise, chamomile).

Beverages: Typical drinks before dinner: *vaina* (a sweet wine beaten up with eggs, sugar, and cinnamon)—regarded as a "sissy" drink and offered only to women; *pisco* sour (*pisco* is a liquor made from grapes); *pisco* and Coke (called *piscola* and considered a lower-class drink); gin and tonic. With meals, men usually drink wine—sometimes beer—while women have soft drinks. It's acceptable for foreign women to have one glass of wine, but no more.

• Other beverages served with meals are juice or soda. Don't drink the juice if water or ice has been added. Don't ask for water. People will regard you as strange.

• In the South, expect to be offered *yerba mate* after dinner to aid digestion. It is a ground herb that steeps in a cup or gourd and is sipped through a metal straw/strainer.

• Note that whiskey is rarely drunk before a meal, but it is always offered as an after-dinner drink. Men often drink whiskey and expect foreign businessmen to do the same, because Chileans regard whiskey drinking as a sign of sophistication.

• Expect to find Coke, Fanta, and Sprite available in Chile.

• Remember that *café con leche* is made by pouring hot milk into a cup that has a single spoonful of coffee in it. *Té con leche* is a small amount of tea with hot milk.

Table Manners

• At a dinner party, expect little snacks such as olives, pickles, and chips with pre-dinner drinks. It's also likely that bread will be served both before and during dinner.

• Anticipate receiving your plate with the food already on it or for service to be buffet style.

• If the dinner is a formal one, never eat anything with your hands. "Finger food" is never served on formal occasions. On all occasions, eat fruit with a knife and fork.

• After the first drink has been poured, expect a toast. One person makes a few comments in honor of the host or the occasion, and glasses are raised while everyone says "Salud" [sah-**lood**] (health). Make eye contact with everyone at the table when glasses are raised.

• Try to force yourself to eat at least a bit of what is served even if you don't care for it. Many Chileans don't understand health food fanatics, vegetarians, and the like. They will be understanding if a medical problem or allergy prevents you from trying something.

• If you're serving another person wine, don't do it with your left hand.

• If asked to pass the salt, never hand it directly to a person. That gesture is considered terrible luck. Put the salt down on the table within the person's reach.

• Don't offer to help clear the table or do the dishes, since most middle-class families have a maid.

• When leaving a party or dinner, spend about ten minutes talking and saying good-bye. Don't just dash out the door.

Eating Out

• Note that Santiago has many foreign restaurants: Chinese, Italian, Mexican, Indian, and Brazilian. You'll also find fast-food spots and vegetarian restaurants. There are many restaurants which serve only *parrilladas* (barbecued cuts of beef and sausages, which may include heart, stomach, intestines, and blood sausages).

• Be aware that *fuentes de soda* (soda fountains) serve juices, soda, and sometimes beer. The lower the class of the soda fountain the more alcoholic beverages they offer.

• Avoid small, sleazy bars. In better neighborhoods you'll find pubs (that's what they're called). Most sell only drinks but some offer *empanadas* or small sandwiches. Often they feature a singer or a play.

• For the best food in small cities and towns, go to a hotel restaurant.

• Note that many five-star hotels have been built in central Santiago, so you need not feel restricted about seeking out one of the excellent restaurants in the area at night.

• Expect to find on the table *ají* (tiny, fiery peppers) as well as *pebre* (a mixture of tomatoes, onions, oil, cilantro, and chili, which is spread on bread).

• Don't join people you don't know at their table, except in fast-food restaurants.

• Be aware that you must pay extra for vegetables, potatoes, lettuce, tomato, and mayonnaise, or extra rolls.

• To attract the waiter's attention, say "Garzón." You may see people clapping to summon the waiter, but Chileans regard that action as rude.

• In ordering wine, remember that *vino blanco* (**blahn**-coh) is white wine, *vino tinto* (**teen**-toh) is red, *seco* (**seh**-coh) is dry, and *dulce* (**duhl**-seh) is sweet.

• Don't be surprised to see minors drinking alcohol. The legal age drinking age is 18, but that limit is never enforced.

• If you order *café*, you'll be served Nescafé. To get brewed coffee, ask for *café café*.

• If you're on business and invited to a meal by a Chilean businessperson, realize that he or she pays. If you issue the invitation, you pay.

• Remember that one person pays for the group even at a friendly dinner. Those who are treated should reciprocate later, since it's unlikely that the person who paid will allow you to pay him your part of the bill. Splitting the check is very unusual and is called "American treat."

Specialties

• Try some of Chile's most popular foods: *caldillo de congrio*, the country's national dish—a soup with conger eel, potatoes, and onions; *humitas*—ground corn, wrapped in corn husks and boiled; *pastel de choclo*—ground corn, meat or chicken, onion, boiled eggs, and raisins baked in the oven; *cazuela de ave*—a casserole of chicken, corn, rice, green beans, pumpkin, carrots and herbs; *bistec a lo pobre*—grilled steak with fried potatoes and sautéed onions, served with fried eggs on top; *sopaipillas*—fried pumpkin fritters, usually eaten in winter.

• Sample some of Chile's many famous seafood and fish treats: *albacora*—swordfish; *camarones*—shrimp; *centolla*—king crab; *cholgas*—mussels; *choritos*—small mussels; *congrio*—conger eel, grilled,

baked, fried, or stewed; *corvina*—sea bass, considered the best quality fish; *erizos*—sea urchins, which are about the size of tennis balls, served raw with chopped onion, parsley, ground pepper, salt, and oil (each urchin has a miniature crab attached to it; Chileans like to pop these into their mouths—live; if you would like to eat *erizos* this way, ask that the crab be left on); *gambas*—large deep-water shrimp; *langostas*—large spiny lobsters served broiled or boiled with butter and lemon; *langostinos*—small rock lobsters, usually broiled; *locos*—a type of abalone, resembling fat clams and served cold in salads with mayonnaise, baked, or in a stew called *chupe de locos; machas*—razor clams, eaten raw with lemon or *machas a la parmesano*—baked with grated Parmesan cheese; *curanto*—mixed grilled seafood.

• Salads (*ensaladas*) are usually cold vegetables with oil and lemon—e.g., chopped peeled tomatoes and onions with coriander, oil, and vinegar. Lettuce is not often an ingredient.

• Many Chilean seafoods (such as sea urchins) have a very strong iodine taste and are always described as an "acquired taste." Chileans are not offended if you don't want to taste them or don't like them.

HOTELS

• Note that you'll find hotels in the top international class only in Santiago and Valparaíso/Viña del Mar. There are good hotels in medium-size cities also. In smaller towns, there are fewer hotels and fewer amenities, but the warmth and hospitality of the smaller hotels may compensate for the absence of luxuries. For example, don't be surprised if the manager has dinner with the guests.

• At upper to middle-end hotels, expect room service, swimming pools, international cable TV, laundry service, and shopping galleries.

• For the least expensive accommodations, stay at a *hospedaje* (ohs-peh-**dah**-heh), a family house with a few rooms for rent, always with hot water and often including breakfast in the room price. Family and guest share a sitting room. *Hospedajes* vary greatly in comfort.

• A *residencial* is a small hotel, often including breakfast in the price. Amenities are basic: a bed, sheets and blankets, a table, a chair. Some have heat; some don't. Many have

hot water, but in the south you'll have to pay for it.

• *Pensiones* offer better amenities and higher standards than *hospedajes* or *residenciales*. Often there's a restaurant, and you'll usually have a private shower and toilet.

• Realize that a motel in Chile is only for lovers, unless it's called a *motel de turismo*.

• In the Lake District, look for chalets, generally run by people of German descent. They have pools, hot water, and restaurants.

• If you plan to stay in a youth hostel, *hostería*, note that for some you need only an International Youth Hostel card, but in others you'll need a Chilean Youth Hostel card. Hostels are usually open only in January and February and sometimes in March.

• Make reservations well in advance for the peak season (Dec. through March) in the coastal resort areas. If you visit the resorts between mid-March and mid-November, ask for off-season rates.

• Don't leave valuables in hotel rooms. Many have locks which don't function; in the south, many don't have locks at all.

• Feel free to ask for extra blankets, even in budget accommodations.

TIPPING

- Tip taxi drivers 10 percent.
- Tip gas station attendants 100 to 200 *pesos*.
- Because of high unemployment, people will offer to wash your windshield, show you where to pull over when you're parking, or guard your car. Tip these people 100 to 200 *pesos*.
- At a movie theater, where you choose your seat when you buy the ticket, tip the usher 100 to 200 *pesos*. At other movie theaters, where seating is unreserved, there's no need to tip.

PRIVATE HOMES

- Don't drop in on people you don't know well. If possible, telephone in advance.
- If you're invited to dinner at someone's home, always arrive 10 to 15 minutes late. If you're invited to a party, come 30 minutes late.
- Don't make dinner plans if you're invited to drinks at a home. Usually you'll be expected to stay to dinner.
- When invited to a meal, send flowers to the hostess in advance or bring a box of chocolates. People don't often bring wine, since it's so inexpensive in Chile. If you're invited to a large party, bring a bottle of whiskey. If you're invited to *once* (afternoon tea), bring pastries or a cake.
- Note that in most Chilean homes TV sets are in the bedrooms. If you become very friendly with someone, you may be invited to the bedroom to watch TV. This is an entirely innocent gesture and has no sexual connotations.
- A woman should not put her purse on the floor. There is a super-

stition that if she does so she will lose all her money.

• Never walk around barefoot in a home.

• If someone has had you to dinner, call and say "Thank you" before leaving the country. Written thank-you notes are not common.

• When staying with a family, adapt to their schedule (getting up when they do, adhering to their meal schedules) and try to participate in activities they invite you to join. If your visit is a long one, bring some token of appreciation—e.g., flowers, a cake—every three days or so.

• If there is no maid and you're staying with a family for a few days, offer to help with setting and clearing the table and doing the dishes.

• Feel free to take a daily shower. Most people shower in the morning; some also shower and change before dinner. Many homes have constant hot water, but some don't. Ask your hostess if the water needs to be heated before showering. There may also be a bidet in the bathroom.

• If you make long-distance calls, be sure to pay for them. When you place the call, tell the operator that you want to know the cost at the at the end of the call, and she'll call back and let you know.

• Should you be home alone when the postman arrives, be aware that he expects a tip of two or three *pesos* per letter. (If no one is home, he will leave the mail but will expect to be tipped the next day.)

• Leave the maid money after asking your hostess if the gesture is appropriate and also how much to leave.

• If you're invited to stay on a farm, be prepared for facilities to be primitive, i.e., no hot water, outdoor toilets. Some farms, however, have very modern facilities.

Gifts: Good gifts are leather appointment books and photo albums, calculators (especially those that store messages), good quality pens, cigarette lighters, or whiskey.

• Don't give yellow roses. They signify scorn or contempt.

• For a girl's fifteenth birthday, give gold or silver jewelry. Don't give costume jewelry—Chileans wear only the real thing.

BUSINESS

Hours

Businesses: 9:00 A.M. to 5:00 P.M., Monday through Friday.

Government Offices: 9:00 A.M. to 4:30 P.M., Monday through Friday.

Banks: 9:00 A.M. to 2:00 P.M., Monday through Friday.

Shops: 10:00 A.M. to 7:00 P.M., Monday through Friday; and 10:00 A.M. to 2:00 P.M. on Saturday.

In large cities, shops are open on Sunday. All malls are open seven days a week, usually from 10:00 A.M. to 9:00 P.M.

Currency

• The unit of currency is the *peso*, whose sign is $.

• Coin: 1, 5, 50, and 10 *pesos*.

• Notes: 500, 1,000, 5,000, 10,000, and 20,000 *pesos*.

• Remember that you can change travelers' checks at a bank only up to 12:00 noon. Hotels and *cambios*, which give better rates than banks, will change such checks later.

• Expect to find ATM machines all over Chile in supermarkets, malls, banks, etc. Look for RED-BANC signs. If your Visa or MasterCard is programmed for use at an ATM, you can take money out without having to worry about exchanging dollars or travelers' checks. (Note: To be on the safe side, don't rely entirely on ATMs. Some travelers have reported having their card rejected by ATMs in other countries.)

Business Practices

• Realize that Chileans take summer holidays in January and February; avoid making business trips during that time.

• For excellent (and free) information about doing business in Chile, write to the Economic Department of the Chilean Embassy in your country.

• Note that if you're dealing with a franchise of an international company you will need to plan fewer trips to Chile than if you are dealing with a Chilean firm.

• Make appointments with businesses or government offices at least two weeks in advance.

• Create a good impression by staying in one of the best hotels.

• Expect to find fax machines in most hotels.

• Using business cards in English is acceptable; however, be sure to put the telephone number of your hotel on the card, so that business colleagues can reach you.

• Keep in mind that in most cases people in top management speak English; Chilean businesspeople are sophisticated and are usually of English, German, Italian, or Spanish descent. If you should need an interpreter, ask at your country's embassy in Santiago. Embassy staff will also be helpful in finding legal advisors for you. Your need for an interpreter will depend on whether you're dealing with a multinational or a Chilean firm.

• Schedule business appointments during the hours 10:00 A.M. to 12:30 P.M. and 2:30 to 5:00 P.M.

• In general, be punctual for business appointments, though it's acceptable to be 15 minutes late.

• Don't be surprised to find businesspeople working long hours—until 7:00 or 8:00 P.M. The more senior a person is or the more responsible her/his job, the later they will get to work in the morning, the longer their lunch hour, and the later they will stay at the office. Senior management doesn't usually leave the office until 9:00 P.M.

• Note that people working in most major urban areas do not go home to lunch; however, they may have a two-hour lunch in a restaurant.

• Remember that the first meeting is an introduction to discuss your company and your position. Most of the time will be spent in nonbusiness conversation. Since most businesspeople ski or fish (the south of Chile is world famous for its trout and salmon), bring up these sports if you know about them. Another good subject at a business meeting is Chilean wines, which are well known in many countries.

• Be sure to inquire about your Chilean counterpart's family.

• Never use "hard sell" techniques. Chileans are conservative and won't react well to them.

• Expect Chilean businesspeople to value truth and honesty. For example, if a product is inferior they want to know why.

• Note that business decisions are usually made by the few people at the top of an organization.

• Realize that major business deals are always finalized in a formal business setting, not in a restaurant or at the golf course as happens in some countries. Be sure to reconfirm any appointment close to the date of the closing of the deal.

• Don't forget that the *worst* offense to a Chilean is the offer of a bribe.

• Women should realize that they can be successful doing business in Chile, since women there are very advanced professionally. Women will be taken seriously without having to be aggressive to prove that they're professional. They will find *machismo* much less blatant than in other Latin American countries.

• Note that Chileans are very open about inviting visiting foreigners to their homes for a meal.

• If you've been to a family's home and return to Chile two or three times, bring toys for the children. The family will appreciate your remembering the sexes and ages of the children.

• Don't expect spouses to be included in a business lunch. For business dinners that are primarily social, it's okay to include foreign and Chilean spouses. (If you've been invited and aren't sure the occasion is social, ask your host.)

• If you want to invite Chileans to a business lunch, ask them to suggest a restaurant. For a dinner, entertain at your hotel's restaurant.

The top hotels in Santiago have outstanding restaurants.

HOLIDAYS AND SPECIAL OCCASIONS

Expect banks, businesses, government offices, many stores, and many restaurants to be closed on the following national holidays. Check with the tourist office to learn about the regional holidays in areas you'll be visiting.

Holidays: New Year's Day (Jan. 1); Good Friday and Easter Sunday; Labor Day (May 1); Battle of Iquique, honoring Chilean hero Arturo Pratt (May 21); Feast of the Assumption (Aug. 15); Day of National Unity (first Monday in September); Independence Day (Sept. 18); Armed Forces Day (Sept. 19); Columbus Day (Oct. 12); All Saints' Day (Nov. 1); Feast of the Immaculate Conception (Dec. 8); Christmas (Dec. 25).

• Watch out for protests on September 11, the anniversary of the 1973 coup.

• Join the Independence Day celebrations on September 18. *Fondas,* stands decorated with leaves, are installed in public parks, where crowds congregate to celebrate and eat *empanadas* (meat turnovers), drink *chicha* (a drink made of fermented grapes), and dance the *cueca* (the national folk dance) to the accompaniment of guitars.

• Two religious celebrations to remember: on November 1, people visit the graves of relatives. On Friday and Saturday in Holy Week, people eat only fish and shellfish—no meat.

TRANSPORTATION

Public Transportation

• On buses, enter from the front. City buses require exact change. Keep your ticket for the inspector who will get on. He will rip your ticket in half and return half to you. Should the bus be in an accident, you'll need your ticket to prove you were on the bus and thus get reimbursed for medical costs.

• Consider taking the subway in Santiago. It's clean, quiet, and the least expensive way to travel. Buy a ticket from a seller in a booth. You can also purchase a multiple-fare ticket for the subway. The fare depends on the time of day. If there is money left on your ticket, it will pop up from the machine after you go through, and you can use it again until the fare you paid for is used up. The subway runs every four minutes from 6:30 A.M. to 10:30 P.M., Monday through Saturday; and 8:00 A.M. to 10:30 P.M. on Sundays and holidays.

• Outside Santiago, look on the windshield of the taxi to find charges displayed there. If you use a nonmetered cab, ask your concierge what to expect to pay, and agree on this amount with the driver before taking the taxi.

• Note that taxis in Santiago, which are black with yellow roofs, run on meters. Don't negotiate ahead of time. Tourist taxis, found at major hotels, tend to charge higher fares. *Do* negotiate the fare first, since there are no meters. *Colectivos* look like the black and yellow taxis, but they have numbers on the roof. They run specially designated routes and often pick up as many passengers as will fit in the car. There's a 50 percent surcharge for rides after 9:00 P.M. and on Sunday.

• Be aware that there is train service only from Santiago south, none to the north. There are four classes: super salon, the most expensive, has carpets, blankets, pillows, reclining seats, and meal service at your seat;

salon provides reserved seats and reclining chairs, but you must go to the dining car to eat; first class offers reserved seats; second class has no reserved seats and is very crowded, usually with people standing in the aisles.

• Think about taking a bus for long-distance travel. Buses usually have numbered seats, toilets, and (sometimes) attendants who serve tea and coffee. Special sleeper buses, *bus cama* (boos cah-mah), also have reclining seats and foot rests. These buses, available only for long journeys, cost twice as much as ordinary buses, but the comforts may be worth the price. The fare includes the price of alcoholic and nonalcoholic beverages, dinner, and breakfast—and, usually, movies.

• Note that on short trips you may have to stand in the aisle. In January and February (the vacation period) and on weekends and holidays, buses are packed.

Driving

• If your stay is only in Santiago, use taxis. You might want to rent a car for traveling around the country, however. Chile is an easy country to drive in. However, if you have an accident while driving and a pedestrian is injured, you will be arrested, regardless of who was at fault. (Chile's legal system is based on the Napoleonic code—you are guilty until proven innocent.)

• Be aware that seat belts are required for every passenger for whom a seat belt is available. If the passengers aren't wearing seat belts, the *driver* will be fined.

• Be especially careful not to drink and drive on weekends. Police sometimes stop cars to give breathalyzer tests to the driver. If you're drunk, you'll have to leave your car, you'll be detained by the police, and you'll have to pay a fine.

• Never try to bribe the *Carbineros* (traffic police). They have a reputation for the highest integrity.

LEGAL MATTERS, SAFETY, AND HEALTH

• Realize that you aren't allowed to bring *any* fruit into Chile (a precaution to prevent the spread of insects) nor to transport fruit from the north of Chile to the south.

• Stay away from street demonstrations. Don't let curiosity move you to see what is happening. All such demonstrations have political motives, and police are known to arrest everyone on the scene.

• Note that the risk of theft is minor. Nevertheless, don't be careless with money or possessions. Pickpockets are a problem in downtown Santiago. Be alert. Don't stroll around alone when everything is closed. Avoid the Plaza de Armas and Santa Lucia Hill.

• Women should travel accompanied if possible, although in general women should not expect unwarranted, persistent advances. As a precaution, women should not wear jewelry when traveling.

• Be aware that some water in Chile has a high bacteria level. To be safe, drink only bottled water with an intact seal. Don't have ice in your drink or juices to which water has been added.

• If you are going to any of the high-altitude locales (e.g., the ski resort Portillo, which is at 9,300 feet), take precautions against altitude sickness. Eat very lightly for your first few days in the area, avoid alcoholic beverages, and don't smoke.

• Realize that some of the beaches in Chile have dangerous riptides. Be sure to ask about any beach you are planning to visit, and be sure to let someone know where you will be.

• For advice on medicine and hygiene products, see "Legal Matters, Safety, and Health" in the Introduction.

COLOMBIA

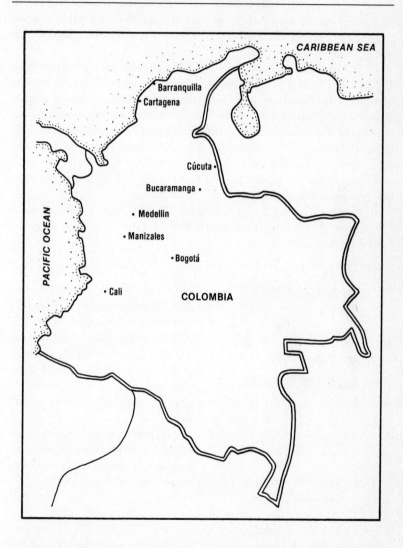

In no other country in Latin America will behaving correctly be so important as in Colombia, where you'll find courtly and traditional behavior, especially in Bogotá. You will also notice a kind of reserve. Don't interpret this formality as aloofness toward a foreigner—Colombians are very reserved with one another. The level of formality depends on the region. In Cali, for example, people tend to be outgoing and not so reserved.

Besides tasting hand-picked Colombian coffee, you can browse through jewelry shops and possibly pick up one of the country's famous emeralds. Or you can visit Bogotá's stunning Gold Museum, with the world's largest collections of pre-Columbian gold, where you most definitely *can't* pick up one of the artifacts.

In September, 1999, the U.S. State Department issued a warning to U.S. citizens, strongly suggesting that they not travel to Colombia because of violence by narcotraffickers, guerrillas, paramilitary groups, and other criminal elements. Citizens of the U.S. and other countries have been victims of threats, kidnapping, domestic airline hijackings, and murders. U.S. citizens planning to visit Colombia should check with the U.S. State Department prior to departure.

Colombia has the world's highest kidnapping rate, with three people a day getting kidnapped.

If you decide to pay a visit to Bogotá, allow yourself time to adjust to the altitude (8,600 feet). Your energy level, blood pressure, and digestion can be aversely affected.

GREETINGS

Language: The official language of Colombia is Spanish.

• Expect men to shake hands with other men and with women. Women clasp one another's forearms; they don't shake hands.

• Among good friends, both men and men and women and women kiss on one cheek. Sometimes good men friends embrace and pat one another on the back.

• Remember that titles are extremely important to Colombians, as they are very conscious of social class. Anyone who has a university degree should be addressed as *Doctor*.

• At parties, expect the hostess to introduce you to others individually. When you leave, say good-bye to each person.

Conversation

• Before you visit Colombia, learn something about Colombian history, art, and literature—and also about soccer.

• Don't make negative remarks

about bullfighting; Colombians regard it as an art.

• To be safe (especially in business conversations), discuss emeralds and coffee. Colombia is a world-class producer of both.

• Never bring up terrorism or illegal drugs.

• Avoid discussing politics, a delicate subject. Businesspeople should be especially wary of political topics.

Telephone

• Note that Colombia's phone system is very modern. However, public phones are frequently broken or don't work.

• To make a call from a public phone, deposit one *peso*, which allows you three minutes. A tone will sound when it's time to deposit more.

• Remember that it's much less expensive to call Colombia from abroad than vice versa. If possible arrange to have people from home call you rather than your calling them. Businesspeople may want to have their offices call them at regular intervals.

• If you have to make a long-distance call, go to a TELECOM office. Go to the counter where you'll be assigned a cabin. Pay after the call. You can make long-distance calls from most hotels, but, before you do, inquire whether there's a surcharge and if so, how much.

• Look for long-distance pay phones outside most TELECOM of-

fices and at airports and bus stations. If you want to use one, have a supply of 50-*peso* coins.

• Expect people to say "¡A ver!"

• When making a business call, never plunge right into business discussions. First, ask how the other person is, and make small talk.

IN PUBLIC

• Don't expect people to wait politely in line—for example, for a bus. You'll have to join the pushing match if you want a place.

• If you're smoking, always offer others in your group a cigarette.

• Some gestures to know about: (1) Tapping the elbow with your hand says that the person you're talking to or about is "stingy." (2) Holding one hand palm down while the other hand makes a sawing motion across it suggests making a deal with the intention of sharing the profits. (3) To indicate the height of a person, hold your palm flat and sideways with the thumb up. The flat palm held downward is used only to show the height of animals. (4) To beckon someone, hold your arm out in front of you, palm down, and move your fingers in a scratching motion.

• Keep in mind that people will hardly ever respond negatively to a request for a favor or to an invitation, whether or not they have any thought of doing the favor or coming to the party. You can often pick up cues from the Colombians. (For example, if you invite people to dinner, they may say, "We'll try to come," meaning that they don't intend to.) Only experience will teach you what people mean. Never pressure anyone for a firm commitment, however. Colombians regard directness by foreigners toward them as insensitive.

• When visiting churches, don't photograph using a flash.

• Feel free to bargain in artisan shops and markets, but not in upscale shops.

• In a shop, if you're paying with cash, rather than a credit card, ask for a 5 to 10 percent discount.

• Note that public toilets are scarce. You'll find them in hotels, restaurants, and shopping malls. In small towns, the bathrooms are not clean and often lack toilet paper. Bring tissues with you. At airports, women stand outside the public toilets selling toilet paper for ten *pesos*.

DRESS

• Remember that Colombians judge people by how they look and how well they are dressed.

• For business, men should wear a dark suit and tie, and women should wear a suit or a dress. Men should arrive for a business meeting wearing a jacket, no matter how hot it is. They will probably be invited to remove it immediately.

• Don't wear shorts on the street or when visiting churches. If you wear jeans, be sure that they are stylish and clean. Never wear grubby jeans.

• In small towns and villages women may wear pants, dresses, or skirts.

• When invited to a meal in someone's home, men should wear a suit and tie and women a skirt or dress.

• The major occasions for formal wear are weddings and graduation parties. The invitation will specify formal dress.

• In the countryside, expect people to wear woolen ponchos, called *ruanas*. In the cities, people sometimes wear them in their houses.

MEALS

Hours and Foods

Breakfast: Not usually a family meal in Colombian homes. Each person eats according to her or his personal schedule. If there is a maid, she prepares breakfast, and will probably offer juice, fruit, eggs, butter, jam, pastry, and coffee. Soup is sometimes served at breakfast. Try *arepas*, which are like pita bread; they are made with ground corn mixed with salt, water, cheese, eggs, milk, and butter, then shaped into small round cakes and pan fried or deep fried.

Lunch: 12:30 or 1:00 P.M. until 2:00 or 2:30 P.M. It's the most important family meal; husbands return from work for it. There will be several courses: soup, a main course of meat with vegetables, rice (a staple served every day), dessert (a home-made sweet), and finally black coffee in a demitasse. Fruit juices and milk are the usual beverages with meals.

Dinner: About 7:00 P.M. In some homes dinner is much the same as lunch but without soup. In other homes, it's a very light meal— soup, toast, fruit, and coffee. While wine is often served at dinners for guests, it's not typically served at a family meal.

Beverages: Local liquors include rum and *aguardiente* (both made from sugarcane). *Aguardiente* is served straight in small glasses. It tastes like "fire water," which is roughly what its name means.

• Colombians make delicious fruit juices with fresh fruit blended and mixed with water—e.g., blackberry, guava, papaya. Avoid these drinks unless you're absolutely certain that they have been made with bottled water.

• Don't drink anything with ice in it, since the ice is made with tap water. If you're eating in an upscale hotel or restaurant, ask if bottled water has been used to make ice or for the fresh fruit drinks.

• Another popular beverage, hot chocolate, is made with hot milk and chocolate bars. To order this drink in a cafe, ask for a *submarino*. You will get hot milk and two sticks of chocolate to stir into the milk.

• Colombian coffee is mild. The small cup of black coffee, the national drink, is called *tinto* (**teen**-toh); coffee with milk is called *café périco* (kah-**feh** peh-ree-koh); a cup of milk with a little coffee added is called *café con leche* (kah-**feh** kon **leh**-cheh).

Table Manners

• When you're invited to a meal in a home, expect several drinks to be offered—mainly Scotch, vodka, gin, port, or sherry. Wine is rarely served before meals. If you don't drink, ask for soda water. At the meal itself, there will probably be wine since a meal for guests is a special occasion (Colombians don't usually drink alcoholic beverages with meals). If you don't want to drink the wine, take one small sip and leave it. If you drink the wine, it's polite to compliment your host on it after the first sip.

• Note that little snacks (e.g., olives, ham, and cheese) will be served with before-dinner drinks.

• Anticipate receiving a plate with food already on it, though in some homes service is family style.

• Don't worry about highly spiced food; Colombian food isn't. If hot sauce is used, it's served separately. However, food tends to be very salty.

• To be polite, leave a small amount of food on your plate to show that you are not ravenously hungry.

• To indicate that you've finished, place your eating utensils horizontally across your plate.

• After dinner at a home during the week, stay until 10:00 P.M. If the dinner is on the weekend, stay until 11:00 or 11:30. If you're invited to a dancing party in a home, expect it to last from about 11:00 P.M. to 5:00 A.M.

Eating Out

• A *café concierto* is a cafe with music (e.g., guitar). You can have drinks, coffee, and light snacks.

• Don't expect to find menus posted in restaurant windows.

• Realize that in a good restaurant, there will be three to four waiters per table. To attract their attention, just raise your hand or make eye contact.

• Remember that wine can be very expensive, since Colombia doesn't produce wine, and it must be imported. Local beer is, however, good.

• At lunchtime, try an *almuerzo executivo* (executive lunch), an option offered by many restaurants. It includes soup, rice, beans and meat, a lettuce and tomato salad, and a beverage for a very reasonable price.

• When you go to a nightclub not in your hotel, take only as much money as you need, be careful not to drink too much, and pay as soon as you're served.

Specialties

• Rice is a staple, to the extent that many homes have electric rice-makers.

• Some main-course specialties: *tamales*—a meat mixture stuffed into ground corn dough, wrapped in banana leaves and boiled; *bandeja paisa*—shredded beef with rice, black beans, and plantains; *sancocho*—chicken, meat, or fish and vegetable stew; *sobrebarriga*—rolled flank steak, stuffed and breaded; *le-chona*—suckling pig; *puchero bogo-tano*—boiled beef, vegetables, and potatoes; *ajiaco*—a sort of stew, made with corn, chicken, white and yellow potatoes, onion, bay leaves, and coriander, served with side dishes of cream, capers, and avocado.

• Also try: *mogollas*—whole wheat rolls; *almojábanas*—corn muffins; *cuajada con melado*—fresh farmer's cheese covered with molasses.

• At the coast, try one of their specialties: *arroz con coco*—rice with coconut, usually served with grilled fish.

• Good choices for dessert: guava paste with milk; *manjar blanco*—soft toffee made with milk, sugar, and spices.

HOTELS

• Remember that on the Caribbean coast, high season is from December 15 to April 30 and June 15 to August 31.

• Note that the top hotels are equivalent to those in Europe in the excellence of the accommodations and service. Reserve at them well in advance because hotels in Bogotá and on the Caribbean coast are often fully booked.

• Be aware that the downtown section of Bogotá is not safe. Even though there are top hotels there, it is better to stay in hotels in the more residential area where many embassies are located. The district is about 15 minutes by taxi from downtown.

• Realize that only deluxe hotels have central heating; however, it's usually not cold enough so that you'll need it.

• In many hotels in small towns, prepare to pay for a room plus meals. There won't be a refund if you miss any meals. However, food is so inexpensive that the additional cost shouldn't be a problem.

• Expect private bathrooms in most hotels except the least expensive. Only more expensive hotels and hotels in colder areas of the country will have hot water.

• Consider bringing a plug for the sinks, since most inexpensive hotels won't have them.

• If you're going into the Amazon area, bring a small flashlight, as electricity frequently goes off.

• Remember that there is a tourist tax of 5 percent on all hotel rooms.

TIPPING

• Don't tip in regular taxis; however, if you rent a private taxi for the day, give the driver the equivalent of one hour's charge.

• Expect 10 percent service charge to be added to your restaurant bill. If it isn't, leave 10 percent.

• Give porters 25 cents (U.S.) for each piece of luggage. At a luxury hotel, give a bit more.

• Tip cloakroom attendants the equivalent of U.S. 25 cents.

PRIVATE HOMES

• Feel free to drop in on friends without telephoning in advance.

• If there is a special soccer game or a popular soap opera (*telenovela*),

don't be surprised if women visitors are brought to the bedroom of the hostess to socialize and watch TV with family and friends.

• If you stay with a family for a few days, ask your hostess what would be an appropriate tip for the maid. Hand the maid the money in an envelope.

• Note that water for a bathroom must be heated in most homes (though some homes have constant hot water). Ask when it's convenient for you to bathe so you won't interfere with the schedule of the family's working members. The hot water heater is not usually lit at night.

• Be aware that most homes have showers rather than bathtubs. Many bathrooms also have a bidet.

• Wear a robe, pajamas, and slippers when you go to the bathroom. Colombians don't like to see people going barefoot and are shocked by foreigners who do.

• Bring your own facecloth, if you use one, and your own soap. Colombians consider soap a very personal item.

Gifts: If you're invited to dinner, send roses in advance, bring whiskey (e.g., Chivas Regal or Johnnie Walker), or bring an imported liqueur—e.g., Grand Marnier or cognac—a bottle of imported wine, or chocolates.

• If you bring flowers when invited to a meal, bring something with them (e.g., chocolates or cigars, if the host smokes), since flowers are so inexpensive.

• To find a unique gift, seek out one of the European specialty shops, which are located in upper-class neighborhoods.

• Don't give personal gifts such as neckties or perfume unless you know the man or woman very well. Colombians are very conservative.

• Good gifts are T-shirts and sweatshirts with logos, cosmetics, and French perfumes.

• If you want to bring a video cassette as a gift be aware that VHS is used in Colombia, as in North America.

• Don't expect your gift to be opened in your presence; in fact, the recipient may never mention the gift.

• Don't expect a thank-you note. The gesture is not customary in Colombia.

BUSINESS

Hours

Businesses: Monday through Friday, 8:00 A.M. to noon and 2:00 to 5:30 or 6:00 P.M. In towns in warmer climates, some firms start at 7:00 A.M. and close earlier.

Government Offices: Monday through Friday, 9:00 A.M. to noon and 2:00 to 5:00 P.M. (In general, government workers prefer to do business with the public in the afternoon.)

Banks: Monday through Thursday, 9:00 A.M. to 3:00 P.M.; Friday, 9:00 A.M. to 3:30 P.M. Some banks are open on Saturday.

Shops: Monday through Saturday, 9:00 A.M. to 12:30 P.M. and 2:00 to 7:00 P.M.

Currency

• The unit of currency is the *peso*. A *peso* is divided into 100 *centavos*.

Coins: 100, 200, 500, and 1,000 *pesos*.

Notes: 2,000, 5,000, 10,000, and 20,000 *pesos*.

• Realize that change is in short supply, especially in the morning in small towns. Carry a supply of money smaller than 1,000 *pesos*.

• Expect major credit cards to be accepted in first-class hotels, restaurants, and shops.

Business Practices

• Plan business travel for some time between March and November. Businesspeople usually vacation in December and January and in Barranquilla during June and July as well. Avoid the five days before Ash Wednesday in Barranquilla; it's Carnival time. Also avoid the two weeks before and after Christmas and the week before and after Easter.

• Realize that it's very important to have a contact in Colombia. If you don't have one, seek assistance from your national Chamber of Commerce or your embassy in Bogotá.

• Send a representative of your company—male or female—who has both high rank and expertise. You will impress Colombian businesspeople.

• Note that Colombian contacts will make hotel reservations, usually in a hotel near their home. They will also arrange for you to be picked up at the airport, picked up for business appointments, and so forth.

• Make business appointments at least a week in advance if you're making them in the country or by phone or telex from outside the country. Allow extra time if you're making arrangements by mail.

• Prepare to spend much more time in Colombia than you think you'll need. What you can accomplish at home in two days will probably take at least a week. Expect to wait several days before you even *begin* to discuss business. Colombian businesspeople will want to know about you, your spouse, your family, your city or town, sports you play, and so on. Don't begin discussing business until Colombians do.

• Arrive at least a day—preferably two—before you begin your ap-

pointments, since you may have a reaction to the altitude in Bogotá. To minimize the altitude's effects, don't drink alcohol, smoke, or eat heavily for a day or two after arriving.

• Men should be sure to wear their hair fairly short.

• If you have several appointments in one day, hire a private taxi, for which you will be charged by the hour. Your hotel will know of trustworthy drivers. If you make several trips to Colombia, it can be advantageous to build up a relationship with a single driver. Be sure to give the driver lunch money if you've hired him for the day.

• Be punctual for business appointments, but don't expect Colombians to be on time.

• Expect to be offered coffee when you arrive for a meeting. Be sure to accept.

• Always start by dealing with people at top levels in companies. A large number of these executives speak English and may resent your bringing an interpreter. If you know that the Colombian doesn't speak English, you should of course bring an interpreter.

• Don't feel that you need to have your business cards printed in Spanish. Be sure, however, that your title is included on your card. Present your business card with the printed side facing the person receiving it. Hold one end of the card between your index and middle fingers so that no words are covered up.

• Be aware that it's very easy to

have materials photocopied in Bogotá.

• Remember that Colombians don't always meet deadlines. They will come through eventually, but you will have to wait patiently without complaining.

• To ensure that people meet your deadlines, tell them why it's important, and keep checking on progress in a friendly, personal manner.

• If you meet workers in factories, shake hands with those near you when you are introduced and again when you leave. Never participate in any manual labor, however, because you will demean yourself in the eyes of Colombians. Status is very important.

• Women should remember that they won't accomplish their goals if they seem aggressive or bossy. When something hasn't been done correctly, be pleasant and patient, and you will usually get what you want.

• Don't change any member of your negotiating team. Colombians want to feel that they are dealing with individuals, not a corporation.

• Don't try to bribe anyone. Some people will regard it as an insult, while others may try to obtain more money from you when they realize that you're willing to offer a bribe. Example: If you're trying to bring a computer through customs, let your Colombian contact deal with the issue; don't try to bribe the customs officer.

• Note that people appreciate it

very much if you say, "You must come visit me in _____." Say it only if you really mean it because people may take you up on your offer.

• Expect to be entertained in business associates' homes; they like you to meet their spouses and families. Don't, however, discuss business when having a meal at someone's home.

• If you must refuse an invitation, be diplomatic and slightly evasive. Otherwise you'll offend.

• Reciprocate hospitality by hosting a meal in a restaurant that serves continental cuisine.

• Good business gifts are Cross pens with the recipient's name engraved on them, pocket calculators (especially solar-powered ones), or a bottle of Scotch.

HOLIDAYS AND SPECIAL OCCASIONS

Prepare for banks, offices, and many stores to be closed on the holidays listed below. Check with the tourist office to find out if any of the country's many regional religious festivals will be celebrated during your stay. As a traveler, you may wish to include such festivals in your itinerary, but you might want to avoid them on a business trip.

Holidays: New Year's Day (Jan. 1); Epiphany (Jan. 6); Saint Joseph's Day (March 19); Holy Thursday, Good Friday, Holy Saturday, and Easter; Labor Day (May 1); Ascension Day (40 days after Easter); Feast of Sts. Peter and Paul (June 29); Independence Day (July 20); Battle of Boyacá (Aug. 7); Feast of the Assumption (Aug. 15); Columbus Day (Oct. 12); All Saints' Day (Nov. 1); Independence Day—Cartagena (Nov. 11); Feast of the Immaculate Conception (Dec. 8); Christmas (Dec. 25).

• Don't plan "fun" activities on November 1. It's a somber day on which Colombians go to cemeteries and decorate graves with flowers.

TRANSPORTATION

Public Transportation

• To get a taxi after you arrive at the Bogotá airport, go to the dispatch booth, where you'll be told the fare and given a piece of paper with the license plate number of your assigned taxi on it. Keep the piece of paper; if you have any trouble, call the taxi company and report the driver. Another way to find a taxi at an airport is to look for a Tourist Police officer, who will tell you how to find one.

• If you need a taxi at night, always telephone for one, because there will then be a record if anything untoward happens. Never just get a taxi on the street.

• When possible, use one of the green-and-white taxis assigned to the major hotels. They are registered with the Tourist Police and are trustworthy. Although they are more expensive than other taxis, they are much safer.

• Realize that Colombia's taxis are the least expensive of any major country. Between 7:00 and 9:00 A.M., noon and 2:00 P.M., and 5:00 and 7:30 P.M., you should telephone for a taxi because they are difficult to find on the streets at those times.

• Be aware that there are two classes of buses in Bogotá, Medellín, and Cali: *buses* (boo-sehs) and *busetas* (boo-seh-tahs). The *buses*, which look like school buses, are often driven by the owners, who pack in as many people as possible to make the maximum profit. If you decide to take one of these buses, enter from the front and exit from the rear. You don't need exact change for your fare, but remember that drivers usually can't change large bills.

• Consider taking *busetas* (minibuses). They are much more costly than the larger buses but also *much* less crowded. Enter from the front, pay your fare (you don't need exact change), and exit from the rear.

• Whatever type of bus you decide to take, avoid traveling during the rush hour; buses are very crowded, and there is a danger of pickpockets.

• Note that for inter-city travel, there are large buses, called Pullmans, with air-conditioning, videos, and bathrooms. Despite the comfort of these buses, you might want to fly between cities if time is of any importance. For example, the bus trip from Bogotá to Medellín takes 11 hours, while a plane takes only 20 minutes.

• Because of the guerrilla warfare in Colombia, be safe and fly from one place to another, rather than take a bus, especially if you don't speak Spanish.

Driving

• Avoid driving at night; you may find animals on the road, potholes, and—sometimes—robbers.

• Prepare to stop at police checkpoints, which are located at intervals along most highways.

LEGAL MATTERS, SAFETY, AND HEALTH

• Be sure to carry your passport with you at all times.

• If you walk or take a bus in Bogotá, wear a money belt. If you take a taxi or are driving yourself, lock doors and close windows. Thieves are known to attack when people are stopped at red lights.

• Be on the lookout for gangs of small children, between 5 and 12 years old. They look innocent but can be dangerous.

• Never leave luggage or packages even for a moment. On a bus, don't put your bags in the luggage compartment; keep them with you. In restaurants, keep packages between your legs.

• Be aware of the following trick: someone with lottery tickets runs by and drops lots of tickets on the ground. If you stop to help him pick them up, a crowd may gather, thus helping someone to pick your pocket.

• Never accept food, drink, or cigarettes from strangers on buses. It's happened that people have been drugged with these items and then robbed.

• Women should expect harassment from men, including the police and the military. Just ignore the harassment and walk assuredly. Colombia is a country in which you'll encounter some of the worst displays of *machismo*.

• No one should go out unaccompanied at night—even in a taxi. Eat at the restaurant in your hotel.

• At night, never go out in a group of fewer than four. Carry your money in one of your shoes. Have a small amount of cash available—the equivalent of U.S. $5.00—in case a homeless person tries to mug you. Ask your hosts, a taxi driver, or the concierge at your hotel which areas are not safe for walking at night.

• The countryside is too dangerous for travel, because of the guerrilla fighting.

• Beware of scams in which people pose as policemen to try to obtain your passport. To avoid having your passport stolen, have a photo-copy made and notarized at home. Have the copy laminated. Leave your real passport in the hotel safe.

• When you arrive in Bogotá, take precautions to prevent *soroche*—altitude sickness, whose principal effect is severe headaches. For your first few days, eat lightly (on your first night, have just a bowl of consommé), don't drink alcoholic beverages, and don't smoke.

• During your entire stay in Colombia, don't drink tap water or eat unpeeled fruits and vegetables or raw shellfish. Never buy cooked food from street vendors.

• Be careful when buying imported liquor. Some bottles have been opened and refilled with other liquids; the bottles could then be dangerous. Stick to rum and beer.

• For advice on medicine and hygiene products, see "Legal Matters, Safety, and Health" in the Introduction.

COSTA RICA

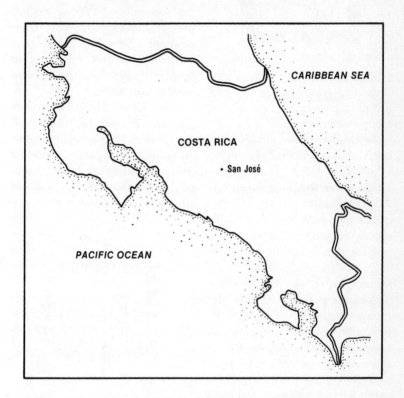

CARIBBEAN SEA

COSTA RICA

• San José

PACIFIC OCEAN

It wasn't until his fourth (and last) voyage to the New World that Columbus discovered "the rich coast" (Costa Rica), where he was convinced he had found a major source of gold for Spain.

In the 20th century, the "gold" is flowing into, rather than out of, Costa Rica. Its stable political climate has attracted large amounts of foreign investment, and not a few fugitive financiers have arrived with their fortunes.

Its geography makes Costa Rica a delight for lovers of flora and fauna. Animals and plants that thrive in countries to the north and south find happy homes in Costa Rica.

In reporting on Costa Rica and its amiable lifestyle for *60 Minutes*, CBS correspondent Morley Safer said that the national motto should be "No sweat."

GREETINGS

Language: The official language of Costa Rica is Spanish.

• Be aware that men always initiate greetings.

• Do not make eye contact with anyone for longer than three seconds. If women continue eye contact, the gesture is considered a sexual come-on—so avoid making prolonged eye contact unless you are trying to send a sexual message. It's especially important for women to avoid eye contact if they are in a bar and trying to avoid unwanted attention. Look everywhere except in a person's eyes. Although *ticos* shift their glance frequently, they are paying attention.

• Remember that men always shake hands with both new acquaintances and old friends.

• Note that when women are introduced to one another they don't shake hands. They pat one another on the left arm. Women tend to kiss one another on both cheeks whether they're just being introduced or have known each other a long time.

Actually, they touch cheeks and kiss into the air.

• Use titles. They are important to Costa Ricans. Some common titles: Doctor (for Ph.D. and medical doctor); architect; engineer; lawyer; professor. (See "Key Words and Phrases" at the end of the book for Spanish equivalents.) Use the title with the last name.

• At large parties, introduce yourself. At small parties you will be introduced by the host or hostess. At either type of party, greet every guest personally by shaking hands or giving a kiss on the cheek. Do the same to each person when you leave.

CONVERSATION

• If you speak Spanish, use *usted* when addressing another person, unless others address you as *vos* (the form used for close friends and intimate relations). The *tu* form is never used.

• Ask about people's children. Both men and women adore children.

• Feel free to discuss politics. Costa Rica is very stable, with a long democratic tradition.

• Ask advice about what to do and see in Costa Rica, especially the nature reserves. Costa Rica has the largest number of wildlife preserves in the world.

• Be aware that people have a strong sense of personal honor; never say anything that could be construed as personal criticism.

• Never ask anyone about his or her salary. It's bad manners.

• Don't use the word *rica* when referring to a person. It has bad connotations. Costa Ricans refer to themselves as *ticos* (**tee-kohs**).

• Don't ask a woman about her job unless you know that she works outside her home. Most women don't.

• If you need to ask someone a favor, always have a brief conversation beforehand. Don't come directly to your request.

• When ending a conversation, don't do so abruptly. For example, don't just jump up and say, "I must be going."

TELEPHONES

• Expect to find telephone booths in cities as well as all along highways. However, in general, they don't work.

• Deposit 10 *colones* per minute in a public pay phone. There are slots for 5, 10, and 20 *colones* coins. Prepaid phone cards are available at many *pulperías* (small grocery stores) and from street vendors. Some cards are for home use. You dial a toll-free number and then enter a code and phone number. The instructions are in English. Other cards are *chip* cards; they can be used only in special pay phones. The home cards can be used at pay phones, but not the other was around—so make sure you know what you're buying. Cards come in denominations of 100, 200, 500, 1,000 and 3,000 *colones*.

• Keep in mind that phone booths do not have phone books. Ask for one at the front desk of a hotel.

• For both local and long-distance calls, go to the telephone office, *Radiográfica Costaricense*, to some private homes where women run phone lines, to corner stores, or use a phone card at a public phone.

• Look for cybercafes in San José and surrounding areas. You can E-mail from there.

• If you'll be in Costa Rica for an extended period and need to set up a phone account, go to RASCA, the national telephone office.

• Keep calls short. *Ticos* don't like to chat on the phone, nor do they like to have their phone lines tied up.

• For any emergency, dial 911, where you will find an English-speaking operator. However, it's faster if you use numbers for specific services. Ambulance—128; Fire—118: Police—117 or 506/295-3000 for an English-speaking operator. For an air ambulance, call 225-4502.

IN PUBLIC

• Note that Costa Ricans don't make distinctions among people based on social rank. All people receive equal respect. However, ex-pect to see a great deal of resentment against both legal and illegal im-migrants from nearby countries who power the harvest of Costa Rica's agriculture. These people, called *nicas*, provide a convenient scapegoat for all society's problems.

• A gesture to avoid: making a fist with the thumb sticking out be-tween the index and middle fingers. It's obscene.

• When waving good-bye, hold your hand in front of you, palm fac-ing you, and wave your whole hand, not individual fingers, back and forth.

• When asking directions, expect to be told how far your destination is from a landmark, because street signs are rare. If you're giving di-rections to someone who's picking you up, tell them how many meters you are from some recognizable place. Most Costa Ricans ignore street numbers. (Street numbers are attached to the sides of buildings near intersections.)

• In restaurants, expect people to make a hissing sound to call the waiter. This gesture is not rude or in any way sexual. However, on the street, hissing takes on a sexual context when men do it to passing women. Women should just ig-nore it.

• Expect to find public bath-rooms everywhere—even in small snack bars in the countryside. Some are kept locked, and you must ask for the key at the counter. *Damas* is for women; *Caballeros* or *Hombres* for men. At some bathrooms, you must pay 2 *colones* to the attendant, who will give you toilet paper. However, to be on the safe side, bring tissues with you. Public bathrooms are usually very clean, except those in bus stations, which should be used *only* as a last resort.

Shopping: Note that there's no bargaining in Costa Rica. If you're buying something in quantity, you can ask for a discount, e.g., "One pineapple costs XXX. How much do you want for three pineapples?"

• To buy anything from canned goods to toilet paper to rope in the countryside, look for a *pulpería*. In the cities you'll find *supermercados*.

great deal, depending on the altitude. In the cities at higher altitudes, nights are cool, and you'll need a sweater or jacket.

• For casual dress, anything except shorts will be acceptable. Women shouldn't wear anything revealing.

• For business, in San José, men should wear a conservative dark suit. A jacket isn't necessary in coastal cities. Women should wear silk or cotton dresses or dressy skirts and blouses, with stockings and high heels.

• There are only two major restaurants in San José at which men must wear ties. Most restaurants are very casual.

• Wear shorts only on the beach or for sports.

• Remember that nude swimming and sunbathing are *extremely* offensive to Costa Ricans. A beach may look deserted, but homes may be right behind it.

DRESS

• To make a good impression, be sure that your clothes are clean, neat, and even elegant. *Ticos* take frequent showers and look nice at all times. Being sweaty is permissible only if you are participating in a sport.

• Note that the climate varies a

MEALS

Hours and Foods

Breakfast: Between 6:00 and 8:00 A.M. In the city, the usual meal is orange juice, bread, and coffee, sometimes with eggs. In the countryside, people eat *gallo pinto* (mixed rice and beans) with sour cream and tortillas, and they drink coffee.

Lunch: 11:30 A.M. to 1:00 P.M. A typical lunch might be *casado* (rice, black beans, salad, meat or egg), *picadillo* (fried vegetables), fried plaintains, fruit, and coffee.

• People stop for the *hora del café* (coffee hour) from 4:30 to 5:30 P.M.

Dinner: About 7:00 P.M. A lighter meal than lunch, it might consist of *olla de carne* (a stew with beef, potatoes, corn, onions, beans, and tomatoes) with rice and beans.

Beverages: Common drinks before dinner at a home are rum and Coke, whiskey and soda, or vodka. Don't have more than one or two drinks. With cocktails

there may be appetizers such as cheese sticks, chips, and ground bean dip.

• Be aware that most of the best coffee is exported. Locals drink their coffee weak and very sweet. Better hotels and restaurants will offer better blends.

• With meals the usual beverages are soft drinks or fresh fruit juices: *fresco de mora* (blackberry juice), *fresco de tamarindo* (tamarind juice), *fresco de carambola* (starfruit juice). Drinks whose name contains *fresco* have water added to them. Don't drink them. If you want juice without water, ask for *jugo*.

• Avoid one of the country's most popular beverages: *horchata*, a crude "aquavit" made from corn. Since you don't know where or how it's been made, don't try it.

• The national alcoholic drink is made from sugarcane. The brand name is *Cacique*; the common name is *guaro*. (This is not a drink upper-class people would serve.)

• A popular morning drink is *agua dulce*, a warm drink made from melted sugarcane and served plain or with lemon or milk.

• Note that it's safe to drink the water in San José but *not* elsewhere. You won't find mineral water; substitute soda water, which is called *soda blanca*.

Table Manners

• Expect the table to be set with forks to the left of the plate, knives to the right, and the coffee spoon above the plate.

• Keep your napkin on the table, not in your lap.

• Remember that people usually start eating as soon as they are served, unless grace is to be said. Watch one of the *ticos* at the table, and follow his/her lead.

• Always compliment your hostess on the flavor and quantity of the food.

• Don't feel obliged to finish everything on your plate, even though people will probably push you to eat more.

Eating Out

• *Sodas* are places offering light meals, sandwiches, coffee, tea, and alcoholic drinks. They serve snacks such as *arreglados*, little puffed pastries stuffed with beef, chicken, or cheese.

• In San José, expect to find a wide variety of restaurants—French, Swiss, Italian, Chinese, and vegetarian.

• Most bars offer little appetizers, called *bocas*. They are usually free, but, if not, they are very inexpensive. Popular *bocas* are *gallos* (tortillas stuffed with meat, beans, or cheese), *tamales* (stuffed cornmeal patties wrapped in banana leaves and then steamed), and *ceviche* (marinated seafood salad).

• At lunchtime, most restaurants serve *casado*, a set meal consisting of black beans, beef or other meat or fish, fried plantain, chopped cab-

bage, and sometimes avocado or an egg.

• When ordering fruit salad (*ensalada de fruta*), be sure to ask if the fruit is fresh. Usually fruit salad refers to canned fruit, Jell-O, and ice cream. Don't eat any fresh fruit that can't be peeled.

• A note for vegetarians: The word *carne* in Spanish means "meat"; however, in Costa Rica it usually means "beef." If you see on a menu or are told *"No tiene carne,"* which means "There's no meat in it," it really means that the dish contains no beef—but it may contain other types of meat.

Specialties

• The national breakfast dish is *gallo pinto*: rice and beans cooked together.

• Two dishes to try are *sopa negra*—black bean soup with a poached or boiled egg on top—and *picadillos*—vegetable puree made of potato or plantains and a bit of meat. *Picadillos* are served either as *bocas* or as a side dish.

• For fish lovers, Costa Rica offers *ceviche* (fresh white sea bass marinated in lemon juice, coriander, and onions) as an appetizer, and *corvina* (white sea bass served grilled, baked, or steamed).

• *Olla de carne* is a soup containing beef and vegetables such as potatoes, squash, yucca, and plantains.

• An authentic Costa Rican dish is *sopa de mondongo*, made from tripe.

• In the province of Limón, rice

and beans are prepared with coconut milk. Another specialty of this area is *patacones*—salty, fried green plantains. Others are Johnnycakes, curried goat, and *ackee* (a small pink-skinned fruit, which tastes like scrambled eggs and is served with codfish).

- For desserts, try *queque seco* (pound cake), *flan* (caramel custard), or *tiramisu*.
- *Palmito* are hearts of palm; they are used in salads or as an elegant vegetable dish.
- *Tamales* in Costa Rica are a filling of pork or chicken, raisins, rice, and olives, stuffed in white cornmeal, all wrapped in banana leaves. To eat them, you unwrap the *tamal*, and discard the leaves.
- *Tortas* are sandwiches of meat or cheese on rolls.

HOTELS

- Note that Costa Rican hotels range from the basic to the luxurious. Luxury hotels usually have excellent food, room service, swimming pools, and flowering tropical plants and bushes. You may also find small hotels that are clean and have helpful management.

- Except the high-season rates to be in effect from December through March. During Holy Week (the week before and including Easter), hotels are packed. Book way ahead if you need a room at this time.
- Some alternatives to traditional hotels: (1) *apartoteles*—rooms with kitchen facilities, offering weekly and monthly rates; (2) *cabinas*—motel-like rooms; (3) *pensiones*—inexpensive basic hotels with no meal service; (4) rooms in a home (usually with meals and laundry service)—find one by calling language schools or checking at the University of San José.
- Be aware that most hotels in San José and the surrounding area don't have air-conditioning because, with the altitude, the nights are always cool.
- If you're staying on the coast or anywhere in a lower altitude, make sure that there is a fan in your room.
- Realize that the small, inexpensive hotels on the coast often don't have hot water—just tepid tap water.
- Be cautious when taking a shower. Most places have a small electrical heater that heats the water as it passes through the shower head. Thus, less water pressure equals hotter water. If a shower is hooked up to an electric heating element, which is switched on when you want a hot shower, **don't** touch anything metal when you're in the shower. You might get a shock.
- Expect to find at least one person who speaks English at most hotels.

• Be aware that some hotels on the coast include meals in the room rate, and you must pay for them, whether you eat them or not.

• Keep in mind that most hotels change travelers' checks, but you can obtain a better rate at a bank. Many hotels accept major credit cards. Ask first. Most places will accept U.S. dollars.

• Ask if it is possible to connect your personal computer in the room. Costa Rica operates on 110 volts, so visitors from the U.S. will not need a converter. However, since there are two types of plug, it is a good idea to bring a two-prong adapter.

TIPPING

• Recall that restaurants add 10 percent service charge.

• Don't tip taxi drivers.

• Give porters and bellhops 75 cents per bag. At better hotels give $1 to $2.

• Tip hotel maids $1.00 per day.

• Give gas station attendants 5 to 10 *colones*.

PRIVATE HOMES

• When invited to dinner at someone's home, leave soon after the meal. People begin work very early because of the heat, and children start school at 7:00 A.M. However, don't just eat and run. Let there be a polite interlude, and then depart.

• Note that few families have maids. If you're staying with a family with no maid, offer to help clear the table, do the dishes, and make your bed.

• Realize that people often take two or three showers or baths a day because of the heat. Your hosts will be offended if you don't take at least one bath or shower a day.

Gifts: When invited to a meal, bring flowers or a good wine. Roses and carnations are popular, but don't give calla lilies—they're for funerals.

• Bring women makeup, perfume, or silk scarves. Bring men shaving cream and aftershave.

• Both men and women enjoy delicacies, e.g., baskets of fancy jams, smoked fish, fancy chocolates, unusual crackers, nuts, mustards.

• Scotch and wine are also welcome gifts. However, some families don't drink liquor, so don't bring it unless you're sure they imbibe.

• Note that teenagers enjoy sports team T-shirts, caps, and designer T-shirts currently in vogue.

• Because many Americans live in Costa Rica and because there aren't many import restrictions, American-made products are easily obtainable and aren't considered special.

BUSINESS

Hours

Business: Monday through Friday, 8:00 A.M. to 5:00 P.M., closing for lunch from 11:00 or 11:30 A.M. to 1:00 P.M.

Government Offices: Monday through Friday, 8:00 A.M. to 4:00 P.M.

Banks: Monday through Friday, 9:00 A.M. to 3:00 P.M.

Shops: Monday through Friday, 8:00 A.M. to noon, and 2:00 to 6:00 P.M. Saturday: 8:00 A.M. to noon. Stores in malls are usually open from 9:00 A.M. to 8:00 or 9:00 P.M. and don't close for lunch.

Currency

• The currency is the *colón* (plural, *colones*).

• Coins: 1, 5, 10, 20, 25, 50, and 100 *colones*.

• Notes: 50, 100, 500, 1,000, 2,000, 5,000, and 10,000 *colones*.

• Realize that the 5,000 and 10,000 *colones* bills are hard to break in taxis and small stores, so ask for smaller bills at banks, at your hotel, or at large stores.

• Remember that it's illegal to change money anywhere other than at banks and some hotels. If you change money on the street, both you and the seller may be prosecuted.

• Change money in San José. In the countryside, there will be fewer ATMs than in San José.

• Remember that it's often difficult to change *colones* into dollars when you leave Costa Rica. Spend them.

• Plan to use major credit cards at most hotels, stores, and restaurants. Less-expensive places will want cash.

Business Practices

• Note that the best months for business travel to Costa Rica are February and March, and September to November. Avoid the two weeks before and after Christmas and the week before and after Easter. December and January are popular times for vacations.

• Be sure to have a contact before you make a business trip to Costa Rica. Look for one through the Costa Rica Chamber of Commerce.

• Stay in the best hotels to make a good impression.

• Make appointments about two weeks in advance with business-people and government officials.

• Be punctual. Costa Ricans honor appointment times much more than businesspeople in other Latin American countries.

• Remember that Costa Ricans are very serious, formal, and European in style. Don't expect the *abrazo*—the bear hug with which men greet one another. One visiting businessman observed, "Meeting some Costa Rican businessmen is the equivalent of meeting an English lord."

• Men should *always* keep their jackets on at meetings.

• Never put your feet up on furniture.

• Have your business cards printed in Spanish and English.

• Don't worry about getting proposals or other materials copied in Costa Rica. It's very easy.

• To make a good first impression, offer a compliment on the beauty of the country, especially the nature reserves. Don't discuss the politics of Central America during your initial meeting because people are likely to remain on the subject and you'll have a very difficult time returning to a business discussion.

• If you will be offering sales literature, have it printed in Spanish as well as English, though most younger businesspeople speak English. Should you need an interpreter, consult the ads in the *Tico Times*, the English-language newspaper.

• Be sure to have a lawyer to get government approval for starting a business. (Costa Rica has one of the highest percentages of lawyers per capita in the world, and many of them are fluent in English.)

• Remember that time estimates for deadlines are not reliable; however, you should never complain about Costa Rica or Costa Ricans because people will be *very* offended.

• When attending an official meeting, a ceremony, or a lecture, expect the speaker to give a long, formal recognition of everyone in the room with her/his title and to explain why they are present.

• Note that foreign investors can own 100 percent of any business or property. In most Latin American countries, foreigners are limited to less than 50% of any business.

• Inviting as it is to be able to own 100 percent of an investment, don't buy large amounts of land unless you plan to live on it or actively farm it. You could have problems with squatters. Once they've stayed on a property for more than a year, they have certain rights of possession, which makes it difficult to evict them.

• Keep in mind that decisions are usually made by the consensus of a group, not just by the top people, as in other Latin American countries. Head officials defer until a consensus is reached.

• Realize that Costa Ricans are notoriously late in paying their bills. Be sure you know in advance the method of payment. It's best to have a contract backed up by a letter of contract or a performance bond from a bank in *your* country.

• Consider the explanation of one Costa Rican government official for the delays in payment (an explanation that says much about attitudes in the country): "We in Costa Rica are all individual farmers. Farms operate on credit. A gentleman would never ask another to pay off a debt during a year with a bad harvest. We in Costa Rica have had bad harvests for the past eight years."

• Women should note that they will have a better chance to succeed in business in Costa Rica than in other Latin American countries.

• Expect business entertaining to be in the evening, since most businesspeople return home for lunch.

• Entertain only the people with whom you are negotiating.

• Invite spouses—both foreign and Costa Rican—to business dinners.

HOLIDAYS AND SPECIAL OCCASIONS

Below are national holidays on which you should expect to find government offices, banks, businesses, and many shops closed. Check with the tourist office to learn if there are any local festivals during your stay. Such festivals may cause everything to be closed in that area.

Holidays: New Year's Day (Jan. 1); Feast of St. Joseph, patron saint of the city of San José (March 19); Juan Santa Maria's Day (April 11—a day honoring Costa Rica's national hero with concerts, parades, and dances); Holy Thursday through Easter Sunday; Labor Day (May 1); Feast of Corpus Christi (the Thursday after the eighth Sunday after Easter); Feast of Sts. Peter and Paul (June 29); Annexation of the Guanacaste Province (July 25); Feast of Our Lady of the Angels (Aug. 2); Feast of the Assumption, Mother's Day (Aug. 15); Independence Day (Sept. 15); Columbus Day (Oct. 12); Feast of the Immaculate Conception (Dec. 8); Christmas Eve and Christmas Day (Dec. 24 and 25); New Year's Eve (Dec. 31).

• Be aware that Good Friday is kept as a day of mourning throughout the country. During Holy Week the entire country, including businesses, basically shuts down. If you will be traveling at that time, be sure to make all the necessary arrangements (reservations, tickets, etc.) well in advance.

• Expect to hear fireworks when a local saint's day is being celebrated. If you hear loud explosions, such a festival probably explains them. Sirens, on the other hand, may mean that an important person has arrived in town.

TRANSPORTATION

Public Transportation

• Note that within cities there are different bus companies with different fares. The more modern buses are slightly more expensive. People queue for buses very politely and quietly. Pay on the bus. You don't need exact change, but drivers won't have change for large bills.

• Be aware that buses are not air-conditioned and can be very hot for long trips.

• Remember that there is no smoking on either city or inter-city buses, no matter how long the ride.

• For long-distance buses, buy tickets in advance at the terminal or on the bus.

• Consider taxis for short distances in cities. They are readily available, clean, and well maintained. As you would expect, taxis are harder to find in rural areas. They are also more expensive outside the cities. There are no meters. Check with someone knowledgeable and find out what the fare should be. After 10:00 P.M., there is a 20 percent surcharge. Taxi drivers tend to be reckless. Don't slam the door when you get out; you will anger the driver.

• Realize that there is no public transportation on Holy Thursday or Good Friday.

• Think about taking a plane for travel between cities. Airfare is reasonable, and people often travel by plane because of the mountainous terrain. The domestic airline is called SANSA. Make reservations in advance, and pay for your ticket by the day before the flight. Be prepared for the plane to land at tiny airports with cattle on the runways.

Driving

• If you plan to rent a car, shop around for the best price. There are many car rental agencies.

• Realize that to rent a car you must be at least 21 years old, have a valid driver's license, and a major credit card in your name.

• When renting a car, make a *very* thorough inspection of the exterior for any dents or other damages. Car rental companies sometimes claim that you owe money for minor damage when you return the car.

• As an alternative to renting a car, check with tour agencies to hook up with van services, usually for three or more people. There's less stress than renting a car, and the van is much more comfortable than the bus. Yet another option is hiring a car and driver for yourself. Rates are usually favorable in relation to renting a car. However, remember that you should *always* agree on the price before starting out.

• Be aware that seat belts are required for the driver and front-seat passengers.

• Keep to between 60 and 90 kilometers an hour (35 to 45 mph) on the highways. Police on the highways use radar.

• Expect little traffic on highways outside the city. There are some excellent highways, but road signs are poor. At some places—when you least expect it—a paved road may become a dirt road covered with rocks. Determine exactly where you're going and what the road conditions are; you may want to rent a Jeep.

• During the rainy season (beginning in late April or early May), watch for landslides and mudslides. Another hazard is fog, which can set in quickly.

• If you happen on one of those rare occasions where a roadblock has been set up by thieves (you will probably see suspicious activity), don't stop. Drive straight on.

• Don't pick up hitchhikers.

• If you need gas in a small town, look for a handmade sign saying *gasolina*. Families sometimes sell gas by the liter.

• Never pay money directly to any policeman who stops you for a traffic violation.

• Note that Costa Ricans drive relatively slowly outside San José, but in the city, be sure to drive defensively.

LEGAL MATTERS, SAFETY, AND HEALTH

• Be aware that it's illegal to change dollars anywhere except at banks and hotels (and only registered guests can change money at hotels). In an illegal transaction, both buyer and seller are liable.

• When crossing the street in San José, remember that pedestrians *don't* have the right of way. Check cars coming from behind you, since drivers tend to shoot around corners.

• Some precautions: Don't wear backpacks in cities as they can be opened easily by thieves. Don't carry wallets in back pockets. Don't wear expensive jewelry.

• Never leave anything in a parked rental car, because there may be a break-in. Most hotels have secure parking lots.

• Don't worry about dining alone in restaurants if you're a woman alone, but don't go into local bars.

• Women alone should use taxis from a hotel, rather than one hailed on the street to avoid inappropriate advances from the driver. Especially after dark, avoid pirate cabs, which have no insignia from a cab company.

• Women should avoid making eye contact with men, if they aren't interested in a relationship.

• If you camp out or stay in a primitive place and must hang your clothes outside, shake out your clothes and shoes before putting them on—to get rid of insects and snakes.

• Realize that riptides occur at several beaches. Don't swim alone, even if you are an experienced swimmer. Ask local people which beaches are safe. Hotel owners sometimes tear down warning signs.

• Don't eat raw vegetables and fruit that can't be peeled. Avoid raw shellfish.

• For advice on medicine and hygiene products, see "Legal Matters, Safety, and Health" in the Introduction.

CUBA

Cuba, once a casual playground for Americans—a quick hop from Miami for a night in Havana—has become more difficult for U.S. citizens to visit since the U.S. imposed an embargo in 1961. Despite the embargo, according to *Fort Worth Star-Telegram* columnist Molly Ivins, Cuba's economy grew 6.2 percent in 1999, and the country has "the best educational system and the best health care in Latin America. Its illiteracy and infant mortality rates are lower than those found in U.S. inner cities." In 1999, Cuba welcomed some 1.65 million tourists, some of them American, who enjoyed basking on one of Cuba's many beaches in front of new hotels.

However, no U.S. airlines and no U.S. travel agents are permitted to book travel for U.S. citizens to Cuba. To arrange to travel to Cuba as a tourist, you will have to use a foreign travel agent and enter through another country. Most U.S. citizens choose Canada, Mexico, or the Bahamas.

Certain classes of U.S. citizens may receive a license to travel to Cuba, including journalists, those engaged in academic research, and amateur or semiprofessional athletes. Travel arrangements for those eligible for a license to visit Cuba can be made by such U.S. organizations as Marazul Tours in New Jersey; Pastors for Peace; Chicago, IL; Global Exchange, San Francisco, California; and the Center for Cuban Studies in New York.

As of August 2000, relations between the U.S. and Cuba are in flux.

Check these Web sites for the current status in relations: travel.state.gov/
cuba.html; *www.state.gov/www/regons/wha/cuba/travel.html;* www.treas.gov.
ofac.

GREETINGS

Language: Cuba's official language is Spanish.

• Don't be surprised to find people very demonstrative in greeting,
even when they are meeting for the
first time. Women usually kiss
women they have just met, and men
may hug each other or offer a very
hearty handshake.

• If you are speaking Spanish,
wait until the other person uses *tu*
(the informal version of "you") before doing so yourself. As soon as you
know a person's first name, feel free
to use it, since Cuba has thrown out
most formalities and social distinction. However, in formal situations
with local government officials, religious officials, and deans of universities, do not use first names.

• Expect Cubans to be very informal in public. They will address one
another as *compañero* or *compañera*

(terms meaning "comrade"—a political declaration). Foreigners are
referred to as *señor* (Mr.) and *señora*
(madam) and *señorita* (a term used
for a woman up to age 30, if it's not
known whether or not she is married). Use these forms of address
when greeting Cubans.

• If you are asking for directions
or some other information, always
greet the person in Spanish (see
"Key Words and Phrases" at the end
of the book).

• At parties, introduce yourself to
others.

Conversation

• Because of Cuba's isolation, expect to find people very curious
about prices and salaries in your
country. You will be approached
constantly by people who want to
talk to foreigners to find out about
your life and to practice their English. They may want to sell you
something or find you a room or direct you to a *paladar* (a small restaurant in a private home).

• If you hear Cubans refer to the
"Special Period," realize that they
are talking about the time when the
Berlin Wall fell, and the Soviet
Union stopped giving aid to Cuba.

• Feel free to discuss rationing
and normalizing relations with the

U.S. However, be aware that people are usually hesitant to talk about politics openly. Be especially careful to avoid political discussions in public places. You could end up embarrassing someone.

• Don't be surprised to be asked personal questions. Feel free to ask them in return.

• **DON'T** use the word *papaya*. It's slang for female genitalia.

• Be careful that you don't criticize the disrepair and the poor physical condition of the infrastructure in the country.

• Avoid discussions of Miami. Some people have relatives there. Others resent the efforts being made in Miami to overthrow Cuba's government.

Telephones

• Be prepared to find local service very poor. Sometimes you won't be able to get a dial tone, because problems with equipment can cut off sections of the city for many days.

• Expect to find only a few working pay phones in Havana. They accept 5, 10, and 25 *centavo* coins. A three-minute local call costs 5 *centavos*. The alternative is to use a phone card. Phone cards, which are paid for in dollars, can also be used for international calls. Public phones are located on street corners and in hotels.

• Look for instructions in English on the telephones' screens.

• Find out about the surcharge your hotel may impose on an inter-national call that is directly dialed. It could be huge. In some hotels, you may have to wait for hours until the international operator is able to connect you.

• Be aware that it often takes a **very** long time for an international call to the U.S. to go through, since it has to be routed through a third country. Throughout the call there may be an echo.

• When answering the phone, Cubans say *"Oigo"* (oy-go), meaning "I'm listening," or *"Dígame"* (dee-gah-may), meaning "Tell me."

• Don't look for a national emergency number, although some cities have 118 for emergencies. If there is an emergency number available, you will find it on pay phones.

IN PUBLIC

• Follow the Cuban custom of offering your seat to handicapped persons, pregnant women, the elderly, and mothers with small children.

• Don't be surprised to find that many streets have two names—one predating the Revolution and the other a post-Revolutionary name.

• If a line starts to form, find out what is being sold—e.g., bread, fruit, etc. If you are interested in purchasing the item, ask the last person in line, "*¿El último?*"—meaning, "Are you the last in line?"

• Look for dollar stores, which are only for foreigners.

• Realize that people expect you to bargain at most markets. You might agree to the price very soon, because prices are so low, and people really need the money.

• Note that it is not legal to bring Cuban cigars into the U.S. (although people often do). It is legal to bring them into other countries that don't have an embargo on Cuban products. Sometimes cheap cigars are sold as though they were a more expensive brand. Thus you need to have a sealed box with official marks on it to insure that you're getting "the real thing."

• Feel free to take pictures of people. Cubans love having their photo taken. If you are able, bring a Polaroid as an extra camera, so that you can give the person a copy of the picture right away. If not, take down the address, so that you can send a copy—and be sure to follow through.

• Don't photograph police officers, police stations, military figures, or military installations.

• To find a public toilet, look for a large hotel. Most towns have public toilets, sometimes with a 10- to 20-*centavo* entry fee. Note that some restaurants do not have toilets for public use. Bring toilet tissue, because there usually isn't any. Don't be surprised if there isn't a toilet seat; they are rare. Flush the toilet only when necessary (e.g., in your hotel room). Put all paper, including toilet paper, in the wastebasket. The fragile plumbing system would not be able to handle the paper.

• Look for public toilets to be identified as *mujeres* or *señoras* for women and *hombres* or *señores* for men.

DRESS

• Expect to see older Cuban men wearing a *guayabera*, a shirt worn over pants. Young people try to dress in the latest fashion.

• Don't be surprised to find Cuban women wearing very tight, rather provocative clothing. If, as a woman, you don't wish to attract men, dress more conservatively.

• Note that Cubans are always neat and clean—even when toiletries are scarce. To show respect, be sure that your clothes are neat and clean. Never be sloppy.

• If you are invited to an event such as an opening of an exhibition at a museum or another more formal event, feel free to dress informally, but, again, be sure that your clothes are clean and neatly pressed.

• Don't wear jewelry. It is considered ostentatious, and you would encourage theft.

• Men should wear shorts only on the beach.

• Be aware that nude or topless bathing is not permitted on Cuba's beaches.

MEALS

Hours and Foods

Breakfast: Between 6:00 and 7:30 A.M. Usually milk, a roll, and coffee.

Lunch: Between noon and 1:30 P.M. There is always rice. Other foods served at lunch could be black beans, fried or boiled eggs or fish or pork (if available), or beef from the ration book (see bullet following "Dinner"), tomato or cabbage and maybe fried plantains (*tostones*). Coffee is served after the meal.

Dinner: Between 6:00 and 8:00 P.M. The food will be the same as at lunch.

• Note that each Cuban family has a ration book, called a *libreta*. Because of the great food shortages, people are able to obtain meat only about once a month. Foreigners who pay in dollars will find a great variety of food in restaurants.

Table Manners

• Don't expect predinner cocktails.

• If you're invited to a meal, wait for your host to seat you.

• If you're avoiding spicy foods, don't worry. Cuban food tends to be very bland.

• Since food is served family-style, help yourself. Don't take more than you think you'll eat. It is impolite to leave food on your plate, especially during times of food shortage.

• Note that Cubans tend to concentrate on the food when they are eating, so there is very little conversation during a meal.

• To eat as the Cubans do, use the fork in the left hand and the knife in the right.

• If you wish to smoke during a meal, excuse yourself and leave the room.

• After dinner, you'll be served Cuban coffee, which is like *espresso*.

• Don't stay longer than two hours after dinner, unless there is a party.

Eating Out

• Be aware that the best restaurants are privately owned and are located in private homes. They're called *paladares* (meaning "palates"). The price usually includes salad, dessert, and sometimes beer. Many are open 24 hours a day and serve Cubans for pesos and foreigners for dollars. The only way to find one is to ask people. (It's as if you decided to open a restaurant in your dining room and advertised only by word of mouth.) If you're staying at a hotel, don't ask for the location of a *paladar*, since the clerk will be a state employee, and the state-run restaurants are in competition with the *paladares*.

• If you know of a *paladar* where you would like to dine on a weekend, try to make a reservation.

• Note that some *paladares* have written menus and others don't. Don't eat in one if there's no menu with prices listed, because some *paladares* in tourist areas charge exorbitant prices.

• Expect to see menus posted outside of tourist restaurants.

• If you don't want Cuban food, seek out an Italian restaurant, though you'll probably find a limited menu of pizza and spaghetti. Almost every town has at least one Chinese restaurant.

• Keep in mind that most coffee stands have disappeared, but there are a few, as well as tea shops called *Casas de Té* or *Casas de Infusiones*.

• Be prepared for the more expensive restaurants to offer continental cuisine. However, it's usually not very good.

• Remember that state-run restaurants have from 1 to 7 grades, 1 being the best.

• Realize that the ubiquitous shortages make it very difficult to find a good meal.

• Even in warm weather, bring a sweater if you're going to a restaurant. The air-conditioning may make the dining room very cold.

• Feel free to seat yourself, but don't try to share a table with people you don't know.

• Be prepared to be patient. Service may be extremely slow.

• Keep in mind that foreigners must pay in dollars in state-run restaurants, even though Cubans pay in pesos.

• At most restaurants, you'll find a typical Cuban dish called *crillo*. The two main types of meat are chicken or pork, served with black beans and rice and fried plantains or bananas. It's not at all spicy.

• If you order fish, expect it to be overcooked.

• Other dishes you'll often find in restaurants are: *cerdo asado*—roast pork; *moros y cristianos* (Moors and Christians)—rice with red beans; *ajíaco*—a stew of meats and vegetables.

• Realize that there are rarely fresh vegetables in restaurants, except for salads, such as *palmito*—heart of palm salad; *col*—shredded cabbage; *yucca*—a starch served like potatoes in different ways; *boniato*—

sweet potato. A common soup is *garbanzo*.

• Don't expect to find fruits and vegetables in local restaurants. They are scarce, and the best dishes sell out early. Most fruits are used in the production of juices. The juices are safe to drink if water and/or ice cubes have not been added.

• Indulge your desire for lobster—it is very inexpensive if you avoid tourist restaurants.

• Expect to find occasional specials such as fish or pork, if they are available.

• Remember the caution against eating anything that can't be peeled or that hasn't been well cooked.

Specialties

• Specialties include *empanadas de carne* (meat turnovers); *ayacas* (corn tortillas filled with meat and spices); *piccadillo* (spiced beef, tomato, and onion)—served as a snack; *fufu* (crumbled pork rinds mixed with cooked plantain—especially popular in Oriente); *lechón asada* (roast suckling pig); *cerdo asado* (roast pork); *bistec uruguayno* (steak stuffed with ham and cheese).

• The most common fish are *corvino* (sea bass), *filet de emperador* (swordfish), and *pargo* (red snapper).

• A popular snack is *tostones* (fried green plantains—a relative of the banana).

• Desserts: popular desserts include *flan* (caramel custard); *tatianoff* (chocolate cake smothered with

cream); *chu* (bite-size puff pastries filled with meringue); *coco quemado* (coconut pudding); *coco rallado y queso* (grated coconut with cheese in syrup); *cucurucho* (coconut and pressed cocoa)—a speciality in Baracoa.

• A sweet sold at street stalls and bakeries is *churrizo* (doughnuts).

• Beverages: Cubans drink coffee called *cafecito*, which is like *espresso*. Coffee served in tourist restaurants is called *café con leche* (half coffee, half milk). *Café americano* is diluted Cuban coffee. Since the "Special Period," coffee is often mixed with other things, such as chicory.

• Soft drinks are widely available. If you ask for water at a restaurant, you'll be brought bottled mineral water. (Always be sure that any bottled water has an intact seal.) Other soft drinks: *Malta Caracas* (a nonalcoholic drink from Venezuela that tastes like root beer); *guarapo* (fresh squeezed sugarcane juice); *batidos* (a fruit drink made by beating milk, ice, and fruit together—this is one to avoid); *refrescos* (chilled fruit juices sold at stalls—drink **only** if you are sure that no water or ice has been added). Hotel shops and other shops sell cartons of a good-quality fruit juice called Tropical Island. The national soft drink is *Tropicola*; it is very sweet but doesn't have much flavor.

• Cuba makes some German-style beers. In dollar stores you can buy some U.S. and Mexican brands.

• Rum and rum-based cocktails are very popular. *Carta Blanca* is a light, dry rum aged for three years; *Carta de Oro* is golden, dry, and aged for five years; *Anejo* is a dark, seven-year-old rum. Ernest Hemingway was influential in launching the *mojito* (rum with sugar, lime juice, soda, Angostura bitters and a sprig of mint, served on the rocks).

• The region of Pinar del Río is known for the liqueur *guayabita* made from rum and guava.

• Both Chilean and French wines are available.

• Note that hard liquors, other than rum, are very expensive.

HOTELS

• Be sure to arrange in advance for your hotel for the first few nights of your stay. Otherwise you will have to make arrangements at the airport, and you'll be assigned one of the most expensive hotels.

• Be aware that check-in time at most hotels is 4:00 P.M., and check-out time is 2:00 P.M.

• Realize that the majority of good hotels are in tourist areas. In other places, the quality of accommodations is poor.

• At a tourist hotel, expect a restaurant, a bar, a cafeteria, a night club, a swimming pool, a beauty parlor, car and bike rentals, and easy access to taxis. Also expect that a safety-deposit box for valuables will be available at the front desk.

• Be prepared to find rooms small and with no carpeting. Lighting wattage is usually low. Almost all rooms have air-conditioning. Only in luxury hotels will you find shampoo, conditioner, and lotion. In better hotels, those designed for foreigners, you would rarely be asked to share a bathroom.

• Prepare for higher prices in the high season (December to April).

• If you choose a budget hotel, check your room carefully before you agree to take it. Be sure that you can lock the door and that no one could get into the room through the window. The lowest class of hotels have short beds and undersized sheets and blankets. You usually have to share a communal bathroom and shower.

• Don't be surprised to see "love hotels," which couples use to have some privacy, since many families and extended families live together in very crowded conditions. Rooms are usually rented for three hours.

• Consider alternate accommodations—*aparthotels*, which are often joined to regular hotels. They offer kitchenettes with dishes, cutlery, and cooking utensils. Some are suites with tables and sofas and chairs. Since many have one or two bedrooms, these apartments are a money-saving alternative for families.

• Another class of accommodations is the *peso* hotel. They are primarily for Cubans and cost less than $1.00 a night. Some appear attractive, but most don't even approach Western standards. To book them, you can't use the state-run tourist organization. Look for the central booking office—every town has one—called *Carpeta*. They will charge a small amount to make the call for you. However, don't be surprised to find that many of these hotels refuse foreigners.

• If you have an adventurous streak and would like to meet Cubans at home, look for signs on private homes that rooms are for rent. The price of the room often includes breakfast and dinner. It's even safe to stop someone on the street and ask if they could suggest a home at which you could stay, or ask a taxi driver, who will usually know people who rent rooms. However, avoid responding to touts on the street who approach you.

• Note that one popular form of accommodation—the youth hostel—is not available in Cuba.

• When you arrive at a hotel, expect to be given an identity card (*tarjeta de huesped*). Don't lose it, because you need it when ordering meals, when changing money, and even when you get into an elevator to go to your hotel room.

• Be prepared for the hotel staff to ask to see your passport. They will not keep it. Ask them not to stamp it.

• Try to pay in advance for the number of nights you plan to stay at a hotel. Sometimes, if you pay for just one night, the hotel clerk may tell you the next day that the room is booked.

• Realize that newer hotels operate on 220-volt current—as does Europe—because many joint business ventures are now being done with Europeans. Some hotels have both 110 volts and 220 volts. Be sure to ask about the current when you check in, should you be planning to use a laptop computer or other appliance that needs to be plugged in. To be really safe, bring a converter with you.

• Bring a plug for the sink, if you'll be staying in anything but a deluxe hotel.

• Many hotel rooms have an empty thermos. Even though the bartender will fill it with cold water if you ask, resist the temptation. Drink nothing but bottled water.

• Don't expect constant hot water. It may be available at only certain times of the day, if at all, and it may be at best tepid. In most large hotels in Havana, water will be available. However, due to electrical shortages and low water pressure, there may not be constant water outside the city. Sometimes there will just be cold water, often not enough for taking a shower. Sometimes, you will find a bucket by the faucet to use in flushing the toilet.

• Be careful when you take a

shower. The units are often electrically powered. You switch it on and leave it on during the shower. However, **don't** touch anything metal, or you may get a shock.

• In most of the large resort hotels, expect meals to be served buffet-style. Sometimes the meals are very good. State-run beach hotels try to have buffets available.

• If you know your next destination, ask the hotel clerk to phone and make reservations.

of tip include lipstick, nylons, and barrettes.

• To museum guides who give a tour, give $1.00.

• Tip hotel guards who watch your car at night $1.00.

• Give drivers of official taxis $1.00. With private taxis, use your own judgment. (See "Transportation" for the distinction between the two.)

• Never offer money to anyone in exchange for preferential treatment.

TIPPING

• Note that service charges are not included in restaurant bills, and tips are not obligatory. However, if you wish to round off your bill to the nearest $1.00, hand the money to the waiter on your way out. Don't leave the tip on the table. If you received special service, each person in the party should leave about 50 cents.

• Leave hotel maids $1.00 per day on the pillow. Don't leave other things (e.g., a nightgown or robe) on the pillow, because the maid may think that it's for her. Other forms

PRIVATE HOMES

• If you know that the people you plan to visit have a phone, phone ahead, so that any problems with work schedules and transportation can be worked out. It is okay to take a chance and drop in if you want to, since neighbors go in and out of one another's homes without calling.

• Expect your host to insist that you eat or drink something during your visit.

• If you use the phone in a family's home, be sure to offer to pay for the calls.

• Should you be a houseguest, include the family when you plan to take a walk or go to a *paladar*.

• Feel free to take a daily bath, but be sensitive to the limited water supply.

• Offer to help with the chores if you're staying with a family. Your host will refuse.

Gifts: If invited to dinner, bring a bottle of wine.

• If you're staying overnight, give soap, shampoo, peanut butter, or chocolate. Books in Spanish (current novels, poetry, children's book) are treasured. Young people enjoy receiving English/Spanish dictionaries.

• Remember that Cubans rarely say "thank you" for gifts, but they are very generous and eager to please.

• If at all possible, bring school supplies, over-the-counter medicines, and calculators to donate to clinics and schools. These items are in short supply in Cuba.

BUSINESS

Hours

Businesses: Open from 8:00 A.M. to 5:00 P.M., Monday through Saturday. Offices are closed every other Saturday.

Government Offices: Open 8:00 A.M. to noon and 1:00 to 5:00 P.M., Monday through Friday.

Banks: 8:30 A.M. to noon and 1:30 to 3:00 P.M., Monday through Friday and every other Saturday from 8:00 to 10:00 A.M.

Shops: 10:00 A.M. to 6:00 P.M., Monday through Saturday and 9:00 A.M. to 1:00 P.M. on Sunday.

Currency

• The unit of currency is the *peso*, which equals $1.00. The rate of exchange does not fluctuate.

• Coins: 1, 2, 5, 10, 20 *centavos*. Twenty *centavos* are also called a *peseta*.

• Notes: 1 (olive), 3 (red), 5 (green), 10 (brown), 20 (blue), and 50 (purple) *pesos*.

• One *peso* = 100 *centavos*.

• Canadians should realize that their currency is rarely accepted in Cuba. They should bring U.S. dollars.

• Bring as much money as you think you'll need. There are no ATMs in Cuba.

• Be aware that state-run entities want only dollars. Bring *pesos* for buses, restaurants, or bars not frequented by tourists. Use *pesos* at agricultural markets. People at crafts markets may accept *pesos*, but they prefer dollars.

• Credit cards not issued by U.S. banks are accepted. If you have a Carnet, Eurocard, MasterCard, or Visa credit card not issued by a U.S. bank, it will be accepted. Thomas Cook Visa travelers' checks in U.S. dollars are acceptable, if they have not been issued by a U.S. bank.

• Don't change money on the street. Not only is it illegal, but you may be given counterfeit money.

• Don't be surprised if, at a bank, people put you at the head of line. It's often a courtesy extended to foreigners.

• Bring U.S. dollars in cash in small denominations—$20 and under—for daily transactions. Be sure to have a good supply of $5 and $1 bills for taxis and markets, because people may not be able to make change. Use larger denominations only for paying hotel bills.

Business Practices

• Avoid trying to do business in July and August. Cuba is very hot during those months, and many people are on vacation.

• Note that the best time to schedule appointments is between 10:00 and 11:00 A.M. The worst time is between 3:00 and 5:00 P.M., because people will be concerned about transportation.

• Note that most of the larger tourist hotels have an office in the Ministry of Communication. This place serves as a post office and provides long-distance telephone service. Some have fax and telex machines.

• Be sensitive to the fact that taxis are too expensive for people without access to dollars, so many businesspeople must rely on crowded buses.

• Be prepared to show that your business will benefit Cuban society by creating new jobs, paying taxes, and expanding the economy. Cubans will be particularly receptive to businesses concerned with the environment.

• Realize that foreigners doing business in Cuba must have a partner—the government—in a joint venture. The government will make decisions on which programs to accept.

• Remember to be on time for meetings, but be prepared for Cubans to be late because of the vagaries of public transportation.

• Bring enough copies of your

proposal for everyone at the meeting. There is a serious paper shortage and there are few photocopying machines.

• Be aware that personal relationships are **very** important. At the first meeting, expect informal conversation over coffee and juice. (Best to decline the juice, because it may have water in it.)

• Bring business cards. Give them to everyone at a meeting—the people who make the decisions and the people who have accompanied them.

• Reconcile yourself to being patient. Bureaucracy will probably be a problem. Also, never speak to anyone in a critical tone.

• Realize that after foreign investments are paid off, the government's portion of the profits goes to subsidize food, free education, and health care.

• Visiting businesswomen should recall that the roles of women and men are the same, so they will have no problems in Cuba.

• Note that business lunches and dinners aren't common, but there will be a reception or dinner after negotiations have been completed.

• After the second meeting, invite your counterpart to a meal in a restaurant. (Both males and females should do this.) Spouses are not usually included in the invitation.

• Never give gifts to government officials with whom you're negotiating, but bring small gifts, such as pens, for businesspeople.

HOLIDAYS AND SPECIAL OCCASIONS

On some of Cuba's holidays, work continues; on others, everything shuts down. The dates for some holidays/festivals are changed frequently (e.g., the Havana International Jazz Festival). It's difficult for U.S. citizens to find out the dates of "floating" holidays, since, at this time, the country does not have diplomatic relations with Cuba. It is also difficult to determine whether banks and shops will be open.

• Liberation Day (Jan. 1—a nonworking day); Victory Day (Jan. 2); Jose Martí's birthday (Jan. 28); Anniversary of the Second War of Independence (Feb. 24); International Women's Day (March 8); Anniversary of the Students' Attack on the Presidential Palace (March 13); Bay of Pigs Victory (April 19); Labor Day (May 1—a nonworking day); National Revolution Days (July 25–27—nonworking days); Day of the Martyrs of the Revolution (July 30); Anniversary of Che Guevara's Death (Oct. 8); Anniversary of the First War of Independence (Oct. 10—nonworking day);

Memorial Day to Camilio Cienfuegos (Oct. 28); Anniversary of the Landing of the Granma (Dec. 2); Memorial Day to Antonio Macco (Dec. 7); Christmas (Dec. 25); (celebration of Christmas was abolished in 1969, because it coincided with the beginning of the sugar harvest, but it was reinstated in 1997 to honor the visit of Pope John Paul II).

• Note that with the advent of socialism, traditional fiestas were abolished.

• Remember that *Carnaval* (similar to Mardi Gras) was renewed in 1997. It is celebrated in late July and at the beginning of August.

TRANSPORTATION

Public Transportation

• Keep in mind that most large towns have inter-city buses, which are very overcrowded. If possible, enter at the front and drop your money into a fare box near the driver. Cubans sometimes get on at the rear and pass their fare up. If you want the bus to stop, yell "Parada!" (Stop) [pah-**rah**-dah].

As of March 2000, Cuba is building more buses—Brazilian bodies with Mercedes engines being assembled in Cuba to alleviate one of the country's serious problems: the availability of mass transportation.

• Expect the bus station in Havana to be chaotic. You probably won't be able to book a ticket on a bus for days. Be prepared to pay in U.S. currency and for the buses to be very run-down.

• Remember that it's almost impossible to make advance reservations on short distance inter-city buses. You'll be given a slip of paper with your destination and position in line. Board when your number is called. (Ask for help if you don't understand Spanish.) Sometimes you'll just wait in line, and board the bus. Fees are paid on board.

• For long-distance travel, choose between two categories of bus: the special air-conditioned buses are faster and more comfortable than the regular buses. Sometimes you must wait as long as a month if the bus will be going on a popular route.

• Don't look for a "no-smoking" area on transportation. You won't find one.

• Sit toward the front on long-distance buses. They often get very hot and smell of exhaust. Bring bottled water and snacks. Stops are rare. Some of the buses have toilets.

• Note that regular local buses are called *guaguas*. They are usually very crowded. The driver only opens the front door when he lets

passengers off. Try to stay in
front. If you are stuck way in the
back, pound the middle or rear
door; if he hears, the driver will
probably open the door and let
you off. The huge "double-
humped" buses, pulled by trucks,
are called *camellos* (camels).

• Be aware that there are two
types of taxi: official and private.
The official (state-run) taxis may or
may not have meters. You'll find
tourist taxis at hotels; they have a
blue "T" on the front door. You
must pay the fare in dollars. Private
"pirate" taxis have yellow license
plates. Negotiate the fare in advance, since these taxis don't have
meters. You must pay in dollars.
The private taxis are often available
for all-day tours or for transporting
businesspeople. In that case, there
will be a set fee.

• Expect to find taxis in the center of town or in front of train and
bus stations. They are usually old
American cars. The fare is cheaper;
drivers want to be paid in dollars.

• If you want a taxi for a long distance and don't mind sharing the
transportation, look for a *colectivo* in
front of the train or bus station. The
charge is per seat, and the bus de-
parts when it is full. A foreigner will
be charged more than a Cuban.

• Be prepared to find only
second-class accommodations on
trains—hard, wooden seats. When
first class is available, you'll find
padded seats, but conditions are
crowded and uncomfortable. Some

routes have a special first class,
which is more comfortable and includes basic lunch-box meals.

• Be sure to bring a jacket or
sweater for a train trip. The air-
conditioning makes compartments
very cold.

• Be aware that there is food on
the 17-hour trip from Havana to
Santiago, but it's of very poor quality. If you're making that trip, bring
your own food.

• Remember that most trains are
sold out days or weeks in advance.
The ticket office, located in cities
and at train stations, is called *Ladis*.
Foreigners must pay in dollars. It's
difficult to purchase many legs of a
train journey in advance. Purchase
your ticket for one leg, and as soon
as you arrive at your first destination, purchase the ticket for the next
leg.

• Consider flying within Cuba.
The cost is not great; however,
flights are frequently booked
months in advance—especially during August and December, when
most Cubans take vacations. Be flexible, because there are frequent
schedule changes.

• Remember that payments for
flights are usually nonrefundable.
Foreigners paying with dollars are
usually given preference for waiting
lists. If you don't arrive on time for
check-in, your seat may be given
away, and you will **not** be given a
refund.

• Don't try to purchase tickets for
buses or trains on short notice, using

pesos. Even with dollars, purchase tickets well in advance, especially for internal flights.

Driving

• Consider driving around Cuba, since there are few cars on the roads, but the road network is one of the most advanced in Latin America. Cuba has the highest driving standards of all the Latin American or Caribbean countries. People must take an intensive driving course. They drive slowly, are respectful of other drivers, and obey traffic signals.

• To rent a car, use your own driver's license or an international driving permit.

• Beware of livestock—bulls, cattle, oxen—and ox-driven carts when driving. Since few people own cars, there will be many people riding bicycles swerving from side to side in both cities and rural areas. Be cautious.

• Be especially wary if driving at night. There are no streetlights and no side rails or markings. Because of the transportation problems, people sometimes sleep right on the road.

• If you see sticks up in the road, remember that they are there to mark potholes. You'll encounter many potholes on country roads.

• Note that there are no seat-belt regulations. (Many cars were built before 1959, pre–seat belt).

• If you rent a car, be aware that gasoline is in short supply and is very expensive. Always keep your tank at least half full. There are hard currency gas stations around Cuba called *Servi-Cupex.* Most are open 24 hours a day. (Cold drinks and groceries are available.) Many local stations are often out of fuel or don't have the "super" required for rental cars.

• If you are fined for a traffic violation, pay when you return your car to the rental office.

• If you see a white sign with a red triangle and the word *Pare,* stop. Speed limits: in cities, 30 mph; on dirt roads and in tunnels, 25 mph; on paved highways, 55 mph; on freeways, 60 mph. If you're stopped for excessive speed, the insurance on a rental car may be invalidated.

• Realize that it's a law that children must sit in the backseat.

• Don't buy black-market fuel. Someone may approach you when you're stopped or getting in or out of the car and try to sell it to you. It may be watered down and do damage to the car, and your rental agreement may be compromised.

• To stay within the law, don't honk your horn.

• Don't worry about parking problems. There are so few cars that it isn't difficult to find a space.

LEGAL MATTERS, SAFETY, AND HEALTH

• Never offer money to a policeman. If one asks for money, get his name and badge number, and file a complaint with the Ministry of Foreign Relations.

• Keep in mind that violent crime is rare. However, the increase in tourism has brought some pickpocketing and petty theft. Women should watch their purses carefully. Both men and women should wear money belts. Keep your money in several different places in case some is stolen.

• Discourage thefts from your hotel room (clothing is a common target) by putting the "Do Not Disturb" sign on your door when you go out. That way a potential thief will believe that someone is in the room.

• Remember to drink nothing but bottled water. Avoid fruit juices and ice. Older travelers to Cuba may remember that it used to be safe to drink the water. However, the embargo on chemicals to purify the water and parts to repair water-treatment plants has created the conditions for water-borne diseases. Bottled water is available in hotels and shops. Be sure that the bottle is sealed, an indication that no one has opened it, used it, and filled it with tap water.

• Be sure to bring tissues, because most bathrooms don't have toilet paper.

• Note that the standard of medical care in Cuba is high, but medical supplies may not exist. If you get sick, you can either go to a doctor and hope for the best or try to leave the country, if you're able.

ECUADOR

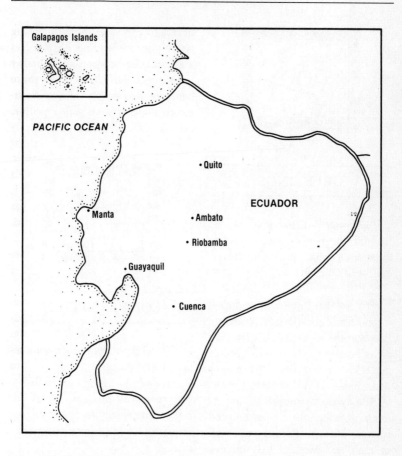

Galapagos Islands

PACIFIC OCEAN

• Quito

ECUADOR

• Manta

• Ambato

• Riobamba

• Guayaquil

• Cuenca

While Ponce de León searched for the fountain of youth, many modern travelers look for a climate that's eternal spring. They'll find it in Quito, whose warm days and cool nights give the city as close to ideal weather as you're likely to find. Venture just a few miles outside Quito and you can straddle the equator, with one foot in the Northern and one in the Southern Hemisphere.

For many travelers, Ecuador is the gateway to one of the world's great adventures—a trip to the Galápagos Islands, the remote archipelago (mostly still uninhabited) where Charles Darwin gathered a great deal of the evidence that led to his theory of evolution, and where you can still see giant tortoises who may have been members of Darwin's welcoming committee.

duced to everyone individually by your host. Depending on the formality of the occasion and whether people are elderly, they either shake hands or kiss on one cheek. At an informal party with young people, everyone will kiss on one cheek.

GREETINGS

Language: Ecuador's official language is Spanish, though the indigenous people speak Quichua, a dialect of Quechua.

• Note that when introduced, when greeting, and when departing, Ecuadoreans shake hands with people of both sexes. Indigenous people don't kiss in greeting. When they shake hands, they do so very lightly.

• Be aware that greetings are often more affectionate between good friends. Women and women as well as men and women kiss on one cheek when greeting and departing. Men shake hands with other men.

• Be sure to use titles in greeting others. They are very important, as they confer status. The major titles are: *Abogado* (lawyer), *Arquitecto* (architect); *Ingeniero* (engineer), and *Doctor* (lawyer or medical doctor).

• At a party, expect to be intro-

CONVERSATION

• Good topics for conversation are family and jobs.

• Avoid bringing up politics, your personal problems, your (or anyone else's) sex life, or any subject implying your country's superiority.

TELEPHONES

• Expect to find a limited number of public telephones—mostly in hotels and at the airports—in Ecuador's main cities. Deposit one *sucre* for three minutes. If you want to talk longer, deposit more money. If you can't find a public telephone, ask to use one in a shop. There will usually be a small fee.

• Look for EMETEL offices to make international calls as well as long-distance calls within Ecuador. The company has an office—open from 6:00 A.M. to 10:00 P.M.—in every town, EMETEL offers only telephone services, but in large towns you can also send telexes and telegrams.

• Realize that collect calls are available only to countries with which Ecuador has an agreement.

• Realize that some telephones accept phone cards, which can be purchased at EMETEL offices.

• Notice that fax machines and E-mail are becoming common in larger cities such as Quito, Guayaquil, and Cuenca. All three have public E-mail centers. First-class

hotels charge about half of what an EMETEL center charges.

• For tourist information, check the green pages of the telephone directory. Some sections are in English.

• Emergency phone numbers: Police—101; Fire Department—102; general emergency—111; Red Cross ambulance—131, 580, and 598.

IN PUBLIC

• Realize that English is understood only in first-class hotels, travel agencies, and airline offices. Most indigenous people are bilingual in Quichua and Spanish, but some speak only Quichua.

• Expect to find two very different cultures in the country's two major cities. Quito, in the mountains and with a large indigenous population, is traditional, conservative, and Catholic, while Guayaquil, on the coast, is a bustling city and the center of Ecuador's economic life.

• Enjoy the variations in local clothing, dialect, and cultures you will see when traveling in different parts of the country.

• If you're planning to travel outside the major cities, remember that rainstorms sometimes cause landslides, closing roads and businesses, and interrupting telephone service.

• Should you be invited to a girl's fifteenth birthday party, expect to be one of hundreds of guests. The party is often held in a club, but sometimes in a home. If the invitation specifies formal wear, men should wear tuxedos or suits, and women long dresses. Bring the invitation with you, as it may be checked at the door. Good gifts are jewelry or clothing.

• Bargain in markets, but not in stores or supermarkets. First check in shops to find out what they charge for the items you would like to buy. That will give you an idea as to how much you can probably lower the price by bargaining at a market.

• Expect indigenous people to be very flattered at being photographed, but be sure to ask first. The only time they don't want to be photographed is if their clothes are dirty and torn from working.

• In a city, expect indigenous people to ask if they can guard your car or carry your bags. If you want their services, tip them the equivalent of a quarter. If you don't, be firm in rejecting the offer.

• Look for public bathrooms in hotels and restaurants. You can also try asking in a shop if you can use the facilities. Bring your own tissues

as many bathrooms don't have any. Some public bathrooms charge for the use of tissue. Lavatories are marked SS.HH (*Servicios Higienicos*). There may be a single lavatory. If there are two, one will be labeled *DAMAS* (Women) and the other *HOMBRES* (Men). Or they may be marked by a picture of a man and a woman.

• Be prepared to see men urinating outdoors, because of the lack of public toilets. Women in towns generally ask to use a bathroom in a restaurant. In villages, women may urinate outdoors as well. When traveling through the countryside, however, prepare to use the woods.

DRESS

• In the coastal areas (Guayaquil, Manta), which tend to be hot, stick to natural fibers such as cotton, linen, and silk. Synthetic fabrics can be very, very hot.

• Realize that clothing is important to Ecuadoreans. Even the poorest people wear clean, ironed clothing. Respect this custom by always looking neat and clean.

• Feel free to wear jeans on the

street. Women can wear pants in the cities. Shorts are appropriate for the coastal cities but not downtown or at public or private offices.

• Business dress in the highlands (Quito, Cuenca) is more formal. Men should wear dark suits, and women, suits, dresses, or skirts, and stockings. On the coast men wear *guayaberas* (shirts worn over the trousers) and women wear sleeveless dresses, because of the heat.

• When invited to an upper-class home in a city, men should wear suits and women dresses.

• Note that formal dress for men is a dark suit and for women a cocktail dress. Long dresses and tuxedos are worn only on very special occasions.

MEALS

Hours and Foods

• A caution: Don't drink tap water or have drinks with ice in them—ALWAYS buy bottled water. Be sure that any bottled water you use has a seal. Do not eat unpeeled fruits or vegetables. If there are no op-

tions, eat cooked food from street vendors if it is **very** hot.

Breakfast: Usually served between 7:00 and 8:30 A.M. (though it may be earlier in families with children in school). The meal is light—juice, bread, coffee, and milk.

Lunch: From 1:00 to 2:00 P.M. It's a substantial meal: soup, chicken or fish (in a restaurant, the main dish is often meat), served with rice and salad or potatoes, fruit or ice cream, and juice.

Dinner: About 8:00 P.M. Usually a light meal of soup and coffee. Office workers who have only 30 minutes for lunch will have a large dinner at home.

• Note that on Saturdays, Sundays, and during vacations, lunch and dinner are usually served later.

Beverages: Common beverages are natural fruit juices, mineral water, and beer. The most common drinks with meals are fresh fruit juices, served unchilled. To order juice, ask for *jugo puro* (hoo-goh poo-roh), *sin agua* (seen ah-gwah) without water.

• Try to stick to soft drinks, natural fruit juice, or beer. People may not boil the water in their homes, so there's a risk of illness with any drink that has cold water.

• Note that many Ecuadoreans make coffee by boiling it for hours and then pouring the syrup into a pitcher to which they add milk or water. Espresso is available only in finer restaurants. Tea or *té* (teh) is always served with lemon and sugar. If you ask for tea with milk, you'll get hot milk with a tea bag in it.

• Herbal teas and hot chocolate are also popular drinks.

Table Manners

• Realize that an invitation to a dinner party is unusual. People are more inclined to have parties that start late at night and go on until 4:00 or 5:00 A.M. Snacks such as canapés and *empanadas* (small turnovers filled with meat, spices, and vegetables) will appear during the party, and the night often ends with guests staying for breakfast. If you leave as early as 1:00 A.M., your hosts will think you're not having a good time.

• In upper-class homes, expect to be offered whiskey before dinner. Appetizers—shrimp, cold cuts, and cheese—will be offered. Don't pass them up, thinking you'll spoil your dinner, because it will be served very late; it may start at 11:00 P.M. or midnight and last until 2:00 A.M.

• In middle-class homes, before dinner expect a local alcoholic drink made from sugarcane (called *trago*). There probably won't be any appetizers, but there will be a hearty meal.

• Women should note that it's not considered polite for them to drink hard liquor, though it's acceptable for them to drink wine.

• Expect to sit at the head of the table if you are the guest of honor.

• In the countryside, note that peasants use spoons instead of knives and forks.

• In a middle- or upper-class home, anticipate being served individually by a maid or your hostess.

• Don't worry if you're not fond of spicy foods. Ecuadorean food is not spicy. If you would like to add some zest to it, you'll find a little dish of homemade hot sauce (*salsa picante*) or *ají* on the table.

• Expect rice as a staple in the coastal area, while potatoes are the staple in the mountains.

• Don't belch or burp in public. All social classes consider this behavior rude.

• If you eat with the lower middle class, the poor, or peasants, finish everything on your plate. Despite the fact that they serve huge portions, they feel that leaving food on your plate means you haven't enjoyed the food, which they interpret as an insult. The upper classes, who (ironically) serve much smaller portions, understand if you leave something on your plate.

• If you're dining in a home for the first time, leave about an hour after the meal is over. Good friends may stay longer.

Eating Out

• Anticipate a variety of international restaurants only in large cities. Quito has the best selection of Italian, French, and Chinese restaurants. Only in Quito and Guayaquil will you find many snack bars and fast-food places for pizza, fried chicken, and hamburgers.

• In Quito, you'll find pastry shops as well as sidewalk cafes where tourists and young people congregate.

• To find a Chinese restaurant, ask for a *chifa* (**chee**-fah).

• A *pollo a la brasa* specializes in fried chicken.

• *Parrilladas* are steak houses or grills. Chicken, liver, pork chops, steaks, and tripe are served on a grill, which is placed on the table. If you don't want the whole mixed grill, ask for just the item or items you do want—e.g., *sólo pollo* (**soh**-loh **poh**-yoh), just chicken.

• Don't plan to read the menu before entering a restaurant. Menus aren't posted outside.

• Enter the restaurant and choose your own table. In local restaurants, you may join others already seated at a table. Only in very expensive French and Italian restaurants are guests seated by a maître d'.

• In Quito and Guayaquil, anticipate finding restaurants open seven days a week, with dinner served until 11:00 P.M.—sometimes later. People don't usually go out to dinner until 8:30 P.M. In small cities restaurants close earlier, usually before 10:00 P.M.

• If eggs are your breakfast staple, note that while they are available, boiled eggs are usually presented barely cooked. Ask for them *bien cocidos* (byen koh-**see**-dohs), well cooked, or ask for scrambled eggs.

• Call the waiter *señor* (seh-**nyohr**), *mesero* (meh-**seh**-roh), or *mozo* (**moh**-soh). The latter two both mean "waiter." Though you will see some people clap their hands over their head to summon the waiter, realize that it's considered rude.

• Be aware that imported liquor is extremely expensive. Drink Ecuadoean beer, or Pilsner, which is very good, or imported Chilean wines, which aren't as expensive as those from Europe. *Pisco* is akin to rum. *Aguardiente* (a drink like schnapps or *eau-de-vie*), anise-flavored and mixed with lemon, is called *paico* (py-koh). Sangria is another common beverage in restaurants. Other popular drinks are Cuba Libre (rum and Coke) and *caipirhinas* (*aguardiente* and lemon and sugar).

• For mineral water, look for *Guitig* (**wee**-teek). It's good and it's fairly inexpensive. If no shops are available, you'll have to ask for it in a restaurant. You can't remove bottled water from restaurants (i.e., to take on a bus or train trip). Bring a canteen, a thermos, or a plastic bottle if you want to take water with you from a restaurant. You can also buy plastic bottles of water or soda.

• Don't suggest separate checks

or splitting the check. Ecuadoreans consider it insulting to pay individually. One person pays for everyone.

• If you eat at a lower-class restaurant, don't be surprised to see children hang around to eat your leftovers. It's a common (and accepted) practice.

Specialties

• Note that the most commonly used herb is fresh coriander leaf; in Spanish, it's known as *cilantro* (see-lahn-tro).

• Soups are called *caldos, sopas,* or *locros. Caldo de gallina* is chicken soup. Somewhat heartier is a *seco,* a stew. *Seco de gallina* is chicken stew, while *seco de cordero* is lamb stew.

• The specialties in coastal towns are three types of fish: *ceviche,* raw fish marinated in lime, onion, and coriander; *corvina,* white sea bass; *trucha,* trout, which is widely available mostly in the coastal region.

• Other specialties: *yaguarlocro,* potato soup with blood sausage; *lechón,* suckling pig; *tostadas de maíz,* fried corn pancakes; *humitas,* corn *tamales,* especially popular at breakfast; *patacones,* fried plaintains; *cuy,* whole roasted guinea pig, which is considered a delicacy.

• In the Sierra, a specialty is *llapingachos,* potato pancakes made with cheese and often served with eggs. These are sold in markets and are safe to eat.

HOTELS

• Select from a variety of accommodations. A *pensión* or a *hospedaje* is often an inexpensive boardinghouse, usually run by a family. A *hostal* can vary from an inexpensive hostel to a moderately priced inn. A *hostaría* is a mid-range comfortable country inn. Hotel can mean anything from a brothel to a luxurious establishment. A lodge is most often in a remote area and usually provides guides, transportation, and meals. A lodge will probably have only kerosene lanterns and cold showers.

• Never rent a room without looking at it first. Be sure that the door locks securely and that the toilet and tub/shower function.

• Don't be surprised if you're charged extra in Quito hotels during the festival celebrating the foundation of the city (the week ending Dec. 5) and the New Year fiesta (Dec. 28 to Jan. 6). During those two periods, hotels are allowed to raise their rates.

• If you're staying in a smaller hotel in the highlands (Quito, for example), check to make sure that there is central heating. If not, make sure your room has a large supply of blankets.

• Expect parking problems if you arrive in Quito by car. To avoid them, choose a hotel outside the center of the city.

• Plan on a 10 percent service charge and a 5 percent tax being added to your bill in first- and second-class hotels.

PRIVATE HOMES

• Don't drop in on anyone during the siesta hour, 1:00 to 3:00 P.M.

• Realize that street numbers often don't go in sequence because houses are numbered according to the original building plot. If you're visiting a house, make sure that the host knows when you're coming so he can leave the entrance gate open. Gates are usually kept locked, and often bells don't work.

• Expect to see guards standing on every street corner guarding the homes. The residents of the neighborhood pay them to stand watch.

• If you're staying with a family in which everyone works, arrange to sightsee on your own.

• Anticipate waiting for a supply of boiled water if you're a very early riser. Maids get up early to boil the day's supply of water for drinking and cooking. Never drink unboiled tap water.

• Should you stay with a family for several days, tip the maid the equivalent of $5.00 (U.S.). The maid will make your bed and do your laundry, which she will usually

TIPPING

• Be aware that better restaurants add 10 percent tax and 10 percent service charge to the bill. If the service has been satisfactory, add another 5 percent for the waiter. Don't leave the money on the table. Hand it directly to the server.

• Tip boys or men who park your car and look after it about 20 cents for several hours.

• Each person in a touring group should tip guides $2.00 to $3.00 a day. Tip the driver about half as much as the guide.

• Give porters the equivalent of 50 cents.

• Don't tip taxi drivers, ushers, or gas station attendants.

have ready for you the day after you give it to her.

• Don't put used toilet paper in the toilet. Put it in the basket next to the toilet.

• Be aware that there is no water or electricity after midnight in some areas. Electricity may go off unpredictably. Be prepared with a pocket flashlight.

• Realize that some bathrooms have hot-water switches for the shower and some have a separate electrical switch that turns on the hot water. The first will give you an instant shower; for the other, you may have to wait a few hours for the water to heat up. Ask your host/ hostess which they have.

• If the family you are staying with isn't wealthy, offer to help by buying groceries. Upper-class families appreciate a token gift.

Gifts: As thanks for an invitation to a meal, bring pastries, chocolates, or flowers. Don't give lilies or marigolds because they are associated with funerals.

• From outside the country, bring women clothing, perfume, nail polish, or hair ornaments. Men like high-tech gadgets, calculators, and after-shave lotion. To teenagers, give T-shirts or sweatshirts with English writing on them, popular music cassettes or CDs, or mousse or gel for the hair (it's very expensive in Ecuador).

BUSINESS

Hours

Businesses: 9:00 A.M. to 1:00 P.M. and 3:00 to 6:00 P.M., Monday through Friday.

Government   Offices: 8:30 A.M. to 12:30 P.M. and 1:30 to 4:00 P.M., Monday through Friday.

Banks: 9:00 A.M. to 1:30 P.M., Monday through Friday. Some banks are open Saturday mornings.

Shops: 9:00 A.M. to 12:30 or 1:00 P.M. and 3:00 to 7:00 P.M., Monday through Friday; and 9:00 A.M. to noon, Saturday.

Currency

• As we write this, Ecuador is in the process of converting its currency to the U.S. dollar.

• Exchange money in major cities because it's difficult to change money in smaller towns, and the rate there is lower. You can also change money at good restaurants and hotels.

Business Practices

• Expect to make several trips to Ecuador to accomplish your business goals.

• Be flexible. People will talk as though actions are going to start right away, when they will actually take time.

• Realize that it's important to have a lawyer or consultant as a contact in Ecuador.

• Avoid business travel during school vacations; they occur from mid-January through April in Guayaquil and mid-July through October in Quito.

• Arrange appointments two weeks in advance.

• Arrive one or two days before your business appointments begin to allow your body to adjust to the altitude, if in Quito or the Sierra. To minimize problems, avoid eating heavily or drinking alcohol.

• Schedule business appointments after 10:00 A.M.

• Be punctual, but be prepared to wait at least 20 minutes for your business meeting to begin.

• Have your business cards printed in Spanish. Bring a supply with you as it will take a week to have them printed in Ecuador.

• Have business proposals and other materials translated into Spanish beforehand, since few people are really proficient in English.

• Note that there are photocopy machines and secretarial services easily available in Quito and Gua-

yaquil, and most good hotels have telex machines.

• Be relaxed and easygoing when doing business. Ecuadoreans are not formal and reserved as businesspeople.

• Realize that time estimates aren't very reliable. It's important to allow a certain margin for delays.

• Women should never be aggressive or argumentative. Be subtle and polite. Speak softly. Dress conservatively.

• Women will find it difficult to pay for a businessman's meal in a restaurant.

• A woman who is entertained by a business colleague should never have more than one alcoholic drink.

• Don't expect to be invited for a social drink after working hours.

• Realize that lunch is the most common meal for business discussions. Dinners are more formal, usually social occasions.

• Don't include spouses in invitations to business dinners. Ecuadoreans consider business a man's affair.

• When you host a meal, take businesspeople to well-known restaurants that specialize in French or international cuisine.

HOLIDAYS AND SPECIAL OCCASIONS

Expect banks, businesses, and many stores to be closed on the following national holidays. Check with the tourist offices to learn about local holidays in regions you plan to visit.

Holidays: New Year's Day (Jan. 1); Epiphany (Jan. 6); Tuesday and Wednesday before Ash Wednesday (Carnival); Holy Thursday; Good Friday; Labor Day (May 1); Pichincha Day, the anniversary of the Battle of Pichincha (May 24); Bolívar's Birthday (July 24); Independence Day (Aug. 10); Columbus Day (Oct. 12); All Saints' Day (Nov. 1); All Souls' Day (Nov. 2); Christmas Eve and Christmas Day (Dec. 24 and 25).

• Note these holidays, since they take place in important areas: Guayaquil Day (Oct. 9); Cuenca Day (Nov. 3); Quito Day (Dec. 6).

• Enjoy dancing in the street in Quito on the night of Dec. 5 (the night before Quito Day).

• If you're walking around during Carnival, wear waterproof clothing. People throw water balloons or pails of water at each other—and especially tourists, the preferred targets.

• Women need to be especially careful during local fiestas, which usually feature dancing and drinking. Men tend to harass single women. If you can find a male escort, you'll have fewer problems.

TRANSPORTATION

Public Transportation

• Note that there are no subways, even in the large cities.

• Be aware that buses are very crowded. Pay the fixed fare (no matter how far you're traveling) as you board. You don't receive a ticket. Buses, which always have a name and number, usually have a fixed route but may detour because of road repairs. One alternative to the crowded buses is a minibus. It costs slightly more.

• Check with the local tourist office about road conditions on the way to your destination. If you want to travel in the afternoon, ask the bus driver and passengers on an incoming bus at the terminal what road conditions are.

- Guard your money **very** carefully on a bus. Expect pickpockets. Wear a money belt, or, as one traveler did, put your bills in your shoe.
- Note that Quito now has an electric trolley that crosses the city. It's safe and dependable.
- Negotiate the fare in advance with a taxi driver, since only some taxis have meters. You can hail taxis on the street, but at night it's better to telephone for one.
- Should you plan to travel by train in the country, check when you arrive to see what is operating. The severe floods of 1983 and the earthquake of 1987 damaged much of the railway system.
- Note that long-distance buses don't have different classes of seating. Tickets are available at the bus terminal sometime between a few days and a few hours before departure. If you buy a ticket, you're assured a seat. Along the way, the driver may pick up people who are going a short distance and who will be packed in—standing. Some companies are better and safer than others; Occidental Tranesmeraldas and Pan Americana are usually reliable.
- If you are traveling a long distance, try to get a larger *executivo* bus. It will be more comfortable than other buses and will have a bathroom on board.

- Consider traveling by plane within Ecuador. Domestic air service is very inexpensive. The small difference in price between planes and buses is well worth the expense. Planes may take a few minutes to make a journey which will take hours by bus.
- Don't expect planes or buses to adhere to (or even to have) schedules. They leave only when they are full.

Driving

- Drive *very* defensively. Ecuadorean drivers are aggressive and pay little attention to driving rules.
- Though seat belts are not required, wear them for safety—especially in the countryside.
- Be aware that people honk their horns constantly.
- As a foreigner, do *not* try to bribe a policeman if you are stopped for a traffic violation.
- Note that there are laws regarding drinking and driving, but they are not strict and are only sometimes enforced when an accident has occurred.

LEGAL MATTERS, SAFETY, AND HEALTH

• If you have something stolen, report it to the police, obtain a copy of the report (to use with your insurance company back home), and put the incident out of your mind. You'll get nowhere pursuing the matter in Ecuador.

• Keep in mind that coca leaves, which are legal in Peru and Bolivia, are illegal in Ecuador.

• Be aware that penalties for drug possession—of even very small amounts of illegal drugs—are much stiffer than they are in the U.S. Sentences can be up to several years.

• Realize the areas of the indigenous peoples are very safe, but in the main cities there have been rapes and muggings of tourists. An additional problem in crowded areas and markets is pickpocketing. Guard your money carefully.

• If a woman has to go out alone at night—and we can't emphasize too strongly that she **SHOULD NOT**—she should carry a metal whistle in her hand.

• Women shouldn't travel alone in Ecuador unless they can speak Spanish. It's best not to travel alone outside cities. If you're traveling in a small group in the countryside, be sure that at least one of the group speaks Spanish fairly well.

• In Quito and in certain sections of Guayaquil, a woman can safely take a taxi alone at night. Ask at your hotel what areas of the city are safe. Guayaquil is more dangerous at night than Quito. There's a very active "night life" in Guayaquil, whereas Quito is more conservative, and people don't go out so much at night.

• Keep in mind that **no one** should **ever** go to beach areas alone at night. The only time you should go—even in a group—is with Ecuadoreans.

• Few Ecuadorean women go to restaurants alone. Most business women prefer to have meals in their hotel.

• Note that Ecuadorean women never speak to strange men. If, as a foreigner, you speak to men—even casually—it will be interpreted as a signal that you are interested and available.

• Indigenous people present no threat to women traveling alone. They remain detached from travelers, from *mestizos*, and the coastal black population as well.

• For advice on medicine and hygiene products, see "Legal Matters, Safety, and Health" in the Introduction.

GUATEMALA

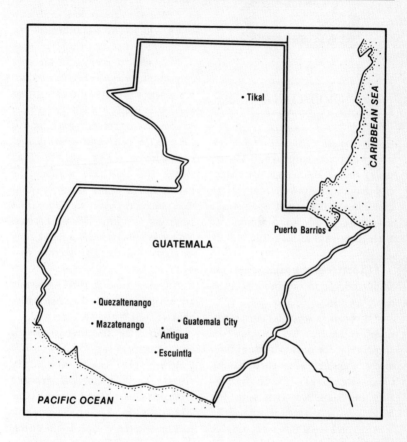

What happened to the Maya, one of the most mathematically so-phisticated civilizations ever? We can date the fall of Rome and the conquest of the Aztecs, but, while the great Maya civilization seems to have slipped away, much of the culture remains. Guatemala holds some of the most intriguing clues they left behind, especially in the greatest of the Mayan cities, Tikal, which the dense jungle made inaccessible until re-cently.

Though the Spanish arrived there in 1523, Guatemala (in contrast with the other countries of Central America) is still largely indigenous in culture and language.

GREETINGS

Language: In addition to Spanish, the official language of Guatemala, many indigenous languages and dialects are spoken. Many Maya children do not speak Spanish, so it's futile to try to communicate with them in that language.

• Expect a handshake when you are introduced to a member of either sex.

• If you are a woman being introduced to another woman, don't be surprised if she pats your right forearm or shoulder rather than shaking hands. Return the gesture by patting her shoulder with your left hand.

• In rural areas don't expect—or give—a firm handshake. Such handshakes are for those from urban areas or those who are Americanized. Men and women usually offer a limp handshake.

• Note that men and woman and women usually kiss when greeting one another in Guatemala City. They do this no matter how close or distant the relationship. Foreigners are not expected to kiss in greeting Guatemalans (unless they wish to) until the relationship is a familiar one.

• Men who are good friends embrace and pat one another on the back.

• Remember that titles are very important, even more so in rural areas where so few people have titles. *Profesor* is used in a village to refer to anyone who teaches anything. *Licenciado* (lee-sehn-**syah**-doh) is anyone with a college degree (e.g., B.A.). Use this title without the name, unless you're asking a question such as "Are you *Licenciado* Rodríguez?" Other titles: *Arquitecto* (architect); *Ingeniero* (engineer); *Doctor* (lawyer or medical doctor); *Profesor* (professor).

• Realize that at parties, people are always introduced individually. Shake hands with everyone.

• Note that in rural areas it's courteous to say *"Buenos días"* ("Hello" or "Good morning"), *"Buenas tardes"* ("Good afternoon") *"Buenas noches"* ("Good evening"), or *"Adiós"* ("Good-bye") to anyone you pass on a street or road. In the cities, don't say anything to passersby.

CONVERSATION

• Learn about Guatemala before you visit the country, so that you can show an interest in the country's people, history, and culture.

• A good subject for conversation is travel—within Guatemala and abroad.

• Talk about children, your hobbies, and your job.

• Don't be surprised if people ask about your job and marital status on very short acquaintance. Personal questions about costs of items and so forth are not meant to be offensive. They are simply matters of curiosity.

• Avoid discussing politics or "the violence" (of which Guatemala has suffered a great deal since 1978). If people are discussing politics in your presence, do nothing but listen. Make no comments. If you're pressed for a subject for conversation, talk about soccer.

• If you are talking to a man and a woman and ask a question, expect the man to answer it. You'll find this attitude especially prevalent in the indigenous population. If you

want to talk seriously to a woman, wait until she is alone.

• Never discuss anything relating to sexuality with a woman when a man is present.

• Do not be surprised if Guatemalans do not look you in the eye when they speak to you. Casting their eyes in a downward glance is a mark of respect, especially when a man is talking to a woman who is a stranger.

TELEPHONES

• Note that in 1996 all telephone numbers were changed to ones with seven digits. TELGUA offices have a formula to help you convert an old number to a new one.

• Look for public telephones in all major departmental cities. In smaller towns, some private homes will have a sign indicating that there is a public phone inside. Very few villages have telephones.

• To make a call, deposit several 10 or 25 *centavos* coins, if you wish to speak longer than three minutes, since you'll be cut off if you haven't deposited enough. Whether the call goes through or not, you will be charged for three minutes, and your money won't be refunded. Connections are often cut off despite the deposit of the required number of coins.

• Look for a button on the face of the phone under the receiver. When using this phone, you must press the button once when your party answers or he/she will not be able to hear you.

• To make long-distance calls, go to a TELGUA office. Give the operator the number you want; listen for your name to be called, and then go to the booth pointed out to you. Pay when you finish your call. Most TELGUA offices are open from 7:00 A.M. to 10:00 P.M. daily; some are open until midnight.

• Note that long-distance calls from a TELGUA office will be very expensive. Have your party call you back.

• Before telephoning from your hotel, check charges. They are often astronomical. You'll have to weigh convenience versus cost.

• Remember that you can't make collect calls to Britain, but you can to the U.S. and Canada.

• Send faxes and E-mail from TELGUA offices, many private offices, or from some of the new cyber cafes that have sprung up recently.

• Emergency numbers for Guatemala City: Police—120; Fire—122; Ambulance—125.

IN PUBLIC

• Speak softly; otherwise people will consider you very rude.

• Carry small change to give to beggars, who are usually physically handicapped people. Guatemalans themselves often give to beggars.

• To gesture "Come here," stretch your arm out, palm down, and give a quick jerk of the wrist, as in a scooping motion.

• To wave good-bye, raise your arm with the palm facing you, and flick you fingers, held together, away from you.

• Note that people frequently point their lips to indicate direction.

• Never fully extend your arm or hand outward with fingers spread, pointing forward. It's an obscene gesture.

• Don't photograph religious ceremonies (unless they are public fiestas) without asking the permission of the people involved.

• Never photograph any private home or property or business without asking permission from the owner—even if you see others taking pictures.

• In certain villages, especially in the lake district, anticipate a request for payment if you wish to take someone's picture. The person will ask for the equivalent of five or ten cents. Don't begrudge the money, since the economic situation—especially for indigenous Mayans—is extremely difficult.

• Expect to bargain in markets, antique shops, and other small shops. Ask the price. Offer half. Wait for a counter offer, and keep going up a bit. If the vendor's final offer is too much, walk away. You may be called back and offered the vendor's lowest price, or he or she may not call you back. If you really want the object, go back and agree to the lowest price the vendor offered.

• Note that the most popular items for tourists are those which are handwoven by indigenous Mayans. When bargaining for them, remember the months of work that have gone into the pieces and the extremely poor economic situations of the people.

• To find a public bathroom in a city, go to the town hall, restaurants, or hotels. In the countryside, go to a service station if you're near one (they often have clean bathrooms).

• Always carry toilet paper or tissues, since most public restrooms don't have any. Because the plumbing systems are poor, it's customary to throw dirty tissue in the trash instead of into the toilet.

DRESS

• For casual occasions, don't wear shorts in the cities or in the highlands. Jeans are popular everywhere. Men should wear pants and shirts (and sweaters in the highlands). Women may wear pants or a skirt and blouse.

• Women should avoid wearing dresses, shorts, tank tops, tight tops, or anything with spaghetti straps. Shoulders should be covered.

• Be aware that, outside the city, scantily clad women are thought of as prostitutes on their way to work.

• For business, men should wear a lightweight suit, in either a light or dark color. Women should wear a dress or skirt and blouse—never pants.

• When invited to a meal in a home, men should wear a jacket and trousers but no tie (ties are considered very formal) and women should wear a dress or skirt and dressy blouse or pantsuit.

• Formal wear—i.e., tuxedos for men—is worn only for certain weddings and diplomatic receptions.

• Note that in the highlands, each village has its own hand-loomed clothing for men and women. If you decide to wear native dress, be sure you're wearing the costume for the correct sex. Otherwise you'll make a fool of yourself. Embroidered pants are for men only, and the blouses called *huipiles* are for women. People feel proud that you choose to wear their hand-woven clothing.

MEALS

Hours and Foods

Breakfast: 7:00 A.M. to 8:00 A.M. The meal usually consists of eggs, black beans, bread, orange juice, and coffee. Breakfast in the countryside would consist of tortillas, eggs, and *chirmol* (see "Specialities").

Lunch: 12:30 or 1:00 P.M. Many homes will have soup, meat with vegetables (usually stewed) or salad, followed by fruit and coffee. Lunch in a traditional home consists of black beans, tortillas, and fried plantains. Lunch is the main meal of the day.

Dinner: 7:00 P.M., 8:00 P.M., or later. The meal will be much the same as lunch, but lighter. There might be black beans, rice, and fried plantains; or corn *tortillas*, tamales, and salad; or eggs with *tortillas* and beans. In rural Guatemala, beans and tortillas make up all three meals of the day. On special occasions, such as weddings, holidays, or death, *tamales* are served. They consist of a corn-based tortilla with beef in the middle, wrapped in banana leaves and boiled. No meal is considered a meal if tortillas aren't served.

Beverages: The most popular liquors are *ron* (rum) and *aguardiente* made from distilled sugar-cane. Note that imported liquors are very expensive, while Guatemalan beer is excellent.

• Common drinks before dinner are *Cuba libre* (rum and Coke) and Scotch.

• In rural areas, people drink coffee or water.

• With meals people drink soda, fruit juices, or beer. Wine is only for elegant meals. After dinner the drinks is always coffee.

• Popular drinks in homes are two hot drinks—*atole de maíz*, made with corn, and *atole de arroz*, made with rice. Both are boiled, so tourists will have no problems with them. If available, these drinks are served at all three meals all over the country.

Table Manners

• Women should never have more than one drink before dinner. In rural areas, it is rare to see women drink at any time.

• In wealthy areas, expect appetizers with drinks before dinner. The appetizers—called *boquitas*—consist of crackers, olives, peanuts, and *nachos* with guacamole.

• Note that female guests sit to the right of the host and male guests to his left.

• Note that in some families a maid will serve each person individually while in others you will help yourself from platters on the table.

• Realize that you're expected to finish everything on your plate. If food is served "family style," take small portions the first time. People will appreciate it if you take seconds.

• After eating a meal, if you are first to leave the table, say *"Muchas gracias"* ("Thank you"). If others leave before you, say to them *"Buen provecho"* (bwehn pro-**veh**-cho), roughly translated as "May it do you good."

• On week nights, stay until about 11:00 P.M. On weekends feel free to stay until midnight.

Eating Out

• In Guatemala, a *restaurante* is a high-class restaurant. A *comedor* is a small eating place serving typical Guatemalan food. A *bar* is a seedy place, where a woman would never go unless she were a prostitute. A *cantina* is a place where a woman can go to have a beer. For pastries to take out, visit a *pastelería*; a *café* offers sandwiches, coffee, tea, and hot chocolate in addition to pastries. For bread and rolls to take out, look for a *panadería*.

• Anticipate a large choice of restaurants in Guatemala City, where there are many German, French, Italian, Mexican, and Spanish restaurants. All cities and some large towns have a Chinese restaurant.

• Don't expect to find any pattern as to whether menus are posted outside of restaurants. Some of the lower-class ones do, and some of the luxury ones don't.

• Men should note that many better restaurants require them to wear a jacket and tie, although dress codes are sometimes not made evident or enforced.

• Note that in less elegant places, groups of three or more people should expect that every meal ordered will arrive at a different time.

• To attract the waiter's attention, raise your hand. If the waiter is male, say *"Joven"* (**ho**-ven) (young man); if female, *Seño* (sen-yo) (miss). At informal restaurants, people summon the waiter or waitress by saying "Tch, tch." Never do it in an elegant restaurant.

• At an inexpensive restaurant, don't expect good coffee. It's usually very weak because it's made with inferior beans; at better restaurants, the coffee is excellent. Note that if you order coffee with milk, half the cup will be filled with hot milk. At some restaurants you'll be served a pot of coffee and a pot of hot milk to mix yourself.

• In rural areas and in poorer areas of the capital, the coffee is a mixture of oats and inferior beans. (The excellent coffee gets exported.)

• Call the waiter to request the check. It won't be brought automatically. To ask for the check, say, "*La cuenta, por favor*" (lah **cooen**-tah, por fah-**vor**).

• Note that there are no set rules or customs about whether one person pays for a group or whether each person pays individually. Offer to pay your share. If one person absolutely insists on paying, let her or him do it, and then reciprocate. If a group goes out for drinks and not a meal, then each person usually buys a "round."

Specialities

• On the Caribbean coast, look for Creole cooking, which includes bananas, seafood, and coconuts. You'll also find *caldo de mariscos*—seafood soup with spices, usually with shrimp and fish.

• Try some of the following special dishes: *plátanos fritos*—fried plaintains; *guacamole*—mashed avocado with onions and tomatoes; *chiles rellenos*—stuffed peppers; *carne guisada*—stewed beef in a sauce; *chuchitos*—corn dough stuffed with meat and sauce and then wrapped in

a corn husk; *chirmol*—a sauce of onions, tomatoes, and spices served with grilled steak; *carne asada*—grilled thin steak served with *guacamole* and *chirmol*; *ceviche*—marinated raw fish with lime, onions, chilies, and cilantro; *pepián*—a tomato-based sauce with raisins, pumpkins, sesame seeds, and ground beef; *pollo jocón*—a sauce of roasted and peeled *tomatillos*, parsley, and garlic, to which chicken is added. It's served with rice.

HOTELS

• For the peak seasons—January, Easter, August, and December—be sure to make reservations well in advance.

• Realize that deluxe and first-class hotels have different prices for Guatemalans and foreigners. Moderately priced hotels, which are often clean and well run, don't raise their prices for foreigners.

• Check a guidebook for names of inns in various towns. Some have fireplaces in rooms, antiques, room service, and swimming pools. They are small and are much more interesting than the large, anonymous hotels and are decorated with Guatemalan art and weavings.

• Before you officially check into a room, inspect it. Check to be sure that there's a secure lock on the door and that the bathroom facilities work.

• Expect international cuisine in the restaurants of deluxe and first-class hotels.

TIPPING

• Note that a service charge is *not* included in a restaurant bill. Leave 10 percent.

• Give porters the equivalent of $1.00 (U.S.) per bag.

• Tip gas station attendants who perform extra service 25 or 50 cents.

• Don't tip ushers.

• Give boys who carry parcels out of the markets 25 cents.

• Urban hairdressers expect about 10 percent as a tip.

• Tip taxi drivers 5 percent.

PRIVATE HOMES

• Since there are no telephones in most of Guatemala, try to arrange a visit in person ahead of time. However, people will still be accommodating if you drop in without notice. The usual time for visiting is after dinner and on weekends.

• If you're staying with a family, be aware that meal times are extremely important, and people will be upset if you are late, especially for the midday meal when fathers usually come home from work and children from school.

• Be sure to offer to pay for international calls made from a private home. Your host will probably not let you. It's not necessary to pay for local calls.

• Since there are different types of heaters for showers, be sure to ask your hosts how to use the one in their house. Don't try to use one without asking; you could get an electric shock. The heating element is often incorporated directly into the shower head; this is why it could give off a shock. In some homes, you need to turn on the shower using a dry towel.

• If you stay with a family for a week or more, and there is a maid, tip her the equivalent of $5.00 for each week of your stay at the end of your visit. Just hand her the money.

Gifts: When invited to a meal, bring a bottle of imported wine or flowers. Don't bring white flowers, as they are associated with funerals, or red flowers, as they signify love.

• From the U.S. or Europe, bring the latest gadgets (e.g., watches, small tape recorders), the latest best-sellers (for people you know read English), or liquor, especially Johnnie Walker Red or Black Label Scotch.

• For business, bring a bottle of cognac or wine—but not on your first visit. (See advice in "Business" section.)

BUSINESS

Hours

Businesses: Monday through Friday, 8:00 A.M. to noon, and 2:00 to 6:00 P.M.

Government Offices: In Guatemala City, Monday through Friday, 8:00 A.M. to 4:30 P.M., or 9:00 A.M. to 3:30 P.M. Rural government offices close for lunch.

Banks: 8:30 or 9:00 A.M. to 3:00 P.M. on weekdays and 9:00 A.M. to 1:00 P.M. on Saturday.

Shops: 9:00 A.M. to 12:30 or 1:00 P.M. and 1:30 or 2:00 to 6:00 P.M., Monday through Friday. Many shops open on Saturday morning and close at 12:30 or 1:00 P.M.

Currency

• Note that the unit of currency is the *quetzal*. One *quetzal* contains 100 *centavos*.
• Coins: 1, 5, 10, and 25 *centavos*.
• Bills: 50 *centavos* and 1, 5, 10, 20, 50, and 100 *quetzales*. One *quetzal* is often called *sencillo* (sen-**see**-yo), meaning single.
• Change money in Guatemala City, where banks give a better exchange rate than do those in other parts of the country.
• Expect to find ATMs at banks in major cities.
• Don't flash around 100 Q bills.
• Note that major credit cards are accepted by large hotels, restaurants, retail stores, airlines, and car rental agencies. They are now becoming accepted even in rural areas.
• Don't be surprised if there is a shortage of small change. If you need change for a tip or a phone call

you may not be able to get it, or someone to whom you hand a bill may say, "I don't have any change."

• Break up your 50 and 100 Q bills when you can. For example, pay at a restaurant with a large bill so that you will have smaller bills. You'll need them to pay for transportation, items at craft fairs, etc.

• Don't accept a torn bill if someone tries to give you one, because many elegant places will not accept one from you.

• Be aware that you cannot change *quetzales* into dollars when you leave Guatemala. Don't change more dollars into *quetzales* than you'll be able to use during your visit.

Business Practices

• Realize that contracts are important. Obtain them through your embassy, A.I.D. (U.S.'s Agency for International Development), or shippers. Sometimes you can make personal contacts at conferences for people in your business.

• Prepare to make several trips to Guatemala to achieve your goal.

• Avoid business trips in January, April, August, November, and December. Many businesspeople vacation in August, and during the two weeks before and after Christmas and the week before and after Easter. Also avoid the two-to-three-day celebration around Independence Day (Sept. 15).

• From abroad, make appointments at least two weeks in advance. If you're in the country, a few days will be enough.

• If you're planning to bring a computer or other electronic device, note that outlets take U.S.-style plugs and run at 110 volts.

• Note that in tourist areas, private business offer fax services, and some offer E-mail and Internet access. It's usually cheaper to use these services than to telephone.

• Be punctual, as businesspeople usually are in Guatemala.

• Don't feel obliged to have business cards translated into Spanish; however, materials for use outside the office (e.g., manuals on how to operate machinery) should be translated into Spanish.

• Remember that you must establish a personal relationship with a Guatemalan businessperson before discussing business. He or she will want to know about you and your background. Be prepared to answer very personal questions—about your family and background. Inquire about your counterpart's personal life, in return. Establishing trust is vital, and nothing productive will occur without it.

• Ask questions quietly, and be patient. Never raise your voice or insult anyone.

• Expect delays. They may be caused by the country's frequent power shortages.

• Note that although there are women involved in business in

Guatemala, it's still unusual to find them in a company's upper echelons.

• Don't bring gifts on your first business trip, but for subsequent trips ask people what they would like from abroad. (One businessman requested American cereal for his children, another asked for unsalted peanuts, and a third wanted razor blades.)

• If a colleague invites you home to a meal, don't discuss business there.

• Note that business lunches and even breakfasts are more popular than dinners.

• If your spouse is accompanying you on business, invite your Guatemalan counterpart and his or her spouse to a social dinner in a restaurant.

to learn if there are local holidays or religious festivals that will result in closings.

Holidays: New Year's Day (Jan. 1); Easter week (Weds., Thurs., and Fri. before Easter); Labor Day (May 1); Army Day (June 30); Assumption Day (Aug. 15); Independence Day (Sept. 15); Revolution Day (Oct. 20); All Saints' Day (Nov. 1); Last Thursday in November (Thanksgiving is now celebrated in Guatemala City); Christmas Eve and Christmas Day (Dec. 24 and 25); Last Year's Day (Dec. 31).

• On November 1, expect people to do anything from flying kites in cemeteries, bringing flowers and picnics to the graves of their relatives—or even going to the movies.

HOLIDAYS AND SPECIAL OCCASIONS

• On the following holidays, banks, businesses, government offices, most stores, and many restaurants will be closed. Before visiting an area, check with the tourist office

TRANSPORTATION

Public Transportation

• Enter local buses from the front. Pay on the bus. You don't need exact change. Keep your ticket because there are sometimes inspectors who check them. The fare collector walks down the aisle and collects the fare after you're seated. He can make change.

• Note that during Holy Week bus fares may be doubled. Avoid travel on Good Friday, when everyone goes home to their family for Easter.

• Don't expect to find subways in Guatemala.

• Use taxis that have meters. The fare will be cheaper than with unmetered taxis, and you will not have an argument about the fare.

• Note that for long-distance travel, there are first-and second-class buses. For first-class buses—called Pullman—you can go to a bus station, buy your ticket, and reserve a seat in advance. First-class buses are usually old U.S. Greyhound buses. They have bathrooms, which usually don't work. Second-class buses, which are like old school buses, don't have reserved seats, and people squeeze on. Buses make bathroom stops and will stop if necessary. If you need to go to the bathroom between stops, however, you probably won't have toilet facilities—just the space behind the bus.

• There are currently no trains running in Guatemala.

• Realize that outside the city, buses will stop anywhere along the side of the road to pick you up. There are no designated bus stops. Make a scooping gesture with your hand, and the bus will pull over. Even if the bus is not going directly to your destination, people will encourage you to get on. When they tell you to get off, and you have not reached your destination, someone on the bus will say, "Wait here for your bus."

• Women should take public transportation only during the day. They should know **exactly** where they are going in order not to look vulnerable. Tell the driver and conductor your destination; try to sit near the driver. Greet people by saying "Buenos dias," as you sit down. If you don't exchange courtesies, people may not be willing to help you.

Driving

• If you want to see the countryside, consider driving, during the day. Roads are good, and there are adequate signs. At hilly locations you will probably notice signs that say *"Frenar Con Motor,"* which literally means, "brake with motor," or downshift instead of using your brakes. Guatemala has many steep hills, and it could be very dangerous if your brakes give out. In the past few years, the road department has constructed runoff ramps, in case brakes fail, so you can take this form of exit and avoid crashing.

• Don't drive after dark. There aren't any street lights. There are drunken drivers. People drive without headlights.

• Stay off the roads on Sundays

and market days, when you're more likely to encounter drunk drivers. Be especially wary in rural areas on Sunday, since that is the "binge drinking" day. Also realize that carjackings and other forms of lawlessness have increased in recent years.

• Always carry your passport. Police may pull over drivers at random to fine them. There are many roadblocks throughout the country. Usually, stopping cars is a routine procedure, but you may be asked to show your passport.

• If you're driving near military vehicles, stay 200 meters in front of or behind them.

• Always park in a guarded car park or at a hotel with a protected parking place.

• In Guatemala City, expect to find individuals who say they are "guarding" all the cars in a certain block or street. In actuality, these are public parking spaces, but they will still try to have you park in one of "their" spots and then pay them a nominal fee when you lock your car. It's not worth arguing, since the people only want spare change.

LEGAL MATTERS, SAFETY, AND HEALTH

• As mentioned above, carry your passport at all times.

• Don't carry pocket knives. They're illegal weapons.

• Note that it's illegal to wear military-style clothing or to bring such clothing into the country.

• If you make several trips to Guatemala and see the same customs official every time, be polite and courteous, but *never* offer him money to expedite matters.

• Beware of pickpockets; men and women should wear a money belt, or men should carry their wallets in their front pants pocket or shoe. A woman should be aware that thieves are known to slash purses.

• Use caution. Muggings and violent crime are on the rise in Guatemala City. Don't walk around at night. Take taxis.

• If you are robbed, be sure to report the robbery to the police. The process will be long, but you'll need the police statement for insurance.

• **NEVER** go hiking alone.

• Be aware that earthquakes are frequent, but they are usually minor. If there is a major earthquake, go outside, or stand in a doorway.

• Remember to drink only bottled, boiled, or iodized water. Use this water when brushing your teeth—and keep your mouth closed when taking a shower. Milk and cheese in inexpensive restaurants are usually not pasteurized, but milk in better restaurants may be. Be sure that any meat you eat is well done. Don't eat fruits or vegetables that can't be peeled, or any uncooked vegetables.

• For advice on medicines and hygiene products, see "Legal Matters, Safety, and Health" in the Introduction.

MEXICO

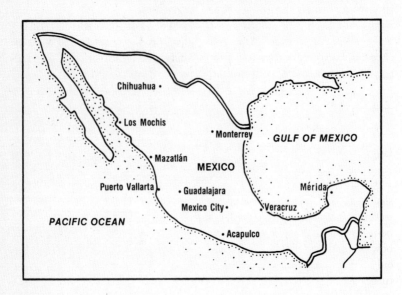

We visit Mexico for many reasons. Some want to worship the sun in Acapulco, Puerto Vallarta, or Cancún. Some go to explore the great Indian civilizations—Maya, Aztec, Toltec—at one of the world's outstanding museums, the Museum of Anthropology in Mexico City's Chapultepec Park, or in the great ruins of Yucatán. Others want the exquisite silver of Taxco and San Miguel de Allende.

Whatever your reason for visiting, it's hard to be disappointed, except by the dreadful pollution in Mexico City. As one visitor commented about the city's air, "It was like vacationing in a tunnel."

Sometimes one can fully forget the air pollution, as at Christmastime when the Paseo de la Reforma is festooned with garlands, or on Sundays when Chapultepec Park explodes with festive people, or when the gardens at Xochimilco are a mass of blooms.

GREETINGS

Language: Mexico's official language is Spanish.

• Note that both men and women shake hands when being introduced to someone of the same sex. A man being introduced to a woman will bow slightly; he will shake hands only if the woman initiates the gesture.

• In cities be aware that among friends, women kiss on the cheek, and men and women who are good friends often kiss.

• Note that Mexican males who are good friends often embrace when they meet. Don't be the first to make this gesture. Allow your Mexican friend to begin.

• Allow Mexicans to take the lead in the use of first names. Use titles with people high in the academic, government, military, or medical hierarchy.

• At a party, bow slightly when you enter the room. Then go to each person and shake hands. Usually your host will come with you to make introductions. When you leave, shake hands with each person,

addressing him or her as *Señor, Señora,* or *Señorita.* This is absolutely essential, even if you haven't talked to the people before.

• In business or with older people, use the title and last name, e.g., *Doctor, Director,* and *Ingeniero* (anyone with a science degree). After you have worked with the person a while, use just the title without the last name. *Licenciado* (lee-sehn-syah-doh) is used very commonly, to refer to any person who has received any degree of higher education.

CONVERSATION

• To make a good impression, learn something about Mexican art and literature.

• Note that Mexicans are impressed by university degrees, so mention yours if you have one.

• Good conversation openers are your home area, your school, your job. Try to find points in common, such as a mutual interest in travel or film.

• Be aware that Mexicans are rather open in discussing personal feelings. They often regard North American reluctance to do so as insensitive or unfriendly.

• Men should not withdraw from a Mexican male's expressions of warmth and friendliness, such as touching you on the shoulder, holding your arm, or touching your lapel. To shrink from such gestures is insulting. However, don't gaze into the eyes of the person to whom you are speaking. It's considered confrontational.

• Realize that the word *indio* is often derogatory, implying social naïveté and backwardness.

• Don't be surprised if Mexicans ask you how much you paid for an item. They like to make comparisons between costs in the U.S. and Mexico. If you don't want to share the information, say that the item was a gift or that you don't remember the cost. If people ask about your salary, you can say that you don't want to discuss the subject, or you can tell them what it is and then describe the cost of rent, food, telephones, etc., in your country.

• Don't criticize the Mexican government or suggest possible improvements in it. Be sure to avoid mentioning illegal aliens or the U.S.'s Mexican War. Be aware that the present-day states of Texas, California, Nevada, Utah, Colorado, New Mexico, and Arizona were part of Mexico until the late 1840s.

• If you're from the U.S., refer to yourself as a North American (*norteamericano*, masculine; *norteameri-*

cana, feminine), or as from the United States (*de los Estados Unidos* [deh lohs ehs-**tah**-dohs oo-**nee**-dohs]). Don't forget that Mexico is just as much a part of the American continent as the United States.

• Be careful of behavior or remarks that could be construed as insults to a person's dignity—e.g., not saying good-bye to a person, expressing distaste for the food, implying to a man in some way that his sister's morals aren't all that they should be. Mexicans consider such remarks serious provocations and would end either a personal or business relationship because of one.

• Steer away from subjects related to money, e.g., salary, prices. Don't ask what someone paid for something.

• Never make denigratory remarks about indigenous people. Mexicans play down racial differences, and Mexican indigenous people exert a strong influence on political and social life. (Only 10 percent of Mexicans are pure Caucasian.) An oddity: While Mexicans will go out of their way to show you the achievements of the Maya and the Aztecs, many don't want you to think that there is any Indian blood in their personal background. Don't say, "You look Indian" or "Are you part Indian?"

• Be sure that you *never* tell an off-color joke in the presence of a woman.

rains or other abnormal weather conditions often cause disruptions.

• Emergency number for police, fire, and the Red Cross—060.

TELEPHONES

• Be prepared to find many of the public phones out of order.

• Remember that LATADEL is a public pay-phone service with phone booths where you pay with coins, credit cards, or telephone cards for local or long-distance service.

• Buy telephone cards at convenience stores, bus terminals, airports, pharmacies, supermarkets, or Sanborn's (a department store with many branches).

• Make calls from a TelMex office during business hours. In small towns look for private telephone offices (available for public use), often set up in the corner of a shop. Private telephone offices and hotels add a surcharge to the cost of the call. Ask at your hotel about the size of the surcharge. The convenience may make it worth paying.

• For international service, consider calling collect. You will avoid hassles.

• Expect people to say "Bueno" when they answer the phone.

• Be prepared for erratic telephone service in small towns. Heavy

IN PUBLIC

• Don't be surprised if someone hisses "psst-psst" to you. It's the common way to get attention and isn't considered impolite.

• In giving someone an item such as money or keys, always hand it to the person. It's very rude to throw or toss it. When paying, always place the money in the cashier's hand rather than on the counter.

• Men should not put their hands in their pockets in public.

• Note that putting your hands on your hips signifies a challenge or threat.

• Be aware that "first come" doesn't always mean "first served." Great deference may be shown to someone because of age, position, or social status. Don't express annoyance at another being served first.

• Remember that asking Mexicans for information will always produce an answer designed to please you by telling you what they think you want to hear, though it may be far from the truth. For example, don't say "Is the train station that way?" because a Mexican will most certainly say "Yes," whether it is or not. Ask "Where is the train station?" and then continue to ask people along the way.

• Be cautious in expressing admiration for objects. The owner may feel obliged to give it to you.

• Note two important expressions about time: To give the time and add *a la gringa* means to be strictly punctual. Time *a la mexicana* implies a less precise punctuality.

• Some gestures to be aware of: (1) To motion someone to come to you, hold your hand out, palm down, and wave in a downward motion. (2) Holding the palm up with the thumb and forefinger extended and a bit apart signifies "Wait a minute." (3) Holding the palm upward and crooking the index finger toward the body (the U.S. gesture for "come here") is vaguely obscene. (4) Avoid the U.S. "O.K." gesture made with the thumb and index finger. It is a vulgarity in Mexico.

• Be prepared for people to stand very close to one another while talking and to touch often. Physical contact between members of the same sex is common. Close friends may embrace and/or walk arm in arm.

• Don't forget that people do not wait in lines. They push to the front. Unless you do the same, you will be left behind.

• Always ask permission before photographing anyone—even vendors, beggars, and children. Be especially sure to ask indigenous people before photographing them, because they often resent being regarded as anthropological objects. Sometimes people ask for a few *pesos*; sometimes they don't.

• Don't photograph the subway in Mexico City, or military installations.

• Note that there are no public bathrooms. If you need one, go to a department store, museum, hotel, or restaurant (even if you're not a customer there). In the countryside bring tissues, because there probably won't be any toilet paper.

Shopping: Remember that you can bargain virtually everywhere, except where there are price tags. Someone who doesn't bargain and pays the first asking price is considered very foolish. Mexicans regard such people as ignorant and even unfriendly.

• Never become angry when bargaining; it's supposed to be a game.

• If you and the seller agree on a price, and you buy the item, you may conclude the deal by shaking hands. If the seller finally accepts your first price, you are honor bound to buy the item.

DRESS

• When choosing your wardrobe for a visit to Mexico, keep in mind that clothing is more conservative than in the U.S. and is strongly influenced by European fashion.

• For business, men should wear dark suits, ties, and black shoes. It is considered fashionable for men to wear white socks with black dress pants and black dress shoes. Women should wear nice dresses or suits accented with jewelry and should be sure to wear makeup and heels. Men shouldn't remove jackets or loosen ties unless their host suggests it.

• Expect Mexicans always to be impeccably groomed with clean shoes, jewelry, and well-groomed hair. Even people of the lowest socioeconomic classes wear decent, well-pressed clothes if they possibly can. When Mexicans see foreigners in torn jeans, bare feet, and with disheveled hair, they consider such people vulgar.

• Realize that Mexicans are status conscious and will be impressed if you wear designer clothing.

• Casual wear for men is shirt and pants; for women, it's a skirt and blouse. Shorts are never appropriate for men or women, except at resorts or at pools. Never wear shorts to restaurants.

• Note that jeans are one step below casual wear. Always well-tailored, clean, and pressed, they are worn mainly when city people go to the country.

• If you're invited to a home to dinner, wear business clothes on a first visit.

• Never wear shorts or halter tops when visiting a church. Some churches have signs indicating that you won't be admitted in such an outfit.

• Note that Mexicans appreciate foreign men wearing a *guayabera*—a shirt worn over trousers, used during the hot summer months. Especially outside of Mexico City, they are acceptable for social occasions, including dinner in a restaurant and even as business wear. There are simple ones for everyday wear and others with lace and heavy embroidery, which are worn for formal occasions.

• Traditional formal wear for men is tuxedos and, for women, long dresses. The major occasions for such costumes are evening and night weddings. Invitations don't specify formal dress, so it's wise to ask the person who issued the invitation what the appropriate dress is.

MEALS

Hours and Foods

• First, a few words on food safety. Don't ever drink tap water. (Many hotels leave sealed bottled water in your room, but be sure that the seal is intact.) If you're not confident of the water quality in the hotel, buy a brand of bottled water with which you're familiar (e.g., Tehuacán) at a supermarket or liquor store. It's safe to drink fruit juices if no water or ice has been added. Don't eat vegetables or fruit that you can't peel. Avoid lettuce and green salads. Avoid all raw shellfish. Don't eat custards or mayonnaise unless you're sure that they have been refrigerated. Never buy cooked food from street vendors. To help adjust to the altitude and pollution, drink large quantities of bottled water, and avoid alcohol.

Breakfast: Between 6:00 to 7:00 A.M. at home. Business breakfasts may be from 7:30 to 9:00 A.M. or 8:30 to 11:00 A.M. The meal consists of bread or tortillas, cereal, rolls or pastry, and coffee; or continental-style biscuits, fruit, and coffee.

There is a second breakfast (usually reserved for weekends) around 11:00 A.M. The meal consists of eggs of many styles with beans and tortillas.

Lunch: Usually the day's largest meal, from 1:30 to 3:30 P.M. Lunch may begin as late as 4:00 P.M. The first course is often soup; followed by a course of meat, rice, vegetables, and beans; followed by a dessert of fruit or *flan* (custard), and coffee. Tortillas are usually served with the meal. Usual beverages are beer, wine, fruit juices (e.g., tamarind juice, watermelon juice), and lemonade.

• Apart from custom, the altitude of Mexico City and its effect on your digestive system make it wise to eat your heaviest meal around midday.

• Around 5:00 P.M., expect *merienda*—a snack of tea, coffee, juices, pastries, and *pan dulce* (sweet bread).

Dinner: A late and light meal. In a home, dinner will be served between 8:00 and 10:00 P.M. There may be a soup, tamales, or beans with cheese. With the meal, people drink water or fruit juice or wine or beer; afterward, they have coffee. (The coffee may be Nescafé.)

• If a salad is served, expect it after the main course.

Beverages: Prepare to be offered a drink of *mezcal* (mehs-**cahl**), a liquor made from the maguey plant, after dinner. It is somewhat like aquavit, grappa, or brandy. Don't be surprised to see a worm in the bottle. When they polish off the bottle, Mexicans often eat the worm!

• To drink tequila as the Mexicans do, follow these four steps (a dish of salt and a slice of lime will be served with the tequila): (1) put a pinch of salt on the back of your left hand, in the hollow between the thumb and index finger; (2) lick the salt; (3) with the right hand, take the glass of tequila and drink it all; (4) suck on the piece of lime.

• Note that popular beverages are coffee, often made with hot milk and cinnamon; chocolate; beer; and tequila, which is made from the maguey plant.

• Remember that the second most popular drink after tequila is brandy and then rum. Cuba libre (rum, Coke, and lime juice) is a favorite.

• Be aware that hard liquor, such as Scotch, gin, or vodka may only be available at tourist restaurants and hotel bars.

• If your beer bottle has an indentation in the bottom, it's to remove the top from another bottle.

Table Manners

• If you're invited to a home to a meal, expect drinks in the living room first—usually a choice of whiskey, Cuba libre (rum and Coke), or *tequila*. Hors d'oeuvres will probably be *chicharrón* (pork crackling with a piquant sauce), nuts, and guacamole with fried tortilla chips.

• If you decide to hold a cocktail party, remember that it's *very* important to have large quantities of hors d'oeuvres.

• If the meal is formal or semiformal, expect courses to be served one at a time. At a casual meal, all the dishes will be put on the table at once.

• Before a meal, say *"Buen provecho"* (bwehn proh-**veh**-choh), which is like "bon appétit," but actually means "May it benefit you."

• Don't be surprised to see people—especially in informal settings—using *tortillas* to scoop up food.

• To eat a *tortilla* plain, salt it, roll it up into a tube, and eat it with your fingers. If you want to put a filling into it, place the *tortilla* in your palm, add the filling, and then fold the *tortilla*. In homes and casual restaurants, people push food onto the fork with a *tortilla*.

• Even when food is put out buffet-style, always wait for an invitation to partake.

• Always wait until the hostess offers you more food. Don't take a second portion yourself.

• Note that people expect you to try some of everything when you're invited to a meal, but they will understand if foreigners don't care for certain dishes such as tripe or hot peppers (or if they can't eat them for medical reasons). There isn't in Mexico the European expectation that you finish everything on your plate.

• When eating spicy foods, relieve the burning sensation by having some rice or *tortilla*.

• Expect your hostess to insist that you stay later, no matter how late the hour. If it is late, and your hostess looks tired, be diplomatic, and bid a gracious "good night."

Eating Out

• Remember that most restaurants are open from 1:00 P.M. to 4:00 P.M. for lunch. The more elegant restaurants do not re-open for dinner until 9:00 P.M., but other restaurants re-open earlier.

• Note that a *cafetería* in Mexico is not a U.S.-style cafeteria; it offers different kinds of coffees. A *pastelería* serves European-style pastries, hors d'oeuvres, coffee, tea, and soft drinks. The familiar restaurant is a *restaurante* (rehs-tow-**rahn**-teh). A *lonchería* is a small inexpensive restaurant, serving late breakfast and lunch (the main meal of the day), usually open from 11:00 A.M. to 5:00 P.M. For tortillas, go to a *tortillería*, where the tortillas are sold by the kilo. You can buy a minimum of a quarter of a kilo, about ten tortillas. *Cantinas* or *salones de cerveza* are bars, open from noon to 1:00 A.M. (closed on Sunday), where

men drink. Women should never enter these bars.

• Choose from a wide variety of teas in most Mexican restaurants: *té de canela* (cinnamon tea), *té de limón* (lemongrass tea), *té de naranja* (orange-leaf tea), *té de pelo de elote* (corn silk tea), *té de yerbabuena* (mint tea), *manzanilla* (chamomile tea).

• Remember that the type of Mexican food familiar north of the border is a poor and monotonous cousin of the real thing; Mexico has a most varied native cuisine (see "Specialties"). In addition, Mexico City abounds in restaurants of many nationalities—French, Italian, British, German, Spanish, Argentine, and Asian.

• When making a reservation at an elegant restaurant, ask if they have a dress code. Very few places do, but it's best to be sure.

• Expect to be able to read a menu before you enter a restaurant. Sometimes it's posted outside and sometimes at the entrance.

• Note that some restaurants offer a *comida corrida* or *menú turistico* for a set price. It consists of six or seven courses served in sequence: cocktail, appetizer, salad, a main dish (beef, pork, or fish) with rice and beans on the side, dessert, and coffee or tea.

• Don't join strangers at their table, except in German-style restaurants, where you're expected to sit on long benches with others whom you don't know.

• Keep in mind that most elegant

restaurants have a cover charge (*cubierto*), but it is usually small.

• Be sure to treat waiters as the professionals that they are. Don't make sounds to call them. You'll hear many people saying "Psst" to the waiter, but it's rude. Beckon with your finger or hand, or say "Joven" (**ho**-ven), meaning "young man."

• Be prepared for slow service. Mexicans like to take their time at meals.

• Expect *tortillas* to be served with most meals. Feel free to ask for more, as there is usually no additional charge. Sometimes, if the staff realizes that you are a foreigner, they will bring you a French-type bread, thinking that you'll prefer it.

• Remember that imported drinks are extremely expensive in fashionable restaurants. To save money, order Mexican liquor (rum or tequila), beer, or wine.

• To order beer, ask for *"una cerveza"* (sehr-**veh**-sah) followed by *"clara"* (**clah**-rah) for light, *"oscura"* (ohs-**koo**-rah) for dark, *"semioscura"* (**seh**-mee-ohs-**koo**-rah) for semi-dark, or *"de barril"* (deh bah-**rreel**) for draft.

• Don't be surprised if your empty beer bottles are left on the table. When you're ready to pay, the waiter will count them and charge accordingly.

• Be aware that the waiter will not bring the check until it's requested. Ask for *"la cuenta"* (lah **kwehn**-tah).

• Expect an argument over the check, since one person always pays for the whole group. Not to show interest in paying for the group is very rude. In practice, however, the oldest person in the group almost always pays. (Paying shows how well he cares for others.) To show your appreciation for being treated to a meal, invite the person who paid to a meal and state in advance that you are treating since the other person treated last time. If a woman plans to treat, she must say so at the beginning of the meal. To save the other person's pride, she could say her embassy or her business is paying.

• When you pay your bill in a restaurant, hand your credit card or money directly to the waiter/waitress. Don't leave it on the table. If you do, he/she will think you are avoiding contact.

• After paying, leave the small change on the table. Check to see if a 15 percent tip has been included in your bill. If not, leave 10 percent or 15 percent.

• Note that most restaurants in Mexico City—and many elsewhere—accept major credit cards.

Specialties

• You'll find some foods served throughout Mexico, while others are regional specialties. The national dish is *mole poblano de guajolote*, turkey in a sauce made with chiles, chocolate, herbs, and spices. *Sopas secas*—literally "dry soups"—refers to pastas or rice with sauce and is often served as a separate course following the soup course. *Guacamole* is mashed avocado with fresh coriander leaf (cilantro), tomato, onion, and chile paste.

• Other dishes found throughout the country: *quesadillas*, tortillas folded like turnovers and filled with cheese (these are a healthy choice in small towns or if you must buy something to eat on the street); *chalupas*, fried flat tortillas covered with shredded chicken or pork, tomato sauce, onions, and white cheese; *tamales*, any of various fillings (e.g., chiles and cheese, *mole poblano*, or pork and sauce) rolled in cornmeal dough, wrapped in corn husks, and steamed; *huevos rancheros*, fried eggs with tomato and chile sauce; *cabrito*, roasted kid; *frijoles refritos*, cooked beans that are then mashed and fried (not really "refried" beans as commonly called).

• *Bolillos* are French rolls served all over Mexico.

• Dishes to try in northern Mexico (Monterrey, Chihuahua): *empanadas de picadillo*, minced beef turnovers with onions, potatoes, and spices; *machaca de Monterrey*, dried beef fried with onions, tomatoes, and chiles, mixed with scrambled eggs and all put into a flour tortilla.

• Along the East coast (Veracruz, Tampico), look for: *jaibas en chilpachole*, crabs simmered in tomato broth and spices; *camarones a la plancha*, shrimp marinated in olive oil, parsley, and lime juice and then grilled; *carne asada a la tampiqueña*, grilled beef tenderloin with grilled zucchini, apples, onions and potatoes, served with enchiladas filled with white cheese and tomato sauce as well as *frijoles* and *guacamole; huachinango a la Veracruz*, red snapper with a sauce made of capers, tomatoes, onion, garlic, lime juice, and spices; *sopa de mariscos*, a seafood soup similar to bouillabaisse.

• Visitors to the Yucatán peninsula can look for these specialties: *huevos motuleños*, a popular breakfast dish consisting of corn tortillas with black beans, ham, fried eggs, and tomato sauce; *sopa de lima*, chicken and lime soup; *papadzul*, tortillas stuffed, rolled, and served with a pumpkin-seed sauce; *pámpano a la yucateca*, a fish, similar to flounder, marinated and broiled; *pollo pibil*, chicken marinated and grilled in banana leaves; *panuchos*, tortillas, filled with fried black beans and hard-boiled eggs, which are puffed during cooking; *coctel campechana marinera*, a cooked shrimp and raw oyster cocktail. In many dishes you'll find *achiote*, the seed of the annatto tree, used for both flavor and color; the hard seeds are soaked and usually made into a paste. Expect to find many meat and poultry dishes wrapped in banana leaves for steaming or baking.

• In the central highlands (Jalapa, Córdoba, Puebla, Cuernavaca, Toluca, and Mexico City), try: *sopa de calabaza*, squash soup with chicken stock, *chalupas de Puebla*, fried tortillas filled with pork and green chile sauce; *pollo borracho* (literally, "drunken chicken"), chicken fried in oil with a sauce of tequila, chiles, orange juice, and sausages; *postre de almendra*, cake filled with almond paste.

• If you travel to the South (Oaxaca, Mitla, San Cristóbal de las Casas), sample: *sopa de frijol negro*, black bean soup; *plátanos en rompope*, a dessert of bananas soaked in eggnog.

• The lakes area (Morelia, Guadalajara), offers: *sopa de albóndigas*, meatball soup; *chayotes rellenos*, a pear-shaped vegetable stuffed with white cheese, egg, and onion; *adobo rojo de lomo de cerdo*, pork loin in a sauce of chiles, spices, and garlic; *flautas de puerco*, pork in a tightly rolled, fried corn tortilla; *blanco de Pátzcuaro*, whitefish from Pátzcuaro Lake—deep-fried fish with onions simmered in oil and vinegar; *chongos*, custard with cinnamon and vanilla.

• Along the southwestern coast (Puerto Ángel, Puerto Escondido, and Acapulco), you can eat: *ceviche*, marinated raw fish with onion, tomatoes, lime juice, chiles, and coriander; *sopa de aguacate*, avocado soup with chicken broth, sherry, and cream; *huachinango con ajo*, red snapper with garlic.

• Visiting the central west coast (Puerto Vallarta, Tepic, Mazatlán), sample: *pisto*, scrambled eggs with ham, zucchini, peas, and green onions; *huachinango en salsa de perejil*, red snapper in parsley sauce; *chilaquiles*, tortilla hash made with cheese, cream, and *salsa verde* (chiles, coriander, garlic, and green tomatoes).

• In the *Bajío* or lowlands (Guanajuato, San Miguel de Allende), expect these special dishes: *sopa de ajo*, garlic soup with a chicken broth base; *enchiladas verdes*, green enchiladas made with rolled corn tortillas with green tomatoes, chiles, chopped chicken, and cream; *flan*, caramel custard.

• Specialties of the northwest (Culiacán, Los Mochis, Hermosillo) are: *sopa de la cena*, a soup of pork spareribs, tomatoes, corn, chiles, bay leaf, onion, and oregano; *carne de res en chile colorado*, beef in red chile; *ensalada de nopalitos, nopal*, prickly pear cactus, onion, tomatoes, chile, coriander, and farmer cheese; *tortillas de harina*, white wheat flour tortillas, common in the north; *chimichangas*, deep fried *tortillas de harina* stuffed with beans, beef, chiles, and spices—and served with *crema* (sour cream) and *guacamole*.

HOTELS

• Choose from a variety of accommodations: five-star hotels are found in state capitals and at beach resorts. Inexpensive hotels range from two to four stars. Some are larger than budget hotels, and some resemble U.S.-style motels. They have heating and air-conditioning. Budget hotels have clean rooms with private bath and double bed. Purified drinking water, soap, towels, and toilet paper may be provided; sometimes you have to ask for them. Guesthouses (*casas de huespedes*) offer rooms with either private or shared bath. *Pensiones* are about the same as guesthouses, but they may also include meals.

• Ask when you make your reservation if your room has air-conditioning. Before checking in, inspect the room to make sure that the air-conditioning and bathroom fixtures function. Also make sure that the room's locks work.

• Book well in advance (at least a month) for the Christmas–New Year and Easter periods. February is the most popular time for resort areas.

• If you're driving, ask if your hotel charges for parking, since many in large cities do, while others offer free parking.

• If you have a reservation, and the clerk at the reception desk says that there are no rooms, wait patiently in the lobby. Don't show anger, but keep returning to the desk and saying something such as, "Have you found my reservation yet? I want to stay here. It's the most beautiful place I've ever seen."

• Bring a flashlight with you as electricity frequently goes off for a brief time. (Some hotels have candles in the rooms for such an emergency.)

• Note that in elevators *PB* (*planta baja*) means the ground floor.

• In better hotels, expect a small, well-stocked refrigerator. You pay for the items used at the end of your stay. Usually they are very expensive. If you're staying in one place for a while, buy your own drinks and keep them in the refrigerator.

• Ask the concierge to get tickets if you wish to attend a bullfight. Seats in the shade are best, though they are also the most expensive. If you prefer to buy the tickets yourself, do so in advance.

• *Never* drink tap water or brush your teeth with it. Buy mineral water, called *agua mineral* (ah-gwah mee-neh-**rahl**), either carbonated, *con gas* (kon gahs), or noncarbonated, *sin gas* (seen gahs).

TIPPING

• Give porters and bellboys the equivalent of 50 cents (U.S.) per bag.

• Tip a taxi driver 10 percent if he has helped you with the luggage.

• Depending on the class of the hotel, tip chambermaids $2.00 to $4.00 per day.

• To ushers and washroom attendants, give 25 to 50 cents. When the change you are owed at a gas station is less than N$1, it's customary to tell the attendant to keep the change.

• Because of the high unemployment rate, people will approach you when you park and offer to watch your car, wash the windshield, etc. Give these car watchers 25 to 50 cents.

PRIVATE HOMES

• Keep in mind that Mexicans usually invite only close friends to their home.

• If you're invited to a meal in a home, plan to stay about 30 minutes after dinner on a weeknight, longer on a weekend. Note, however, that Mexicans don't measure a social engagement by time— if everyone is having a good visit, feel free to stay longer.

• Sometimes, especially in the homes of humble people, you may be offered food or drink that the family doesn't actually have. If you accept, they may have to ask a family member to run out to the store

to buy it. To avoid embarrassing the family, decline offers of food or drink.

• Never go into a kitchen in a home unless you are invited. The room is the private domain of the woman of the house.

As a guest, feel responsible only to show a great deal of appreciation and to compliment your host and hostess. Reciprocate their hospitality by inviting them to a restaurant, if you will be in the community long enough.

• Be reserved in admiring any object in a home. If you are very enthusiastic, your host may feel obliged to give it to you.

• If you are a guest in a home, don't walk barefoot or put your feet on a table.

• If you're staying with a family ask about—and observe—the meal times. Be sure to get up and have breakfast with the family so that the servants don't have to serve you separately.

• When visiting a family, plan to go out for a few meals in order to lessen the imposition on them. Tell them the night or morning before, since most people buy fresh food every day. Or, you might invite the family to a restaurant to a meal.

• If you want the maid to do some task for you (e.g., your laundry), tip her about $2.00. Put the money in her apron or pocket, rather than handing it to her directly.

• When you leave, after staying with the family for a few days, tip the maid the equivalent of $1.00.

Don't ask your hostess' advice about the amount or she'll tell you not to give a tip.

• Observe the way the family treats its servants, and act accordingly. In some homes the relationship is more formal than in others.

Gifts: When invited to a meal, bring European or American chocolates, imported wine or champagne, or pastries.

• If a business acquaintance invites you to dinner at home, send flowers ahead of time or bring them with you.

• Avoid marigolds, as they are used to decorate graves. Avoid giving red flowers, since they are used for casting spells.

• If you are invited to a fifteenth-birthday party for a girl, note that it's equivalent to a "sweet sixteen" party in the U.S. After a Mass in a local church, there is usually a large gathering at home or in a restaurant for male and female guests to celebrate the young woman's entrance into society. Appropriate gifts are jewelry or religious medals.

• Good gifts from abroad: CDs of pop music for teenagers, classical music for older people; something special to your area of the country—e.g., patchwork from Pennsylvania Dutch country. Good gifts for children are computer software, T-shirts, and baseball caps.

BUSINESS

Hours

Business: 9:00 or 10:00 A.M. to 1:00 or 2:00 P.M. and then 2:00 or 3:00 P.M. until 6:00 or 7:00 P.M., Monday through Friday.

Government Offices: 8:00 A.M. to 3:00 P.M., Monday through Friday.

Banks: 9:00 A.M. to 1:30 P.M., Monday through Friday. In large cities, most banks are open until 5:30 or 6:00 P.M. Some of the larger banks have branches open on Saturday from 9:00 A.M. to 2:30 P.M. and on Sunday from 10:00 A.M. to 1:30 P.M.

Shops: 10:00 A.M. to 1:00 P.M., and 3:00 to 8:00 P.M., Monday through Saturday; except in Mexico City, where there is no lunch-hour closing.

Currency

Note that N$ stands for new *pesos*.

• Remember that the *peso* is divided into 100 *centavos*.

• Coins: 5, 10, 20, and 50 *centavos*, and N$1, N$2, and N$5. Coins smaller than one *peso* are scarce, so payment is usually rounded off to the nearest *peso* or 50 *centavos*.

• Notes: N$10, N$20, N$50, N$100, and N$200.

• Expect many shops on the U.S./Mexican border and in beach resorts to accept U.S. dollars. Stores in smaller towns usually accept only *pesos*.

• Use credit cards and travelers' checks in most tourist area. However, in small shops, inexpensive restaurants, and in small towns and villages, they will probably not be accepted. A credit card must be used to rent a car. Most Pemex stations (gas stations) do not accept credit cards.

• To insure safety, use ATMs only during business hours in public, well-lighted places.

Business Practices

• Anticipate several trips to Mexico to complete your business satisfactorily. The first visit is a sort of "field trip," to secure contacts and make initial approaches to the companies with which you would like to deal.

• Don't plan business travel to Mexico between December 12 (Feast of the Virgin of Guadalupe) and January 6 or during Holy Week. If you'll be dealing with elected government officials, check to make sure that there's no upcoming election, during which they might be away from their offices campaigning.

• Before you initiate business, be in touch with the Commerce Division of the Mexican Consulate in the nearest large city to find out about Mexico's rather strict laws on foreign investment.

• When you make an initial contact, have your letter written in Spanish, but mention that you don't speak Spanish (if that is the case).

• Make your first contact with the top person in the company. The initial approach should be from a top manager in a foreign firm to a top manager in a Mexican firm. The foreign top manager should make the trip to Mexico accompanied by members of the firm's staff.

• Remember that it helps enormously to have a contact in Mexico or a letter of introduction. If you don't, write to your country's Chamber of Commerce in Mexico City. Other sources of contacts: your bank, which may have a correspondent in Mexico; the Confederation of National Chambers of Industry, to which most large businesses belong and which can tell you names of top managers in Mexican firms; your embassy in Mexico.

• Note that all of the country's major businesses have offices in Mexico City.

• Make appointments as least two

weeks in advance; however, don't be surprised if government officials reschedule appointments at the last minute.

• After setting up an appointment from abroad, let your Mexican counterpart decide the time and place of the meeting. He may suggest a breakfast, lunch, or dinner meeting.

• Plan to arrive a day or two before your first scheduled appointment to acclimate yourself to the altitude and to reconfirm appointments. To minimize difficulties from the altitude, eat lightly, and don't drink alcohol or smoke.

• On a business trip, be sure to stay at the best possible hotel. It is one element in enhancing your prestige in the eyes of Mexicans. They will also notice in what restaurants you eat, how you dress, what kind of watch you wear, and so forth.

• Be aware that business offices officially open at 9:00 A.M., but you probably won't find anyone there at that time.

• Try to make appointments for some time between 10:00 A.M. and 1:00 P.M. A second choice is late afternoon. In Mexico City, and Monterrey, allow 30 minutes more than you think you'll need between appointments; there are constant traffic jams.

• Don't be surprised if people schedule appointments at uncommon hours—e.g., 8:30 P.M.

• Consider it a plus if a Mexican colleague suggests a breakfast meeting at 8:00 or 8:30 A.M. It will probably be at your hotel, the meeting will probably be short, and there won't be any drinking—so you won't suffer the effects of altitude on one who drinks or overeats.

• Note that executives and managers do not work on Saturdays, though many factories are open for half the day or all day.

• On the second or third meeting with Mexican businessmen, men should be prepared for an *abrazo*— an embrace accompanied by two or three pats on the back and a handshake. Such a gesture does not, however, mean that you can call the person by his first name. Don't use first names until your Mexican colleague initiates it.

• If people tell you that they would like to meet again in eight days (*ocho dias*), they mean in a week—e.g., if you're meeting on Tuesday, they mean the following Tuesday.

• Expect the first and possibly second meeting to be a social discussion. Mexicans want to know about you and your background before getting down to business. In the first conversations, mention how much you like Mexico, how charming the people are, and what you plan to see in the country. If you work at building a personal relationship before discussing business, you will counter the stereotype of North Americans as too direct and aggressive. Mexicans really want to hear about your family, since family is so important to Mexicans as a huge support system as well as a core of social relations.

• Realize that you cannot be too polite in both formal and informal situations. Mexicans think of people from the U.S. as brusque. Dispel this image by your willingness to engage in conversation at the beginning of a business meeting.

• Don't forget that Mexicans are sensitive to criticism, favoring harmony at work and preferring to avoid personal competition. Never state that something is done better or more efficiently in your country. Never discuss religious or political topics, and avoid mentioning historic problems between Mexico and your country, if these exist.

• Women in business may not be accorded the same respect as a man. It's very rare to find a woman in a top management position in Mexico. A businesswoman should behave in an extremely professional manner.

• Expect Mexicans at the managerial level to be fluent in English. (Many also speak French.) If you need an interpreter, go to your country's Chamber of Commerce in Mexico City. You can also write to them in advance with questions or to arrange for an interpreter.

• Be on time for business appointments, but expect your Mexican counterpart to be 30 minutes to an hour late. Never complain about this tardiness. Bring work or a book for the waiting period. On the other hand, don't be surprised if your Mexican counterpart is punctual. Many businesspeople have been educated in the U.S.

• Allow more time for a meeting than you think you will need, because courtesies are essential. Everyone who enters shakes hands with everyone. Then the speaker is introduced. After the presentation, the speaker and the host make the rounds of the room, saying an individual good-bye to each person. The first fifteen and last ten minutes of a meeting are devoted to courtesies. Never show impatience with them.

• Be sure to show respect to people in high rank and to elders. Mexican managers receive great respect because of their position, their age, or their influence.

• Realize that you'll be at a disadvantage if you aren't related to someone in the company with which you're dealing. Kinship is an important factor in Mexican business.

• Remember that government and business are a close community. If you offend someone, you may have problems doing business with another company, since word travels fast.

• Keep in mind that the buyer in a Mexican transaction is accorded very high respect—very much as in Japan.

• Remember that parties at a meeting first exchange business cards. Have your cards translated into Spanish. Be sure to have your university degree following your name, and also indicate your position with the company. Example:

> John Smith, Ph.D.
> Director, _____

Have your cards printed in the U.S., since it takes a long time in Mexico.

• Have proposals, catalogues, or instructions translated into Spanish in your own country. (Be sure to use professionals for this job.) Mexican businesspeople will appreciate your effort. In addition, people at different levels of the company may have to deal with the materials, and they may not know English well.

• Don't worry if you need extra photocopies of your materials. There are photocopy shops everywhere in Mexico City.

• When preparing your presentation, keep in mind that Mexicans are impressed with scientific appearance. Have computer printouts, charts, graphs. If appropriate, use three-dimensional models.

• To achieve your goals in a Mexican company, start at the top. Don't, however, be put off if you're sent to meet with a lower official. Such a suggestion may simply be an opportunity for you to speak with the company's expert in your field. Always arrange for a follow-up appointment with a top manager.

• During a business meeting, be prepared for many interruptions, such as telephone calls or people

coming in. Never show irritation. Be patient. Mexicans believe that people are more important than time schedules. If a business associate or a visitor drops in, give her or him your full attention. Put aside whatever else you might be doing.

• Keep in mind that there is little long-range planning in Mexican business. They seek to make high profits in a short time. If you are proposing a project that will take years to complete, Mexicans may not be interested.

• Avoid direct questions when negotiating. People will never say "No; we can't do that" and may agree to do something impossible.

• Develop a strategy for getting a candid response, since businesspeople will often tell you what they think you want to hear. Avoid questions that will produce a "yes" or "no" answer, as in:

Foreigner: What do you think of this product?
Mexican: I think it's wonderful.

To get the candid response, your next question should be, "Are there any small changes you think should be made?" Ask questions in different ways, and ask three or four follow-up questions to obtain the candid response. Skill at this tactic comes with experience.

• Be flexible regarding deadlines. People do not usually meet deadlines, even those to which they have agreed. If you need something in a month, say you need it in two weeks, and you *may* get it on time.

• Don't agree to a proposal quickly. Haste in decision-making is considered unbecoming. Say that you will think the arrangement over.

• Don't expect decisions to be made during or immediately after a presentation.

• Realize that Mexicans usually don't like detailed contracts. Agreements may be oral at first, then followed by a written contract.

• Don't try to finalize a transaction by letter or on the phone. Mexicans want a face-to-face meeting.

• Try to appear strong and confident (but not aggressive) to gain the respect of Mexican workers. Mexicans at all levels tend to believe that *gringos* are naive.

• Remember that Mexicans tend to stand very close to others and to make physical contact. If you withdraw physically, you may unintentionally establish a social or emotional distance.

• If you're going to Villahermosa, the oil center, book well in advance, as there aren't many first-class hotels.

• If you're doing business in Monterrey or Mexico City, expect a mixture of U.S. and Mexican business styles; most senior executives there have had training in the U.S.

Business Gifts: Good business gifts: a clock for the office, calculators, paperweights, a coffee-table book with photographs of your area, Scotch, cognac, art books.

• On a second trip to Mexico, bring a gift, e.g., perfume, for the secretaries of important persons. Say, "My wife sent this to you." If you're a businesswoman, you can also give an article of clothing, e.g., a blouse.

• Note that government secretaries who help you in any way—typing, arranging an appointment with an important person—expect a gift of, say, the equivalent of 50 cents or a dollar.

• Never give gifts of silver, which are considered appropriate only for tourists.

Business Entertaining: Realize that breakfast or lunch are the best meals at which to discuss business. During the negotiating process, mutual invitations are essential. Business breakfasts may start at 8:00 A.M. Lunches often start at about 2:00 P.M., and last for over two hours. Always reciprocate these invitations.

• Don't expect to do business at dinner. This time is for socializing. Remember that most fine restaurants don't start serving dinner until 9:00 or 9:30 P.M., so have a snack in the afternoon.

• Don't be surprised if younger executives suggest meeting at about 7:00 P.M. Such an invitation usually involves drinks and snacks after business.

• If a Mexican businessman invites you to dinner at home, send a bouquet of flowers to your hostess ahead of time. Impress on the florist that the flowers must arrive on time. If you know that the family has children, bring gifts for them, e.g., electronic toys or candy. Always arrive 30 minutes late for dinner. Compliment the family on their home, the meal, and so forth. Don't be too effusive about any specific object or your host may feel obliged to give it to you.

• If you are a single man doing business in Mexico, don't invite your counterpart's spouse to a meal. If your spouse accompanies you, then you can include your counterpart's.

• If you extend either an oral or a written invitation, never mention the time when the event is ending. To do so would violate Mexican ideas of hospitality and contradict their flexible ideas of time.

• A foreign businesswoman should never make business dinner appointments with her male counterparts unless they are accompanied by their spouses.

• A businesswoman who wishes to entertain Mexican businessmen at lunch should arrange for the meal to be in her hotel's restaurant so that the check may be added to her bill and not presented at the table. If it is, men will not allow her to pay.

• Be sure to entertain Mexican businesspeople at a prestigious restaurant. Suggest three or four of the best, and ask your guests to choose.

HOLIDAYS AND SPECIAL OCCASIONS

Expect banks, offices, and many shops to be closed on the following days since they are national holidays. Individual localities sometimes celebrate additional holidays. Consult the tourist office to find out about holidays in the region you'll be visiting.

Holidays: New Year's Day (Jan. 1); Epiphany (Jan. 6); Constitution Day (Feb. 5); Flag Day (Feb. 24); Birthday of Benito Juarez (March 21); Holy Thursday, Good Friday, and Easter; Labor Day (May 1); Battle of Puebla (May 5); Navy Day (June 1); Independence Day (Sept. 16); Columbus Day (Oct. 12); Anniversary of the Revolution (Nov. 20); Feast of the Virgin of Guadalupe, Mexico's patron saint (Dec. 12); Christmas Day (Dec. 25).

• Keep in mind that there are 175 additional holidays celebrated in Mexico, most of them religious. Be sure to show respect for these celebrations. Don't drive your car through a procession.

• If a holiday falls on a Tuesday or Thursday, be aware that the adjacent Monday or Friday is often a day off also.

On September 15, at 11:00 P.M., the President appears on the balcony of the Palacio Nacional in Mexico City and recites Father Hidalgo's revolutionary cry for independence. This is followed by the ringing of church bells and by fireworks. The next day features bullfights and general merriment.

• Expect celebrations on the Feasts of All Saints and All Souls—November 1 and 2 (they are religious holidays; offices and shops are open). Incorporating the pre-Columbian feast of the dead, All Souls' Day (*Día de los muertos*) is an occasion for family picnics in cemeteries, decorating graves with marigolds to cheer the dead. People give one another cookies in the shape of skeletons or other symbols of death. Engaged couples give each other coffins made of sugar with the names of their loved ones on them. To enter the spirit of the occasion, give friends chocolate skulls with their names inscribed on them.

• Anticipate major celebrations for another religious festival, the Feast of Our Lady of Guadalupe, on December 12.

TRANSPORTATION

Public Transportation

• When you arrive at Mexico City's airport, go to the transportation desk, where you can book a taxi or arrange for a shared minibus that stops at individual hotels.

• Consider taking the subway in Mexico City as an alternative to buses and taxis; the traffic in this city is often horrendous. To find it, ask for the *metro*. Avoid the subway during rush hours (8:00 to 10:00 A.M., and 5:00 to 7:00 P.M.); during those times certain cars are reserved for women and children. Ask for subway maps in subway stations, at information booths, tourist offices, and some hotels. Pay for your fare at a booth, and use small change, since the ticket seller won't be able to change large bills. The fare is the same, no matter what your destination. Guard purses and wallets from pickpockets.

• In general, buses in cities are for the more hardy and adventuresome visitors, as they are *very* crowded. Enter at the front and exit at the rear. Pay in small change; however, you don't need exact change. Again, beware of pickpockets.

• Note that *colectivos*, sometimes called *peseros*, are taxis (usually green and white) which take as many passengers as will fit and travel on designated routes. You have to flag them down on the street. Sometimes drivers hold fingers out the window to show how many places are available. The fare is based on the distance traveled. State your destination when you get in, and pay when you get out.

• Don't take taxis that you flag down on the street. Only use *sitio* taxis, which you or your hotel call. These are the only taxis that are safe. Taxis on the street may have been stolen and used to rob passengers. At the airport, use the prepaid taxis.

• Realize that there are many options for long-distance buses, offering different amenities. *Primera clase* (first class) has toilets, heat, air-conditioning, reclining seats, and assigned seats. For shorter trips, there may not be heat or air-conditioning. *Expresso* costs 25 to 35 percent more than ordinary first class. *Ejecutivo* (executive) buses have wider seats, video, toilets, and sometimes beverage service, for double the first-class fare. All three types of buses run on time.

• Note that even smaller bus terminals have public bathrooms, telephones, and cafes.

• Be aware that in more remote areas, buses, referred to as *segunda clase*, may be old school buses. They stop all along the route to pick up or drop off passengers anywhere along the way; therefore, they do not adhere to a strict schedule.

• Remember that you can make reservations in advance for luxury buses, but not for others.

• When traveling on an express bus for a long distance, bring water, food, and toilet paper.

• Note that smoking is prohibited on the majority of buses, but this rule is often ignored.

• If you're considering costs, keep in mind that first-class trains cost the same as first-class buses. However there is usually only one train a day, while there are several bus departures, and trains may be up to a day late.

• Know that a few years ago, fourteen train routes were renovated, providing all first-class service. Many have been discontinued, because they could not keep up with the competition from the bus companies. Most of the better train lines run through the north.

• Keep in mind that the first-class trains have *primera*—regular first-class coach; *primera especial*—first-class reserved and air-conditioned; *camarote*—single sleeper with toilet; *alcoba*—double sleeper with toilet.

• If you're taking an overnight train in the winter, bring a blanket or sleeping bag. It's also a good idea to bring toilet paper.

• Buy your ticket well in advance, if possible; however, on some routes tickets aren't available until an hour before the train arrives at the station.

• Be careful about getting off the train before you reach your destination. Sometimes it's hard to tell when the train will take off again.

• You may bring your own food and drink, although in many first-class trains there are dining cars where you are likely to get safe food.

• If you're traveling at night, whether by train or car, bring a flashlight.

Driving

• Try not to drive in Mexico City. Traffic is extremely congested at all times.

• Don't drive at night. It's especially dangerous because of robberies, people on bicycles, potholes, and so forth.

• In the rainy season in rural areas, use caution, because there are potholes and mudslides.

• Note that there are two kinds of roads, the *cuota*, which is a toll road, and *libre*, a regular road. Always take the *cuota*. Keep the receipt for the tolls. If your car breaks down, you will need proof that you have paid the toll to get a road crew to help you. Tip them $1.00 to $2.00 for small jobs and $5.00 to $10.00 for larger jobs.

• Note that no one obeys posted speed limits. Drive with the flow of the traffic.

• Be aware of the "Watch for Cattle" signs. Livestock are a major cause of automobile accidents in Mexico.

• If your car breaks down, raise the hood as a signal for help. If you break down on a tourist route, look for the *Auxilio Turístico*—sometimes known as "Green Angels"—in green pickup trucks (marked "Tourist Assistance" in English and Spanish) equipped to handle breakdowns. They patrol tourist routes between 8:00 A.M. and 8:00 P.M. daily. They often make repairs on the spot and can handle simple medical emergencies.

• If you return to your parked car and find the license plate missing, realize that this means you have parked illegally and that a local policeman has taken the plate. To get it back, go to the local police station where you will have to pay a fine.

• Don't park in "No Parking" zones even when you see that many other drivers have. (The cars probably belong to people of influence, e.g., politicians, journalists, doctors.)

LEGAL MATTERS, SAFETY, AND HEALTH

• Be sure to get a tourist card before you enter Mexico. It is available from travel agents, Mexican consulates, or at the border. Keep it with you at all times. You have to present it when you leave the country. Note on it any expensive items you're bringing with you into Mexico, e.g., cameras and watches.

• Dress conservatively when you cross the border into Mexico by land. Don't dress like a hippie or you may be taken aside for a long period of questioning.

• Don't try to bring videotapes into the country.

• Realize that "sexy" magazines will be confiscated at the border.

• Be aware that nude bathing is illegal and is also *very* offensive to Mexicans.

• Don't carry expensive cameras or wear expensive jewelry. Keep most of your money in the hotel safe.

• Be especially careful at bus and train stations and at airports. Most robberies take place there.

• If you plan to go Chiapas, check with your consulate in Mexico City beforehand, because of past confrontations between peasants and paramilitary groups.

• Women should not go out at night unless with an escort or on a tour. Never go to a bar alone. Before you go out, ask at your hotel which city areas are not safe.

• If you're planning to swim, ask locals which beaches are safe; some have treacherous undertows.

• Note that hotels and restaurants serve purified drinking water. However, if you have the slightest doubt, order bottled water. Be sure that the bottle has an intact seal on it. If it doesn't, the bottle may have been filled with tap water.

• For information on medicine and hygiene products, see "Legal Matters, Safety, and Health" in the Introduction.

PANAMA

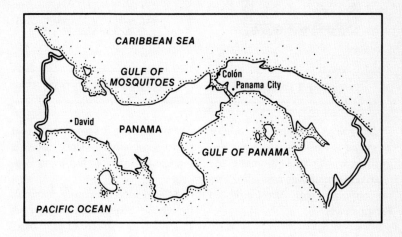

Robert McCulloch called his book about the Panama Canal *The Path Between the Seas*. And indeed most of us associate Panama with the 50-mile path between the oceans dug and hacked out of the jungle by men of many races and nationalities.

The construction of the canal had several side effects. Members of the many peoples that worked on the canal—of Caucasian, Black, and Asian origin—have remained in Panama and lived there together in reasonable harmony through this century.

The canal itself offers visitors a wondrous sight as the locks are flooded to enable ships to move through (often with a margin of only inches on either side of the ship) from one ocean to another.

GREETINGS

Language: Panama's official language is Spanish, although English is widely spoken among the relatively small business elite and the population of Afro-Caribbean Panamanians.

• When people are introduced (whether men or women), they shake hands.

• Note that women friends in the city kiss on one cheek in greeting and departing. Men and women shake hands or kiss on one cheek, and men shake hands with other men.

• At large parties, don't expect your host to introduce you individually. Go from group to group and introduce yourself.

• Remember that titles are important: *Licenciado* (lee-sehn-**syah**-doh) for someone with a B.A.; *Doctor* for a Ph.D., lawyer, or medical doctor; *Arquitecto* for an architect; and *Ingeniero* for an engineer.

CONVERSATION

• Be sure not to say anything that could give offense, since there is some anti-American feeling in Panama.

• Good subjects: family, common friends or acquaintances, interests and hobbies, basketball and baseball.

• Ask people for suggestions on what to see and where to dine.

• Avoid discussions of local politics, the former Canal Zone, and race.

• Don't get confused when talking to locals. They refer to Panama City as simply *"Panama."*

TELEPHONES

• You will find public phones on the street and along highways. Look for them also in shopping malls, or ask if you can use the phone in a shop. A few older phones still require coins. They are being phased out. Newer phones require phone cards, which are sold everywhere.

• To make a long-distance call, go to a Cable and Wireless office (still sometimes referred to as EN-TEL). You can make collect calls there, but you can also make them from a public phone using a credit card.

• If you need to send or receive a fax, go to an ENTEL/C&W office. For a small fee, a fax will be held for a month.

• For E-mail, look for one of the increasing number of cybercafes in Panama City. Many upscale hotels also offer E-mail and fax services.

• Emergency phone number for Police—104; for Fire—103. Telephone numbers for ambulances are found on the first page of the Panama telephone book.

IN PUBLIC

• Realize that the only place you are likely to find English-speaking clerks will be in high-class stores, which cater to the wealthy.

• Be sensitive to people's feelings about being photographed. Many Kuna people, especially older ones, don't like it. Younger ones may expect payment. Ask first.

• Remember that you aren't allowed to use flash equipment in museums or churches.

• Expect to find public bathrooms only in public buildings, hotels, restaurants, and bars. Bring your own tissues with you. Bathrooms are usually marked *caballeros* for men and *damas* for women.

DRESS

• For casual wear jeans are acceptable for men and women, but neither sex should wear shorts on the street. Be sure your jeans are clean and stylish—not ripped.

• Be aware that shorts, tank tops, and halter tops are prohibited in churches.

• Note that shorts are not permitted in any government building.

• If you plan to visit a dance club in Panama City, remember that many will not admit men who are wearing collarless shirts or sneakers.

• Women should not wear revealing clothing.

• If your business is with general managers of a corporation or with someone in banking, stocks, or accounting, expect them to wear suits. Low-level managers and those in retailing or manufacturing wear *panabrisas*, shirts (like the *guayabera*) worn over pants, not tucked in. A foreign businessman should always wear a suit on his first visit but may later wear a *panabrisa*, if that's what his counterpart is wearing.

• For business, women should wear a dress or a skirt and tailored blouse.

• When invited to a home for the first time, men should wear a suit and women a dress or dressy pants.

• When visiting the San Blas islands (which stretch along the Caribbean coast from Colón province to the west and Colombia to the east), women should not offend the Kuna people living there by wearing bikini tops or short-shorts.

• Realize that it's against the law to drive without a shirt.

MEALS

Hours and Foods

• Note that Panamanians eat three hearty meals a day; in homes of the wealthy meals are prepared by a maid.

Breakfast: 7:00 or 8:00 A.M. A typical breakfast might consist of sausages, *patacones* (see "Specialties"), small, thick corn tortillas, called *tortillas de maíz*, and fried dough, called *hojaldres*. In Panama City, people sometimes have eggs in addition to one of the above. Coffee is the usual beverage.

Lunch: Noon. The meal may begin with soup, followed by steak or chicken with rice and plaintains (fried or baked). There will always be beans—*guandú* (pigeon peas) or red kidney beans—cooked together with rice. A salad is served with the main course.

Dinner: 7:00 P.M. You'll probably have meat (chicken, pork, or steak) prepared with a sauce and served with rice, and a salad.

• Don't be surprised to be served potato salad and rice at the same meal. Rice is an important part of all meals.

• Expect dishes to be spiced with *cilantro* (fresh coriander leaves) and many other herbs and spices.

• Note that the most common dessert is fruit. Sometimes, however, there will be cake, pie, cheesecake, or chocolate mousse.

Beverages: Everyday beverages are water, soda, lemonade, fresh fruit juices (guava, papaya, strawberry, mandarin), or beer. On very special occasions there will be wine.

• Common drinks before dinner are Scotch on the rocks, rum and Coke, gin and tonic, and vodka and orange juice.

• After dinner comes coffee, usually espresso.

• Tea is available in cities, but it's difficult to find in smaller towns.

• The drink of the *campesinos* (the peasants in the countryside) is *seco* (distilled from sugarcane), milk, and ice. If you enjoy it in the country (however, you probably shouldn't unless the ice is from bottled water), don't order it in the city. People will think you're odd.

• The most popular drink is *chicha* (fruit juice, water, and sugar). Favorite flavors are *naranja* (orange), *lemonada* (lemon), and *arroz con piña* (rice with pineapple). Enjoy this drink in Panama City, since the water there is safe to drink.

• A nonalcoholic drink to which people attribute health-giving properties is *chicheme* (made of sweet corn, milk, vanilla, and cinnamon).

Table Manners

• Note that for company, drinks are served before, during, and after meals.

• While there is usually no appetizer course, expect snacks of *ceviche* (marinated raw fish) or cheese and crackers.

• Anticipate food service by a maid. At an informal meal she will place platters on the table from which you may help yourself. At a more formal meal she will serve each person at the table.

• Note that the father sits at one end of the table and the mother at the other. If you're the guest of honor, wait for your hostess to seat you.

• Remember that you'll please your hostess by eating everything on your plate, but if you really don't like something, it's okay to leave it.

• To signal that you have finished, place your knife and fork vertically and parallel on your plate.

Eating Out

• Expect a wide variety of restaurants in Panama City: French, Spanish, Italian, South American, Japanese, and Chinese, as well as those serving only Panamanian food.

• Note that a *restaurante* is a restaurant, a *panadería* offers bread and rolls to take out, a *pastelería* sells pastry (primarily to take out), and a *bar* is a more elegant bar than a *cantina*, which is a drinking place usually in a lower-class neighborhood. (Unaccompanied women do not go into *bars* or *cantinas*.)

• In rural areas where there are no restaurants, feel free to approach someone and offer her/him money to prepare a meal.

• If you see the word *carne* (meat) on the menu, recall that it usually means beef.

• Summon the waiter by saying *"Mozo"* (**moh**-soh) or *"Señor"*; call the waitress *"Señorita."*

• Remember that the person who invites also pays.

Specialties

• For appetizers, try *ceviche,* marinated raw fish; or *carimañola*—boiled, mashed *yuca* (cassava) wrapped around ground beef with spices, and then deep fried.

• Some special meat dishes: *ropa vieja* (literally "old clothes")—shredded beef, green pepper, and spices served with plaintains and rice; *empanadas*—fried meat pies; *lomo relleno*—steak stuffed with herbs and spices.

• Also sample: *arroz con coco y titi*—rice with coconut and small dried shrimp; *sancocho*—a stew of chicken, *yuca*, onions, potatoes, corn, and coriander leaf; *patacones*—fried green plantains.

• For desserts, consider *arroz con cacao*—chocolate rice pudding, and *buñuelos de viento*—fritters served with syrup.

• Remember that seafood, such as lobster and shrimp, is considered special and is usually eaten only in restaurants.

• There are many varieties of fish. The most popular is *corvina* (sea bass), prepared in many different styles.

• The Caribbean cuisine of the West Indian population of Panama City and Colón and Bocas del Toro consists of rice, fish, and seafood cooked in coconut milk, lime, and spices. One popular dish is *saos,* pigs' trotters (feet) marinated in lime and chiles. Another is *fufu,* a stew of fish, manioc, and plantains cooked in coconut milk.

HOTELS

• Besides the luxury hotels in Panama City, consider *apartoteles*, residential hotels that provide kitchens with stove and refrigerator, sitting room, and maid service.

• Note that in the 1990s B&Bs became popular. They range in quality from middle comfort to luxurious.

• Make reservations very far in advance if you plan to be in Panama during the Carnaval celebration.

• Check your hotel carefully before accepting a room. Sometimes the same price is charged for rooms with very different amenities. Be especially careful if you are staying in a very inexpensive hotel. It may be a brothel.

• If you're staying in one of the cheapest hotels, be prepared for hot water to be available for a limited number of hours—if at all.

TIPPING

• Give porters at airports and hotels $1.00 (U.S.) per bag.

• Note that restaurants and hotels don't include service in their charges. Add 10 to 15 percent to the bill— 15 percent in better restaurants.

• Don't tip taxi drivers. They have specified rates, depending on the number of zones they cross.

PRIVATE HOMES

• Feel free to drop in on people. They won't be offended.

• After having a meal in someone's home, feel free to stay until 1:00 or 2:00 A.M. Panamanians love parties.

• If you're invited to a party, don't arrive on time. In fact, you can be up to two hours late and no one will mind. Etiquette is somewhat different for a dinner party. If there will be many guests, arrive up to an hour late. If you (or you and your spouse) are the only guests, appear about 30 minutes late.

• When staying with a family, remember that everyone *always* eats together. Ask the time of meals, and be sure to be on time.

• If you make long-distance calls from a home, offer to pay for them.

• Check with your hostess to see if the bath water has to be heated. Feel free to take one or more daily baths, since Panamanians do.

• Ask your hostess where to do your laundry; she will probably tell you to leave it out for the maid to wash.

• If the family has a maid (and most middle- and upper-class families do), don't offer to help clear the table or do the dishes. If there is no maid, offer to help.

• After staying a week, you might want to tip the maid. Give her about $5.00. Don't ask your hostess about tipping; she may not like the idea.

• If you stay with a family for several days or a week, consider inviting them to a meal in a restaurant. A woman may make previous arrangements with the maître d' to pay with a credit card, so there won't be a conflict over the check.

Gifts: Note that you don't need to bring a gift if you're invited to dinner. It's polite to reciprocate

by inviting your hosts to a restaurant. If you can't do that, bring a bottle of good wine or of Scotch.

• From abroad bring wine, CD's, chocolates, fancy bed linens and towels.

BUSINESS

Hours

Business: 8:00 or 9:00 A.M. to 4:00 or 5:00 P.M., Monday through Saturday.

Government Offices: 8:00 or 9:00 A.M. to 4:00 or 5:00 P.M., Monday through Saturday.

Banks: 8:00 A.M. to 3:00 P.M., Monday through Friday. Some are open Saturday morning.

Shops: 9:00 A.M. to 7:00 P.M., Monday through Saturday.

Currency

• Note that Panama has no paper money of its own. They use U.S.

bank notes, which are called *Balboas*.

• Coins are the same size and shape as U.S. coins, but the engraving is distinctive. Coins are: 1 *centesimo*, 5 *centesimos* (called a *real*), 10 *centesimos*, 25 *centesimos*, and 50 *centesimos* (called a *peso*), and 100 *centesimos* which equals 1 *balboa*, written *B/1* or 1$ U.S. Panamanian coins are used interchangeably with U.S. coins.

• Note that prices may be written in $ or *B/*.

• Realize that in cities there are now Clave systems (ATM machines) all over, most with armed guards to keep them safe.

• Be aware that only travelers' checks in U.S. dollars are accepted, and some banks only accept American Express travelers' checks. Shops and restaurants rarely accept travelers' checks.

• Be prepared for difficulty in getting change for U.S. $50 and $100 bills. People may not have change, or they may suspect forgery.

• Keep in mind that the only bank that will exchange foreign currency (e.g., pounds, Canadian dollars, francs, yen, marks, etc.) for dollars is at the airport. If you want to exchange foreign currency after leaving the airport, you'll have to go to an exchange house (*Casa de Cambio*).

• If you're traveling into the countryside, bring a supply of small bills. Village vendors may not be able to change U.S. $10 bills. If you have small bills, you won't have to keep going to a bank to change money.

• Use credit cards, if you wish, in Panama City and in large shops and hotels in other areas. Outside the capital, use cash.

Business Practices

• Make appointments from abroad at least two weeks in advance.

• Don't start talking about business immediately. Panamanian businesspeople want to get to know you first.

• To make the best impression, have any materials you'll be using translated into Spanish.

• If you're planning to bring a laptop, note that the voltage is 110 volts, but a socket may be 110 or 220 volts. Find out which one the socket is before you plug in anything electric. Sockets are two-pronged. Power outages are common, so, if you bring a laptop computer, attach it to a surge protector.

• Note that Panamanian women are moving into higher managerial positions, so foreign businesswomen shouldn't have any problem.

• Foreign businesswomen should not attempt to treat a Panamanian businessman to a meal in a restaurant. He will never allow her to pay the bill.

HOLIDAYS AND SPECIAL OCCASIONS

The following are national holidays on which you'll find businesses, banks, government offices, and many shops and restaurants closed. Check with the tourist office to learn if there will be any local festivals or religious celebrations during your visit.

Holidays: New Year's Day (Jan. 1); Day of National Mourning (Jan. 9); Carnival (four days preceding Ash Wednesday); Good Friday through Easter Sunday; Labor Day (May 1); Panama City Day (Aug. 15), All Souls' Day (Nov. 2); Independence Day (Nov. 3); Flag Day (Nov. 4); First Call of Independence (Nov. 10); Independence from Spain (Nov. 28); Mother's Day (Dec. 8); National Remembrance Day (of U.S. invasion of Panama in 1989) (Dec. 20); Christmas (Dec. 25).

• Be aware that crowds are very unruly during Carnival. Attend the festivities only with a Panamanian.

TRANSPORTATION

Public Transportation

• Look for corners with marked signs for *chivas*, the buses that go along regular routes in cities. Pay when you exit. When the bus nears the stop at which you want to get off, say *"Parada"* (pah-**rah**-dah). It's sometimes hard to find the signs, all of which read *Chivas*.

• Note that most people drive between cities. Buses vary in comfort from cramped, old U.S. school buses, to minibuses, to modern air-conditioned buses. Cities and larger towns have bus terminals. Everywhere else, buses depart from the main square or street.

• Be prepared for constant changes in bus schedules.

• Keep in mind that taxis don't have meters. Agree on the fare in advance. Cost is generally based on distance traveled and number of passengers. Larger taxis are more expensive than smaller ones, and taxis in front of large hotels are more expensive than those you hail in the street.

• Expect regularly scheduled flights and reasonable fares for service between Panamanian cities. Book these in advance.

Driving

• Note that road conditions are variable.

• Use your foreign license for periods of up to thirty days.

• Be sure to wear your seat belt. You can get a ticket for not doing so.

• Realize that locals rarely stop at stop signs. When two cars meet at an intersection, the larger one usually goes through—very fast—and the driver of the smaller car has to be prepared to slam on the brakes.

• Note that oncoming cars with flashing headlights may be signaling a road problem ahead. Slow down.

• Remember that most hotels have their own parking lots, but, if you park on the street, hire someone to guard your car. There are always people around asking to do this. Give them small change.

• Look for many gas stations on main roads and in most towns, many open 24 hours a day. There are fewer stations in rural areas, so keep your tank full if driving in the countryside.

LEGAL MATTERS, SAFETY, AND HEALTH

• Remember that you can bring in only one each of items such as calculators, cameras, and radios. If you have more, you will have to pay duty.

• Be very cautious in Panama, where violence is common. Colón, on the Atlantic coast, is considered a dangerous city. If you must drive there, keep doors locked and windows closed.

• Note that there may be curfew regulations in Colón.

• Don't go out walking after dusk.

• Don't get in a taxi if there is anyone other than the driver inside.

• Check with your hotel to find out which neighborhoods are safe to walk in.

• If you have a problem, look for the tourist police, who wear white arm bands and are usually on bicycles. They are more likely to speak English than the regular police.

• Don't wear expensive jewelry or watches.

• Women should not go out

unaccompanied, and should be especially careful of purse snatchers.

• Women should always take taxis after dark. If you're staying with a family, ask someone to drive you to your destination and pick you up.

• Realize that you can safely drink the water in Panama City; the same water supply serves the Canal Zone. Outside that city, drink only bottled water.

• If you swim, be very careful of the riptides, which can carry you far away from shore. These currents are usually found at fine, white sand beaches. The muddy beaches are usually safe.

• For advice on medicine and hygiene products, see "Legal Matters, Safety, and Health" in the Introduction.

PARAGUAY

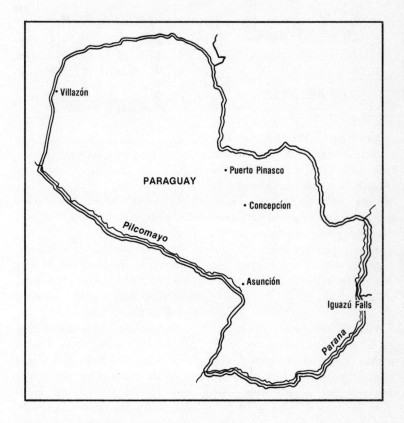

·Villazón

PARAGUAY

· Puerto Pinasco

· Concepcíon

Pilcomayo

· Asunción

Iguazú Falls

Parana

✳ Paraguay and neighboring Bolivia share the distinction of being the only South American countries without coastlines.

If you saw the Jeremy Irons/Robert De Niro movie *The Mission*, you will recall the attempts of Jesuit missionaries to build utopian communities with the indigenous people. The Jesuit experiments took place in several spots in South America, but most notably in Paraguay. Though most of the many missions constructed by the Jesuits and the Indians have been destroyed, travelers can visit a few remaining ruins in such towns as Itapúa.

GREETINGS

Language: The official languages of Paraguay are Spanish and Guaraní. Guaraní is the language of the indigenous people. Government officials *must* be able to speak Guaraní. Thanks to radio and television, more indigenous people now understand and speak Spanish.

People will be very impressed if you, as a foreigner, learn a few words of Guaraní.

• When introduced, men shake hands with other men and with women. Two women introduced by a mutual friend may kiss each other on both cheeks; otherwise, they shake hands.

• Among good friends, women kiss other women, men and women who are related kiss (if not related, they shake hands), and men shake hands with other men or embrace.

• At parties, shake hands with everyone when you arrive and *especially* when you leave.

• Remember that titles are important. Greet a medical doctor, a Ph.D., or a lawyer as *Doctor*, and a person with a college degree as *Li-*cenciado (lee-sehn-**syah**-doh). Other titles are *Profesor* and *Arquitecto* (architect).

CONVERSATION

• Be aware that people will stand very close to you while conversing. Don't back off.

• Discuss family, sports, and current events. Paraguayans are very proud of their hydroelectric dams, so you can make a good impression by asking about them.

• Before offering opinions in a political discussion, try to feel out the Paraguayan's views. People who are in the "wrong" political group often encounter problems. However, for the first time in its history, Paraguay is trying hard to make democracy work.

TELEPHONES

• To use public phones, purchase a phone card at ANTELCO (the central telephone office) or at a convenience store. You can dial right into AT&T for long-distance or international calls.

• Realize that not many people have telephones, especially in rural areas.

• For long-distance or international calls, go to ANTELCO, the central telephone office. You can make collect calls from there or from your hotel, but check first to see whether the hotel imposes a surcharge on such calls.

IN PUBLIC

• Some gestures to note: (1) crossing the index and second fingers (the North American "good luck" sign) is offensive; (2) the American "okay" sign (thumb and index finger in a circle) made with wrist dropped and fingers pointing toward the ground is obscene; (3) tilting the head backwards means "I forgot"; (4) flicking the chin with the top of the index finger means "I don't know."

• To be polite, ask permission when photographing people. They usually enjoy being photographed, but the picture will be posed. For candids, bring a telephoto lens.

• Don't photograph anything associated with the military or the police.

• Feel free to bargain in markets and in places that are half shops and half stalls. Don't bargain in established shops.

• Expect to find public bathrooms only in hotels and restaurants. In very rural areas, facilities are extremely simple. In the countryside, public bathrooms are almost always unclean and unsanitary;

in the larger towns, the level of sanitation varies. Bring tissues as there probably won't be any. Do not put used tissues in the toilet. Put them in a wastebasket next to the toilet, provided to hold the tissues. If you put the tissues in the toilet, it is likely to overflow.

DRESS

• When planning your wardrobe, consider the climate in Paraguay. There may be sudden changes from warm to cold during much of the year. From December to March, temperatures range from 77 to 110° F.; from the end of March to June the nights are cool; and from June through September the temperature is usually mild with some cold days.

• For casual wear, jeans are acceptable for both men and women. Don't wear shorts in cities.

• Women should not wear short skirts or revealing attire.

• For business, men should wear a conservative dark suit and tie and women should wear a suit, dress, or skirt with jacket or blouse.

• If invited to a meal in a home, women should wear a dress or skirt and blouse. Men should wear pants with shirt and sport jacket.

• Note that formal dress is worn only for a reception in a private social club, or to the opera, theaters, and weddings. The invitation will indicate if the dress will be formal. In that case, men should wear a dark suit and women should wear a dress or a Chanel-style suit.

MEALS

Hours and Foods

• First, a word of caution. Don't eat raw vegetables or fruit that can't be peeled. Drink only bottled water. Don't use ice cubes.

• Note that in the cities, Paraguayans eat two large meals a day, and they usually eat meat twice a day.

Breakfast: 7:00 A.M. Coffee with milk or *cocido con leche* (*yerba maté* with milk) are the usual beverages. This is accompanied by *galletas* (a kind of roll) or *chipas* (a very gritty bread made of corn flour, cheese, *mandioca* starch, and eggs) or *sopa paraguaya* (a type of pudding, made with mashed corn, milk, eggs, cheese, and onion—eaten with the hands as bread is, or with a knife and fork).

Lunch: 12:30 P.M. Some alternatives: *Milanesa* (fried breaded beef often served with an egg on top) and sometimes a lettuce and tomato salad; or *so'yosopý* (a Guaraní word meaning beaten meat), a hearty soup made with cornmeal, beef, oregano, and garlic and served with *sopa paraguaya* or, in the countryside, with *chipas*. *So'yosopý* soup is usually accompanied by *mandioca* (cassava, a rather bland tuber) which has been boiled in salted water. Lunch may be followed by a dessert: usually ice cream, but sometimes *dulce de guayaba* (guava paste) served with a white cheese called *queso blanco*.

Dinner: Sometimes a barbecue in the back yard, similar to an Argentine *parrillada* (barbecued beef). Outside the cities, people may have a light evening meal, perhaps just soup and bread.

Beverages: With meals you may be offered soda, Coca-Cola, or fresh fruit juices with ice and water added. Foreigners should avoid the juice, because the water isn't safe. In the countryside, soda is served only for special occasions.

• One of the most popular beverages is *mate*, the drinking of which is a social event. Dried, crushed *yerba mate* leaves are put into a cup made out of a gourd. Boiling water is poured over the *yerba mate*, and the gourd is handed to one person who drinks from it through an aluminum, silver, or gold straw (which acts as a filter to keep the leaves in the gourd) and returns it to the person with the kettle. It is refilled and the gourd is passed to another person who drinks and returns it to the person with the kettle. You have to acquire a liking for the bitter taste of *mate*. This ritual may last for hours. When you've had enough, say *"Muchas gracias."* If you don't want any at all, say, "I have *'gringo'* taste," or "I'm not used to it." *Mate* made with cold water is called *tereré* (teh-reh-**reh**).

• *Tereré* is served from a thermos, and the ritual is the same as for *yerba mate* (one person drinks and then hands the gourd to the person with the thermos, the gourd is refilled, and it is passed to the next person).

• Note that in the countryside, *mate* in one of its forms is drunk four times a day: in the morning when people awaken, the hot version; *tereré* is taken at 11:00 A.M. before lunch and around 3:00 P.M. during a work break; *mate* is drunk around 5:00 or 6:00 P.M. This consumption is an integral part of the culture.

• Other beverages: *Caña* is a kind of rum. And there are several brands of beer and wine made mostly by German immigrants.

Table Manners

• Realize that people usually show up for dinner or parties about two hours late. It's a custom that's simply understood. If actual time is important to you, ask people if they mean "North American time" or "Paraguayan time."

• Don't expect drinks before dinner, but beer or wine will be served at a formal meal and juices at everyday meals.

• If you're the guest of honor, anticipate sitting at the head of the table. There is no rigid rule about seating, however.

• In upper-class homes expect a maid to put food onto individual plates in the kitchen and then serve it. As soon as you finish, more food will be offered or the next course will appear.

• Realize that your hosts will expect you to eat a great deal and to finish everything on your plate. More sophisticated people won't "push" food as much as others may.

• Be aware that the only vegetables served will be a lettuce or cabbage salad with oil and lemon.

• During the week, stay about one hour after dinner; on weekends feel free to stay two hours or more. People enjoy chatting, listening to music, and drinking after dinner.

Eating Out

• Realize that there are a variety of places to get food:

Parrilladas serve barbecued beef along with innards, and wine, beer, and soft drinks.

Copetines are like convenience stores with tables. You'll probably find a blackboard listing the day's specials. There will be four or five tables, where you can have *empanadas* (turnovers filled with meat or cheese), sandwiches, soda, and beer. You can also buy food to take out. To find a *copetín*, look for a lighted Pepsi-Cola sign.

A *bar*, higher class than a *copetín*, is a snack bar where you can buy sandwiches, *empanadas*, coffee, or alcoholic beverages to eat there or to take out.

A *cafetería* is not a U.S.-style cafeteria; it's a place to buy coffee beans in bulk.

For bread and rolls go to *panaderías*.

Finally, expect to find many Chinese, Korean, and Japanese restaurants.

• Note that restaurants usually serve lunch between noon and 2:00 P.M., and dinner from 8:30 to 11:00 P.M.

• Look for menus in restaurant windows. Some restaurants post them.

• To summon the waiter, say *"Mozo"* (**moh**-soh).

• Realize that some dishes such as hamburgers and veal cutlets are served with a fried egg on top. If you don't want the egg, say *"Sin huevo"* (seen **weh**-boh).

• Don't expect a main course to

be "garnished" with potatoes, rice, or vegetables. You must order them separately. Sometimes *mandioca* is served. Eat it with knife and fork.

• Expect beef to be plentiful in Paraguay, although it can be somewhat tough.

• When ordering beer, remember that it comes in large bottles—more than a pint.

• Note that the person who asks for the check usually pays it. Offer to pay your share, but you'll probably be refused. Reciprocate by inviting your host to a meal.

Specialties

Some special dishes from Paraguay: *so'yosopý*—a soup made of ground beef, cornmeal, garlic, and herbs; *bori-borí*—a soup made of vegetables, meat, cheese, and corn balls; *sopa Paraguaya* (a national dish)—not a soup but corn bread with cheese and onion; *locro*—a maize stew; *asado*—beef grilled over an open pit; *parrillada*—mixed grill of steak, sausage, and innards; *croquetas*—croquettes of pork, chicken, or beef; *surubí* (the national dish)—catfish, a delicacy prepared in a variety of ways; *palmitos*—hearts of palm, another delicacy; *mbaipy heé*—a dessert made of milk, corn, and molasses.

HOTELS

• Be sure to make reservations well in advance for the high season—June through August.

• Note that inexpensive hotels don't accept travelers' checks.

• If you're on a budget you may consider one of the less expensive small hotels, which are quite comfortable. They are clean. Sometimes you'll have a private bath; at others, baths are shared. Usually there is constant hot water. Breakfast may be included in the room's price. If you need laundry service, ask the maid to do it (for a small fee).

• At breakfast, expect toast or bread rolls, butter, jam, and one pot of hot coffee and another of hot milk. If you like eggs for breakfast, ask for them.

TIPPING

• Give porters the equivalent of U.S. 50 cents per piece of luggage.

• Tip taxi drivers 10 percent of the fare.

• Note that a service charge is not added to the check at restaurants. Leave 10 to 15 percent of the bill.

• Give doormen, attendants, and others who perform small services the equivalent of U.S. $.50.

• U.S. bicentennial quarters or Kennedy half dollars will please very much when given as a tip.

PRIVATE HOMES

• Feel free to drop in on people, but if you don't know someone well, phone in advance. You'll find phones only in the homes of the upper classes, however. Never drop in on people from 12:30 to 3:00 P.M.—afternoon meal and siesta time.

• When you go to someone's home, clap your hands to announce your arrival. Someone will come to greet you, and then you enter the house. This custom prevails in both cities and country. You will probably be invited to sit on the front patio or porch. In cities, people may have a small living room to which you may be invited.

• Offer to pay for any long-distance calls you make from a private home. It isn't necessary to pay for local calls.

• Note that some homes have constant hot water, while others have no hot water at all, since Paraguay is very warm during most of the year. Ask your hostess if there is hot water. Check with your hostess about operating the hot-water heater. You could get a shock. Some places have gas heaters and some electric.

• Don't be shy about bathing daily. Paraguayans take a bath every evening.

• Don't feel obliged to tip the maid if you've stayed with a family.

Gifts: Note that a gift isn't expected if you're invited to dinner, but flowers, wine, or whiskey will be welcome.

• From abroad bring small appliances, e.g., transistor radios, small tape recorders, pocket calculators with memory, or photographic books of your area.

• For young people, bring a Walkman or cassettes or CDs of American pop music.

• Because Paraguay's economy is based on contraband, realize that you can purchase items from all over the world at a cost lower than in the country of origin. You might want to wait until you get to Paraguay before making purchases.

BUSINESS

Hours

• Remember that summer in Paraguay is from mid-November to mid-March.

Businesses: Monday through Friday, 7:30 to 11:00 or 11:30 A.M., and 2:30 or 3:00 to 5:30 or 6:00 P.M.

Government Offices: Summer hours are Monday through Saturday, 6:30 to 11:30 A.M. Winter hours are 7:30 A.M. to noon.

Banks: Summer hours are Monday through Friday, 7:00 to 11:00 A.M. Winter hours are 7:00 to 11:30 A.M.

Shops: Monday through Friday, 6:30 or 7:00 A.M. until noon, and then from 3:00 or 3:30 until 6:30 or 7:00 P.M. Saturday, 7:00 to 11:30 A.M.

Currency

• Note that the currency is the *guaraní*—plural, *guaraníes*. Coins: 50, 100, 500 *guaraníes*. Bills: 500, 1,000, 5,000, 10,000, 50,000 and 100,000 *guaraníes*.

• In Asunción, better shops, hotels, and restaurants accept major credit cards, but you won't be able to use them outside the capital.

Business Practices

• Plan business trips from June through October. Business vacations in Paraguay are usually taken December through February, and in May during the Independence Days holidays. Avoid the week before and after Easter, and the two weeks before and after Christmas.

• Realize that most business is conducted in Asunción, the capital.

• Try to make appointments in the morning. That's the time when you're most likely to find people, especially government officials, in their offices.

• Be sure to make appointments

in advance with people in business and government. From abroad, make arrangements two to four weeks in advance.

• Bring business cards printed in English on one side and in Spanish on the other. Have any sales literature available in Spanish.

• To make a good impression, compliment Paraguayans on the country's hydroelectric dams. The dams were built in conjunction with Brazil and Argentina.

• Cultivate patience. Decision making is a slow process. Decisions are made by an organization's top people.

• Keep in mind that Paraguayans are hesitant to purchase products that can't be serviced locally. Therefore, it is essential to guarantee support and service in Paraguay after a sale has been made.

• Realize that being a woman may have its advantages in doing business, since Paraguayan men don't like to confront or offend a woman.

• Note that most businesspeople eat the noon meal at home and then have a siesta. Business entertaining therefore usually takes place at night at one of the large hotels.

• If you want to give a businessperson a gift, offer a wristwatch with alarm or calculator or an electronic calculator. For a "super gift," bring a video cassette recorder.

HOLIDAYS AND SPECIAL OCCASIONS

Expect most banks, offices, shops, and many restaurants to be closed on the following national holidays. Check with the tourist office to learn about any local festivals that may occur during your visit.

Holidays: New Year's Day (Jan. 1); Feast of San Blas, patron saint of Paraguay (Feb. 3); Heroes' Day (March 1); Holy Thursday; Good Friday; Labor Day (May 1); Independence Days (May 14 and 15); Corpus Christi (the Thursday after the eighth Sunday after Easter); Chaco Armistice (June 12); Founding of Asunción (Aug. 15); Constitution Day (Aug. 25); Victory of Boquerón Day (Sept. 29); All Saints' Day (Nov. 1); Feast of the Virgin of Caacupé (Dec. 8); Christmas (Dec. 25).

• Don't be surprised at the sound of firecrackers everywhere on New Year's Eve.

TRANSPORTATION

Public Transportation

• Note that there are no subways.

• Pay when you get on a local bus. You don't need exact change. Keep the ticket you'll receive in case an inspector gets on the bus for a check. When you want the driver to stop, whistle, yell, or pull the cord above the window to alert the driver. Exit at the rear.

• Be aware that long-distance buses are extremely inexpensive. First-class buses, called *ejecutivos*, are faster, deluxe buses, with reclining seats, foot rests, tea and coffee services, and toilets. Buy your ticket a day or two in advance, since all seats are reserved.

• Note that taxis are very inexpensive, and you'll find 24-hour taxi stands in Asunción. Some taxis have meters, and others don't. Agree on the fare before you get in.

• Don't expect to take a train. There is a very slow and outdated system used only for freight. Paraguayans don't use trains as a means of transportation.

Driving

• To rent a car, you'll need an International Driving Permit as well as your driver's license.

• Avoid driving at night, because you may encounter cattle and high-wheeled wooden oxcarts.

• Realize that there are few signs, and the cattle in the countryside don't respond to a tooting horn. However, there are only a small number of roads going to any one place, so it's not difficult to find your way around. People are very helpful and will often go out of their way to direct you to a destination.

LEGAL MATTERS, SAFETY, AND HEALTH

• Be aware that it's illegal to take colonial antiques (items from the time of the Spanish conquest in the 1500s and 1600s) out of the country.

• Never publicly criticize the government. You could end up in prison.

• Women alone won't be harassed but should expect to be

questioned about being alone, and as to the whereabouts of their husband. To avoid lengthy explanations, say that your husband is joining you on the following day. In the city, it's usual to see women alone on public transportation going to and from work. However, in the countryside, it's unusual to see women alone.

• Women should not make eye contact with men they don't know and should avoid conversation with strange men on buses.

• Don't flaunt large amounts of money or expensive jewelry.

• If you're taking any medication, bring an adequate supply because brand names and dosages may differ.

• Note that contraceptives for males are available over the counter.

• For further advice on medicine and hygiene products, see "Legal Matters, Safety, and Health" in the Introduction.

PERU

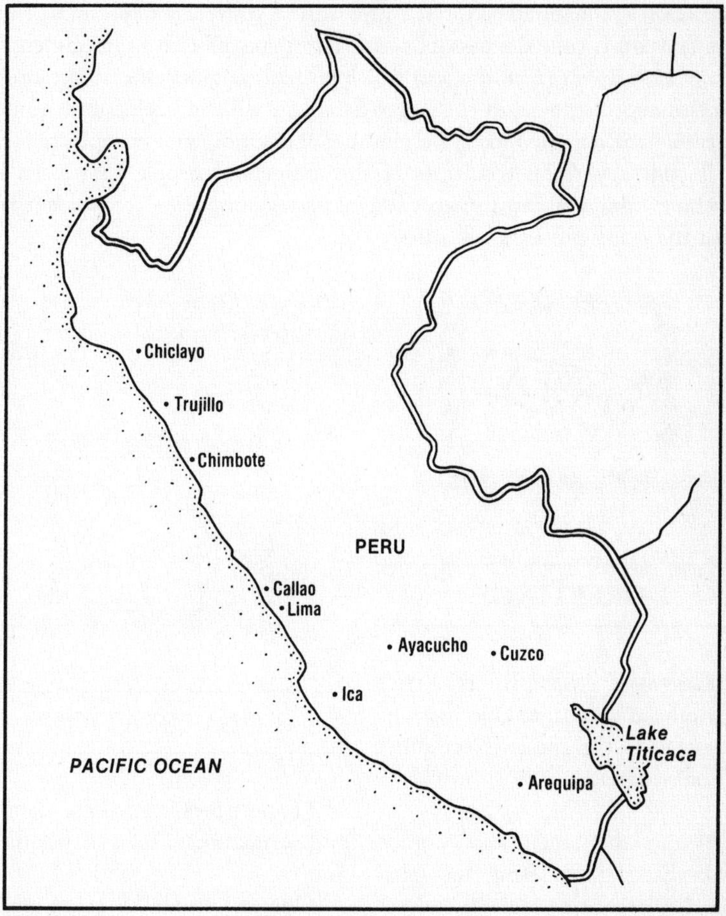
Chiclayo
Trujillo
Chimbote
PERU
Callao
Lima
Ayacucho
Cuzco
Ica
Lake Titicaca
PACIFIC OCEAN
Arequipa

Nothing will more vividly show the difference between the Spanish and Incan cultures than visits to Lima and Machu Picchu.

When Francisco Pizarro founded Lima in 1535, he insisted on a city with no influences of the Incas, whom he had recently defeated. Though the city now has many skyscrapers (and a great deal of smog), colonial Spanish architecture is still plainly evident.

Shrouded in the clouds, Machu Picchu was unknown to Europeans until 1911. Machu Picchu, a great Inca center, is now a famous site, which writer Lynn Meisch described as "beautiful beyond words, an absolutely magical place."

To get to Machu Picchu, you will probably go through Cuzco, the oldest continuously inhabited city in the Americas. A stop there sometimes brings on a bout of altitude sickness, but hotels start you off with a complimentary cup of *mate de coca* (coca leaf tea) which will alleviate its effects. Because of the thinness of the air in the Cuzco area, you will find colors much more intense—the red-tiled roofs, the clothing of the indigenous people, the sky.

If your appetite for cultures of the indigenous people isn't sated by Machu Picchu, you can also visit several places along Peru's coast identified with the many pre-Incan cultures.

titles are: *Doctor, Profesor, Arquitecto* (architect), *Ingeniero* (engineer).

GREETINGS

Language: Spanish is Peru's first official language; Quechua, the language of the Incas, is the other official language.

• Note that men and women shake hands in greeting and parting. Men embrace close friends or pat them on the back. Women kiss one another on the cheek. Sometimes when two women are introduced, they will kiss one another. The same is sometimes true of men and women.

• Greet officials or elders with their title plus last name. Principal

CONVERSATION

• Expect people to discuss family and occupation as soon as they meet you.

• Expect people to stand much closer to you when speaking to you than they would in North America. Don't back away or others will feel offended.

• Organize your ideas on your country's government and on technology. People will ask you about them.

• Ask advice on sights to see and places to eat.

• If you're chatting with women, bring up fashion, a subject that interests most Peruvian women.

• Avoid discussing salary, how much you paid for something, or Peruvian government and politics.

• Don't make any remarks about Peru's government, even if you hear complaints and criticisms of it.

• Never ask people about their ancestors. Peruvians feel more comfortable being associated with their Spanish colonial heritage than with their indigenous heritage.

TELEPHONES

• Make local, long-distance, or international calls from public telephones with coins or telephone cards. Buy cards from street vendors or at pharmacies.

• Note that the telephone company, Telefónica del Peru, has been privatized. Look for offices in large and medium-size cities. Make collect calls to North America and some European countries from Telefónica offices. You can also fax and telex abroad there.

• When people answer the phone, expect them to say "Aló."

• If you can't find a public telephone, ask a restaurant or shop owner if you may use the phone. Most will allow you to make a local call.

• Note that you can make long-distance and overseas calls from your hotel, but be sure to check first to find out whether there is a surcharge for such calls, and if so, how much.

• When making a long-distance call from a private home, tell the operator to call you back with the charges for the call. You don't need to pay for local calls made from a private home.

• Emergency numbers: Police—105; Fire—116.

IN PUBLIC

• Anticipate a warm welcome in Peru. Foreigners are considered very special people.

• If you need directions, expect to ask several people before you find where you're going. Even if they don't know the correct directions, people will pretend that they do—to save face.

• Always offer cigarettes to others when you light one for yourself.

• Don't be surprised to see women walking arm in arm with other women or men with men, and don't be surprised if a person of the same sex takes your arm.

• To beckon someone, wave your hand back and forth while holding it vertically, palm facing out.

• Realize that people don't queue. Be prepared to fight for your position in any kind of line—e.g., for transportation or in a shop.

• Never show impatience or offer criticism in public. Officials may be nearby and may understand English.

• Expect Peruvians to throw their paper, bottles, and garbage into the streets. People may tell you to do likewise. However, it's better to use the trash barrels in public areas and in bathrooms.

• Don't bargain in boutiques or government-owned craft shops, called *Artesanías del Perú*. Try bargaining in other craft shops and in markets. You'll find it easier to get a lower price if you offer cash and/or U.S. dollars.

• Be discreet in photographing indigenous people. Some object to having their picture taken, and some may become angry if you don't offer a tip.

• Don't photograph airports, military installations, or industrial plants.

• If you need a bathroom, go into a restaurant. It doesn't matter that you're not a customer.

• Realize that toilets in the countryside may be portable toilets or perhaps just a hole in the ground. Bring tissues.

• Don't put used toilet paper in the toilet, because it may overflow when you flush. Put it in the receptacle next to the toilet.

DRESS

• For casual attire, men can wear slacks and a polo shirt, and women a skirt or pants and a blouse. However, men should not go shirtless in populated areas.

• Note that in the highlands, people tend to be more conservative about dress, but it's acceptable for foreigners to wear shorts on hiking trails. In general, in the tropical lowlands, both men and women may wear shorts.

• For business in winter men should wear dark wool suits and in summer dark lightweight suits or blazers and slacks. Women should wear a dress or a skirt, silk shirt, and a jacket.

• When invited to a meal in a home, men should wear a sports jacket and tie and women a dress or skirt and blouse. To a party in a home, men should wear suit and tie and women a dress or skirt and blouse.

• If an invitation says that dress is formal (as it often is for official government parties or private, elegant parties), men should wear tuxedos, and women should wear cocktail dresses.

• Because nights are cold in the highlands, bring a warm jacket or heavy coat for a visit there.

• Don't wear clothing of indigenous people. They will think you are making fun of them, and others will think you odd.

• Women should avoid wearing what is considered men's clothing— e.g., a poncho or a man's hat.

MEALS

Hours and Foods

• First, a word of caution. Don't drink tap water. Don't eat raw vegetables or fruits that can't be peeled. Avoid raw shellfish. When you order a drink, always say *"sin hielo"* (seen **yeh**-loh), which means "without ice."

Breakfast: 7:30 to 9:00 A.M. A simple meal: rolls with ham, cheese, or jam and *café con leche* (coffee with milk).

Lunch: 12:30 or 1:00 P.M. to 3:00 P.M. The meal usually begins with a pasta course, followed by steak, chops, chicken, or fish with salad and rice. Finally there will be fruit and demitasse. Infusions of herbs (e.g., *yerba Luisa*) are popular rather than coffee. With the meal, you'll drink wine, lemonade, or soft drinks. Many people mix wine and water.

Tea: 6:00 P.M. People have cake and cookies with tea.

Dinner: 8:30 or 9:00 P.M. The first course may be a soup with noodles, followed by a *guiso* (vegetables pureed with spices) served with rice. The meal ends with coffee or an herb tea (e.g., chamomile).

Beverages: Popular drinks before dinner are *pisco* (grape brandy) or a *pisco* sour (grape brandy, lemon, sugar, and beaten egg whites), which is much stronger than its sweet taste would lead you to believe; also popular are campari and whiskey.

• With meals people drink beer, wine, fruit juices, Coke, Inca Cola (a yellow carbonated soft drink that tastes like bubble gum), and *agua mineral*, bottled, carbonated mineral water.

• Another common beverage with meals is lemonade. Many people boil water before making lemonade, but if you're embarrassed to ask if they have, ask for a bottled soft drink.

• Remember that beer in Peru has twice the alcoholic content of U.S. or European beer.

• Hot chocolate is a popular drink.

• Expect two kinds of coffee to be available: *espresso* (a strong cup of Italian-style coffee) and *americano* (a large cup of American-style coffee).

Table Manners

• Note that people never have more than one drink before dinner or before the midday meal on Sunday. If invited to dinner, you'll be served a drink with appetizers: olives, peanuts, pâté, cheeses, or huge Peruvian corn kernels on toothpicks with a dipping sauce—either one of avocado or one called *a la Huancaína* (white cheese with evaporated milk, hot peppers, onions, salt, and pepper).

• If invited to a meal, arrive 30 minutes later than the invitation states. Most dinner invitations are for 9:00 P.M. Dinner probably won't be served until 10:30 P.M., so it's a good idea to fortify yourself with a snack before setting out for the dinner party.

• Note that the table is set with forks to the left of the plate, knives to the right, and dessert and coffee spoons above the plate.

• Remember that the host and hostess usually sit next to one another. A male guest of honor sits to the right of the hostess and a female guest of honor to the right of the host.

• Anticipate one of two types of service: the maid may serve food directly onto your plate, or food may be served family style.

• If fish is served, use the fish knife and fork provided. A fish knife looks rather like an oversized butter knife, while a fish fork has one oversized tine.

• Don't be surprised to be served rice and potatoes at the same meal. Potatoes are considered a vegetable, not a starch.

• If beer is served in large bottles (about 64 oz.), serve yourself and then pass the bottle to others in your group.

• Don't be surprised if someone pours a glass of beer without asking if you want any. If you don't want it, be *very* firm.

• Realize that people eat enormous quantities of food at meals. (They don't snack between meals as North Americans often do.) Your hosts may press you insistently to eat more. Don't give in if you're full.

• Don't feel obliged to finish everything on your plate—in fact, it's polite to leave a little food—but do at least try everything or you'll offend your hosts. Leaving a bit shows that you're "stuffed" and satisfied.

• Keep your hands above the table. Don't put your hands on your lap.

• To indicate that you have finished eating, place your utensils either diagonally across the plate or vertically on the plate.

• Stay about 30 minutes after the meal ends. Your hosts may press you to stay, but they're usually just being polite. Leave anyway.

Eating Out

• Look for *pastelerías* (pastry shops): some offer places to sit and eat your pastries with tea or coffee; others sell pastries to take out.

• Men who want drinks or a light meal can visit a *picantería*. It will offer beer and native meals such as *ceviche*, *chicharrón* (pork crackling), *papas a la Huancaína*, and *olluquito con charqui* (potato with dried meat).

• Note that *chicha* describes two kinds of drink. One is made from fermented corn and is alcoholic; the other is a soft drink made from corn. The alcoholic variety, *chicha morada*, is purple.

• Look for menus in restaurant windows. Many places have them.

• Take advantages of the special menus some restaurants offer. At lunch you may find a *menú* or *menú fijo* (both terms mean the same thing), a fixed-price menu at a reasonable price.

• If you're eating in a nice restaurant, don't be surprised to find two or three waiters hovering at your table—though they are never intrusive. With subtle touches they make

you feel pampered, e.g., even bringing a woman a little table on which to place her handbag.

• Don't eat *ceviche* (raw fish marinated in lime juice).

• Be aware that if you ask for *té con leche* (tea with milk), you'll get a cup of hot milk with a tea bag in it.

• Keep in mind that the person who issues the invitation to a meal expects to pay.

Specialities

• Some fish and seafood specialties: *ceviche*—raw fish marinated in lime juice with onions and spices; *corvina*—sea bass, the best Peruvian fish; *chupe de camarones*—shrimp stew; *causa a la limeña*—a potato puree mound with shrimp salad, typical of Lima. Two favorite dishes of those on the north coast is *cabrito*—roasted kid, and *seco de cordero*—roasted lamb.

• Meat specialties: *anticuchos*—skewered beef hearts, marinated and grilled; *sancochado*—meat, legumes, and vegetable stew with garlic and spices; *lomo saltado*—chopped steak fried with potatoes, onions, and tomatoes, served with rice.

• The staples of highland cooking are potatoes and corn. *Causa* is made with yellow potatoes, lemons, hard-boiled eggs, peppers, olives, cheese, corn, and an onion sauce. *Choclo con queso* is corn on the cob with cheese.

• A popular potato dish: *papas a la Huancaína*—potatoes with spicy cheese and chile sauce.

• Avocados are the base for

several specialties: *palta rellena*—avocado stuffed with chicken salad; *palta a la jardinera*—avocado stuffed with vegetable salad.

• Jungle cuisine consists mainly of fish, especially *paiche*, served with hearts of palm, yucca, and fried bananas. Other dishes are *sopa de motelo*—turtle soup—and *sajino*—roast wild boar.

• For dessert, try *suspiro a la limeña* (condensed milk, eggs, sugar, cinnamon, lemon juice, and Port wine) or *mazamorra morada* (a purple gelatin dessert made from purple corn).

• Other desserts include *cocada al horno*—made with coconut, egg yolk, sesame seeds, wine, and butter; *pastelillos*—made with yuccas with sweet potato, sugar, and anise, then deep-fried, dipped in powdered sugar, and served hot; *turrón*—Lima nougat.

HOTELS

• Realize that all hotels have a plaque identifying the type of establishment: H=hotel; Hs=hostel; HR=hotel *residencial*; P=*pensión*. The plaques do not rate the qualities or facilities at the establishments. A hotel has 51 rooms or more; a hostel has fewer than 50 rooms. Most midrange hotels have restaurants for breakfast, lunch, and dinner; many budget hotels serve breakfast, but not other meals.

• Be aware that cheaper hotels may not provide water during the middle of the day.

• Note that a room with air-conditioning usually costs an additional 30 percent.

• Remember that the high seasons are June–August, Christmas, and Holy Week.

• For accommodations other than the massive, anonymous hotels in central cities, seek out *pensiones* or *hostales* (oh-**stah**-lehs). They are small, family-run hotels in suburbs, and they are usually clean and comfortable. They range in price from reasonable to expensive.

• Planning to stay at youth hostels? Remember that you need a membership card from your country, though some hostels in major cities don't enforce this requirement.

• Keep in mind that the cheapest hotels may not have hot water at all hours. In addition, some hotels charge extra for hot showers, and some don't even have showers. Ask when you arrive.

• When under the shower, don't touch anything metal, or you may get a nasty shock. The shower head is hooked to an electric heating element. Be sure to dry yourself carefully before turning off the shower.

• Note that even the least expensive hotels can arrange to have your laundry done. At better hotels, the charge for this service may be very high.

• If you're traveling on business and will need to communicate with your home office, stay at a first-class hotel, where you'll be able to send a telex.

PRIVATE HOMES

• Note that the typical time for visiting is at tea time—6:00 to 8:00 P.M. After tea, people go home to dinner.

• Phone before visiting.

• If you have a letter of introduction from a Peruvian, anticipate a warm and fulsome welcome.

• Offer to pay for long-distance calls both within Peru and to other countries.

• If you're staying in a middle-class home, feel free to take a daily bath or shower. There will be a constant supply of hot water. Be sure to ask for instructions about operating the shower. Turning things on in the wrong order could lead to electric shock.

TIPPING

• Give porters the equivalent of U.S. $1.00 per bag.

• Don't tip taxi drivers.

• Restaurants add a 10 percent service charge. If the service is outstanding, add 5 percent.

• Tip cloakroom attendants and high-class hairdressers the equivalent of U.S. 50 cents to $1.00.

• Give car-wash boys the equivalent of U.S. 30 cents.

• Tip car "watch" boys the equivalent of U.S. 20 cents.

• Don't feel obliged to spend all your time with family members. They won't mind if you go sightseeing on your own.

• Compliment the maid on the food she has prepared.

• If you stay with a family for several days, give the maid the equivalent of $4.00 to $5.00 Hand the money to her, or put it in her pocket.

Gifts: When invited to a meal, bring wine, liquor, or chocolates if you wish. Your hosts won't expect anything.

• If you give flowers, give roses. Other flowers are so inexpensive that they don't seem like a gift. You can send roses ahead. There is no delivery charge.

• Bring perfume, scarves, elegant neckties, or costume jewelry (many people don't wear real gold for fear that it will be stolen).

• Don't give clothing made of nylon or polyester. Peruvians prefer natural fabrics.

BUSINESS

Hours

Businesses: Monday through Friday, 8:30 A.M. to 12:30 P.M., and 3:00 to 6:00 P.M. Some have continuous hours from 9:00 A.M. to 5:00 P.M. Most are closed on Saturday.

Government Offices: January to March, Monday through Friday, 8:30 to 11:30 A.M. Closed afternoons. During the rest of the year, Monday through Friday, 9:00 A.M. to 12:30 P.M. and 3:00 to 5:00 P.M. (Hours change frequently, so check ahead.)

Banks: Monday through Friday, 9:00 A.M. to 12:30 P.M. and 3:00 to 6:00 P.M. Some banks in Lima do not close for lunch.

• Note that all banks close on June 30 and December 31 for balancing. If that day falls on a Saturday or Sunday, banks may close one day before or after.

Shops: Monday through Saturday, 9:00 or 10:00 A.M. to 12:30 P.M. and 3:00 or 4:00 P.M. to 8:00 P.M. Some supermarkets do not close for lunch. Some shops are closed on Saturday; most are closed on Sunday.

• Be aware that almost everything closed from 1:00 to 3:00 P.M. There isn't a siesta as such, but people usually return home for lunch during those hours.

Currency

• The unit of currency is the *sol* (*s/*), divided into 100 *centimos*.
• Coins: S/O.10, S/O.20, S/O.50, S/1, S/2, S/5.
• Notes: S/10, S/20, S/50, S/100, S/200.
• When you change money, ask for some small bills, as there is a shortage of change in shops, post offices, taxis, and railway stations.

• Use major credit cards in cities, but don't expect them to be honored in smaller towns.

• Keep your paper money in good condition, as no bank or person will accept a U.S. dollar bill that looks damaged, torn, or old.

• Shop around for the best rates, especially when changing travelers' checks. Change money or travelers' checks at banks, at *casas de cambio* (exchange places), or in first-class hotels, restaurants, and shops. Banks often charge a higher commission and limit the amount you can change. *Casas de cambio* are usually open from 9:00 A.M. to 6:00 P.M., with a few hours off for lunch. They will offer you the best rate of exchange.

• If you pay in dollars at hotels, restaurants, or shops, you'll get change in Peruvian currency. Stores that deal in imported goods will welcome dollars.

• Traveling through areas with small towns, keep in mind that U.S. dollars are often the only currency you can exchange. Another reason for keeping a supply of small bills.

Business Practices

• Don't plan business trips to Peru during January to March, when most businesspeople vacation. Also avoid the two weeks before and the week after Christmas, and the week before and after Easter.

• Be aware that it's important to have contacts in Peru. See the "Business" section of the Introduction for suggestions on acquiring them.

Contacts in the diplomatic world are especially valuable. They can arrange invitations to embassy parties at which you can gather valuable information.

• From abroad, make business appointments at least two weeks in advance. Don't consider arriving in Peru and making impromptu calls at business or government offices.

• Try to schedule appointments in the morning.

• To enhance your image, stay in the best hotels. It isn't necessary, however, to eat at the best restaurants.

• Have business cards printed in both English and Spanish. If you haven't brought a supply, you can have them made locally in two to three days.

• If, for business or personal reasons, you want to keep in touch via E-mail, don't worry. There is Internet access in all important tourist centers. Many schools and hotels have E-mail access, and many towns have cybercafes.

• Note that a morning appointment may produce an invitation to lunch, so it's wise not to make a second morning appointment at another company.

• Be as subtle as Peruvians in negotiating. Don't confront people directly. Ask many, many questions, but avoid questions that would produce a "Yes" or "No" response, since Peruvians will tell you what they think you want to hear rather than what they really believe.

• Don't suggest an appointment

between 1:00 and 3:00 P.M., as many businesspeople take their lunch break during that time. However, a Peruvian may suggest lunch. More businesspeople now go out to eat in restaurants instead of returning home, so the lunch period may be shorter.

• Be punctual, though Peruvians usually aren't. Foreigners are expected to be on time.

• To impress Peruvian businesspeople, include charts and visual aids in your presentation.

• Realize that private enterprises are usually more reliable in time estimates and contracts than government offices.

• Women should realize that it will be *very* difficult for foreign businesswomen to succeed in Peru. Upper-class Peruvian women—if they work—have "second-economy" jobs. For example, they may hire goldsmiths to make jewelry and then sell it from their homes, or they may have knitters working in their garages and then sell the sweaters from their homes.

• For business gifts, bring inexpensive cameras, calculators, or good pens (e.g., Cross, or other major brands).

• Note that lunches are more appropriate for discussing business while dinners tend to be social.

• When planning to entertain for a business discussion, invite only those with whom you have been negotiating directly. When a deal is completed, feel free to invite everyone who has been involved in a project.

• Remember that Peruvian businesspeople like to be entertained at luxurious restaurants. Ask either the secretary of a top person in the Peruvian firm, or call the tourist office to get the names of the restaurants that cater to luxury dining.

• Include Peruvian wives in an invitation to a strictly social function, even if you are alone. If you have a co-worker whose wife has accompanied him, invite her, or ask the Peruvian businessman to invite someone else from the company with his wife. Do this so that the women can talk together.

HOLIDAYS AND SPECIAL OCCASIONS

Expect to find banks, offices, and many shops closed on the days listed below. Many local areas have holidays. Check with the tourist office to learn what they are.

Holidays: New Year's Day (Jan. 1); Easter; Labor Day (May 1); Sts. Peter and Paul (June 29); Independence Days (July 28–29); Saint Rosa of the Americas (Aug.

30); National Heroes' Day (Oct. 8); All Saints' Day (Nov. 1); Immaculate Conception (Dec. 8); Christmas (Dec. 25).

TRANSPORTATION

Public Transportation

• When you take a local bus, pay when you get on. You don't need exact change. The fare is the same for all destinations within city limits. When you want to get off, yell "Baja" (**bah**-hah).

• Note that there are three types of taxis. Hotel taxis are black sedans. They are more expensive than others but they are also more reliable. They have set fares. Most taxis don't have meters. Ask at your hotel what the fare should be, and negotiate in advance.

• If you're in Lima, consider taking *colectivos*. They are small cars, accommodating about five passengers, that run along set routes and that are faster than buses. Fares are based on distance. They'll stop whenever you want to get off.

• Keep in mind that in Lima, the

weeks before and after Independence Day (July 28–29) and before and after Christmas and New Year's Day, it is almost impossible to get bus tickets for travel outside that city. Book tickets well in advance, and realize that rates are more expensive at those times.

• When you purchase your ticket, ask whether the bus has nonstop service. Some do, but others make stops along the way.

• Note that some of the long-distance buses have reclining seats, movies, and bathrooms.

• If you're traveling with one of the better companies, have your luggage locked under the bus. You'll get a receipt so that you can claim it at your destination.

• If you get off the bus at a rest stop, bring all your carry-on bags with you.

• For longer trips, be sure to take bottled water and some food. You can buy food at stops along the way. Be sure the hot food is very hot and the cold food very cold.

• Be aware that heating on buses doesn't always work. If you're traveling at a high altitude it can become *extremely* cold. Bring warm clothes and maybe even a blanket. Air-conditioning doesn't always work either; if you're traveling in the lowlands, it can get very hot.

• Expect buses to stop for three meals a day. If you want to be sure your food is safe, however, bring your own.

• On better buses, look for toilets, but be aware that they often don't work.

• Realize that trains have several classes. First class has compartments (no heat) with two bunk beds and a sink, a dining car, and a bathroom, which everyone shares. Better than first class is Pullman class, where the cars are heated, the sleeping compartments have bathrooms, and the food tends to be of better quality. Second class is crowded and uncomfortable.

• Avoid night trains, because of the prevalence of thieves.

• Buy train tickets a day in advance.

• Recall that train schedules may change radically during the rainy season (November–April), trains sometimes being canceled for weeks or months.

• Bring one large bag rather than several small ones. One is much easier to watch.

• If you hire a car and driver to take you around the country for several days, agree in advance whether you are responsible for paying for his food and hotel room or whether it's included in his price.

• Realize that air travel within Peru is inexpensive. Try to take a morning flight; they tend to be more punctual than later flights. Be sure to reconfirm flights. Be at the airport at least an hour before the flight, since weather conditions sometimes cause flights to leave *early*. Remember that there are no separate sections for smokers and that some flights have

seat assignments but others do not.

Driving

• Note that you must be at least 25 years old to rent a car.

• Expect an on-the-spot fine if you are stopped for a traffic violation. Police may expect a bribe.

• When you stop for gas, get out of the car to make sure that the gauge on the pump is set at zero. Gas is measured in gallons.

LEGAL MATTERS, SAFETY, AND HEALTH

• Remember that coca leaves for chewing or making tea are legal, but cocaine is not.

• Keep in mind that Peru's drug laws are *extremely* harsh. People can spend weeks in prison waiting for a trial and then serve a long jail sentence.

• Be very careful when crossing the streets. Cars do not respect the rules.

• Beware of pickpockets; try to avoid crowds where they can easily disappear. Carry most of your money in travelers' checks.

• Don't wear gold jewelry or expensive watches, or robbers may rip them off.

• Never accept food, drink, or cigarettes from other passengers on buses or trains. The objects might be drugged.

• Single women should note that taking a taxi at night can be just as dangerous as walking.

• If you have luggage, take taxis to bus or train station before 8:00 A.M. or after dark. Be very cautious. Stations attract thieves.

• Realize that no object of archeological interest may be taken out of Peru.

• When traveling to high altitudes, spend the first day resting. Avoid alcohol and cigarettes, and eat very lightly. On your second day, don't rush—walk slowly. If you get true altitude sickness, ask at your hotel (even if it is a small one) if they have a supply of oxygen. The only real cure is to descend to a lower level. Many hotels serve guests *mate de coca* (tea made with coca leaves), a brew that is supposed to ameliorate the effects of altitude sickness.

• Bring sunscreen from abroad. The type made in Peru is not effective.

• Contraceptives are also available in major cities, but the choices are limited.

• Do not drink tap water or drinks with ice. Drink water from bottles that have an intact seal.

• Do not eat fruits and vegetables that cannot be peeled.

• For information about medicine and hygiene products, see "Legal Matters, Safety, and Health" in the Introduction.

URUGUAY

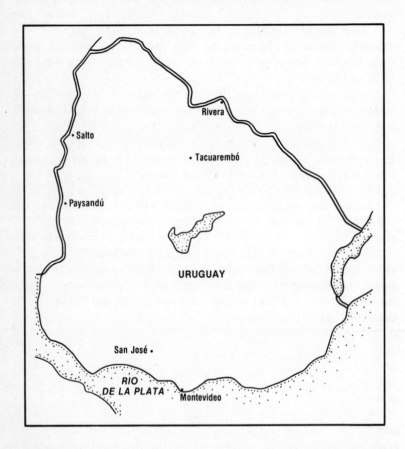

Huddling next to gigantic Brazil, Uruguay, South America's small-est country, makes up for its size with some impressive qualities. It has the highest literacy rate in South America, not to mention the longest life expectancy on the continent.

Uruguay has a European culture, a quiet style of life, and an extensive welfare system. Up until the sixties, it was often likened to Switzerland for its political stability and social and economic progressiveness. Economic setbacks have eroded the country's standard of living, however, and some once affluent families now search for bargains when they shop.

Unlike landlocked Switzerland, Uruguay boasts 250 miles of beaches, including one of the continent's playgrounds for the rich, Punta del Este, Uruguay's South American Riviera, which continues to fill with vacationers—and the good life goes on.

GREETINGS

Language: The official language of Uruguay is Spanish.

• When young people are introduced, note that girls kiss girls and boys kiss girls, while boys shake hands with other boys. When adults are introduced, the custom is to shake hands with members of both sexes, unless they are good friends. In that case, they greet one another as young people do.

• Remember that titles are important. Use *Doctor* for university graduates other than engineers (*Ingeniero*) or teachers (*Profesor*).

• When you leave a party, feel free to say one "good-bye" to the group, unless you've had a long conversation with someone. In that case, say an individual "good-bye."

CONVERSATION

• Good subjects for first conversations are sports—especially soccer—and international politics.

• Ask for suggestions about places to visit, interesting sights, and good restaurants.

• In a first conversation, don't discuss family.

• If you're a young person talking to other young people, prepare for a "one-upmanship" game about the courses you're studying.

TELEPHONES

• Buy tokens, called *fichas* (tokens), at shops, bars, or restaurants. To make a local call, deposit one token for a three-minute call. After that time, a tone sounds, and you must add more tokens. You may also use a phone card, available in denominations of 50, 100, 200, 300, and 500 *pesos*.

• To make a long-distance call, go to ANTEL, the telephone company, which has many offices throughout the country. However, it's less expensive to make a collect call or a credit-card call than to pay local charges.

• Send faxes from ANTEL offices.

• When people answer the phone, expect them to say "¡Hola!"

IN PUBLIC

• Gestures to remember: (1) thumbs up with other fingers closed means okay; (2) touching all the fingers and thumb of the right hand together signals doubt. (3) The North American "okay" gesture is considered vulgar.

• Be prepared for people to converse in close proximity as well as to touch shoulders and pat arms when introduced.

• Don't feel obliged to write a thank-you note for an invitation or a favor. People don't expect them.

• If you're a gambler, note that there are many casinos. Don't change money in one, however, because the exchange rate isn't very good.

• Try bargaining in small shops and markets but not in large department stores.

DRESS

• Casual wear for men is a sports jacket, shirt, and pants, and for women pants. Women shouldn't wear shorts though men can wear shorts for sightseeing. Women may wear jeans in the city but not to a good restaurant, to a social event, or to the theater.

• For business, men should wear dark suits and ties and in winter three-piece suits. Women should wear a skirt, blazer, and good shoes. In winter, women should wear a fur coat if they have one. During the winter, wear nylons; they aren't necessary in the summer.

• To a formal occasion (e.g., a wedding, a girl's fifteenth birthday party, the theater), men should wear a dark suit and women a cocktail dress.

• In choosing your wardrobe, remember that Uruguayans don't usually wear bright, splashy colors for everyday dress. Bring clothes in subdued colors.

MEALS

Hours and Foods

Breakfast: 7:00 or 7:30 A.M. A light meal—usually toast with butter and cheese. The beverage will be coffee or tea.

Lunch: 1:00 P.M. A typical meal might be *churrasco* (steak—Uruguay is known for its excellent beef) with potatoes and salad, or veal cutlet *milanesa* with French fries. They would be followed by fruits or cake and coffee.

Dinner: About 10:00 P.M. A meal similar to lunch, but lighter. There might be *arroz con leche* (rice with milk), chicken, or tortillas (made of eggs, cheese, and spinach, these tortillas are really omelettes, not Mexican tortillas).

Beverages: With lunch, expect wine, soda, mineral water, and juices. With dinner, wine and soda are the usual drinks. Before dinner, people drink whiskey and martinis. A popular drink between meals is *mate*, a kind of herb tea sipped from a gourd that is passed from person to person. Drink it only if it's hot, which means that it has been prepared with boiling water.

Two other popular alcoholic drinks are *clérico*, a mixture of white wine and fruit juice, and *medio y medio*, a mixture of white wine and sparkling wine.

Table Manners

• Expect drinks before dinner to be accompanied by small appetizers, e.g., chips, nuts, or—at an elegant meal—caviar. Drinks and snacks are usually served in the living room.

• If you don't want an alcoholic beverage before dinner or with your meal, ask for a soda.

• Expect beef to be featured at almost all meals.

• Don't feel obliged to finish everything on your plate, but do try a little of everything.

• To indicate that you've finished, place the knife and fork vertically on your plate.

• If you're invited to dinner in someone's home during the week, leave after coffee. On weekends, you can stay later. Use your judgment on how the conversation is going, and leave when your host and hostess seem tired.

Eating Out

• *Confiterías* are tea shops. *Coctelerías* are places for cocktails and hors d'oeuvres. *Parrilladas*, the most common restaurants in Uruguay, are grills where beef is the main dish. *Heladerías* serve ice cream. A *bar* is a sidewalk cafe where you can have soft drinks, beer, and sandwiches.

• Remember that imported whiskey is expensive; local whiskeys cost only half the price.

• If you order a *copetín* (coh-peh-teen) you'll get a drink made with whiskey, and a selection of appetizers will be included in the price of the drink.

• Note that dinner hour at restaurants is from 9:00 P.M. to midnight. Some informal restaurants begin serving at 7:30 P.M.

• Don't expect to find menus posted in the windows of elegant restaurants.

• To get the waiter's attention in an elegant restaurant, simply raise your hand. In an informal restaurant, say *"Mozo"* (**moh**-soh), which means "waiter." Though you'll see some people making a kissing sound to attract the waiter's attention, don't do it—it's rude.

• If you're dining with people of the upper classes, expect one person to pay for the group. Among the lower classes, people usually pay individually.

• Note that better restaurants often accept U.S. dollars in payment.

Specialties

• Try some of Uruguay's beef dishes: *asado*—barbecued beef; *puch-*

ero—beef with beans, bacon, sausages, and vegetables; *lomo*—the best cut of steak.

• Other meat specialties: *milanesa*—veal cutlet breaded and fried; *chivito*—a sandwich with steak, lettuce, egg, melted cheese, and olives; *chivito al plato*—steak served with a fried egg on top, potato salad, green salad, and French fries. *choripán*—sausage baked in dough; *morcilla dulce*—a sweet blood sausage made with orange peel, raisins, and walnuts; *buseca*—a spicy soup with oxtail, beans, and peas; *carbonada*—a stew of meat, rice, peaches, pears, and raisins.

• Sweets include: *yemas*—crystallized egg yolks; *chajá*—a dessert made of sponge cake with cream and jam; *dulce de membrillo*—a quince preserve; *espuma de mar*—angel cake with whipped cream; *dulce de leche*—milk simmered with sugar and vanilla.

Thousands of South Americans vacation in Uruguay during those months.

• Note that hotels in beach areas lower their prices after April 1, but some of them close their dining rooms. During Carnival week, hotel prices go up 20 percent.

• At better hotels, ask if payment in American dollars is acceptable.

TIPPING

• Give taxi drivers 10 percent of the fare.

• Tip porters the equivalent of U.S. $1.00 per piece of luggage.

• Note that all restaurants add a service charge, but an additional small tip is expected.

• Tip 10 percent at cafes.

HOTELS

• If you're planning to visit Uruguay between December and April, book your hotel well in advance.

PRIVATE HOMES

• Never drop in on people you don't know well. Always telephone in advance.

• Don't be surprised if people entertain you with a meal in a restaurant followed by coffee in their home.

• If you're invited to stay with a middle-class family, remember that they have probably been going through hard economic times. Don't expect luxury.

• Don't be surprised to find that upper- and middle-class families have more than one maid. However, it's better to make your own bed, keep your room neat, and do your own laundry.

• If the home does not have a maid, offer to help set and clear the table and do the dishes. Your offer may still be refused.

• Expect constant hot water in most upper- and middle-class homes. Ask your hostess if the water needs to be heated for a bath, a process that will take from 30 minutes to an hour.

• If you stay with a family, give the maid a small gift (e.g., costume jewelry—not money).

Gifts: When you're invited to a meal, bring roses, the choicest and most appreciated flower.

• From abroad, bring something unusual for the house, such as a clock that gives the time in different places around the world.

• For young people, bring tapes or CDs of American popular music. They also enjoy T-shirts or sweatshirts with the insignia of U.S. universities.

• Bring older people tapes or CDs of classical music.

BUSINESS

Hours

Business: Monday through Friday, 8:30 A.M. to noon, and 2:30 to 6:30 P.M.

Government Offices: From mid-March through mid-November, Monday through Friday, 11:00 A.M. to 5:00 P.M. From mid-November to mid-March, Monday through Friday, 7:00 A.M. to 1:00 P.M.

Banks: Monday through Friday, 10:00 A.M. to 4:00 P.M.

Shops: Monday through Saturday, 8:30 A.M. to 12:30 P.M. and 2:30 P.M. to 7:00 P.M. Food shops open Sunday morning.

Currency

• Remember that the unit of currency is the *peso uruguayo*, which replaced the *peso nuevo* (N$ is the abbreviation for the *peso nuevo*) in 1993. Older banknotes of N$5000 and N$10,000 are still in circulation but are gradually disappearing. If you see an object with a price tag of N$10,000, for example, deduct the last three zeros and you'll have the current price of $10.

• Coins: 50 *centismos*; 1 *peso*, and 2 *pesos*.

• Notes: 5, 10, 20, 50, 100, 200, and 1,000 *pesos*.

• Use major credit cards at better hotels, shops, and restaurants.

• Be aware that Uruguayan ATMs will not accept North American or European ATM cards or credit cards.

Business Practices

• Plan business travel to Uruguay between May and November. Vacation period is January through April. Avoid the two weeks before and after Christmas, Carnival period, and the week before and after Easter.

• Stay in a prestigious hotel, because people will often judge you by the place where you stay.

• Have business cards printed in English and Spanish. You can have them printed locally in two or three days.

• Be sure to have sales literature available in Spanish as well as English.

• Expect to find very sophisticated businesspeople, most of whom are of Spanish, Italian, or German ancestry.

• Be aware that Uruguayans understand U.S. business methods better than people in other Latin American countries. They realize that North Americans are practical and straightforward and that they like to proceed quickly in business.

• Don't be surprised to find that an executive's workday in Uruguay is a very long one.

• Realize that decisions will be based on a group agreement of the people at the top as well as on the personal relationships you have cultivated.

• Note that business lunches are more common for discussions that are strictly business. Business dinners are usually held in the restaurants of major hotels.

• If you are entertaining a Uruguayan, choose a Chinese, French, or fine Uruguayan restaurant.

HOLIDAYS AND SPECIAL OCCASIONS

Expect to find businesses, government offices, banks, and many restaurants and stores closed on the following national holidays. Check with the tourist office to learn if there are any local or religious festivals which will lead to closings.

Holidays: New Year's Day (Jan. 1); Epiphany (Jan. 6); Carnival (three days before Ash Wednesday); Holy Week; Day of the Landing of the 33 Easterners (April 19); Labor Day (May 1); Battle of Las Piedras (May 18); Anniversary of the Birth of Artigas (June 19); Constitution Day (July 18); Independence Day (Aug. 25); Columbus Day (Oct. 12); All Souls' Day (Nov. 2); Christmas (Dec. 25).

• April 19 celebrates the beginning of the struggle for independence in 1825. Thirty-three Uruguayans who had started an expedition from Argentina returned to their country and began the struggle against Portugal. (Uruguayans call themselves *orientales*,

"Easterners," in reference to their country's location, east of Rio de la Plata.) May 18 commemorates a major battle in the fight for independence.

• During Holy Week and Easter Week, experience the traditional folk music and traditional gaucho activities such as barbecues. Most businesses close.

• June 19 honors the birthday of Artigas, a leader in the fight for independence associated with Simón Bolívar.

• On December 24 and 31, expect firecrackers and fireworks to be set off throughout cities or towns.

• Be cautious during Carnival and wear waterproof clothing. Young people throw water at everyone.

TRANSPORTATION

Public Transportation

• If you take a local bus, look for small signs on corners to mark bus stops, and be prepared for pushing and shoving in line. Enter from the front. You'll be asked your destination because the fare is based on zones. Keep your ticket as inspectors frequently board buses to check them. Don't pull the cord (which usually doesn't work) before you want to get off; instead, say "psst" to the conductor.

• Note that there are taxis and *coches*, unmetered cars for which you should be sure to agree on a fare in advance. If you have a choice between a taxi (usually a black-and-yellow Mercedes) and a *coche*, remember that the taxi has a meter and is usually much cheaper.

• Look for taxi stands in Montevideo. You can also telephone for a taxi or hail one on the street. Taxis use meters. There will be a small additional charge for luggage.

• Realize that passenger train service has been discontinued in Uruguay.

• For long distances, consider taking a bus. Buses for long trips have reclining seats, air-conditioning, and bathrooms. Buses that make trips of 100 kilometers or less don't have such amenities.

Driving

• Be aware that Uruguayan drivers don't signal when turning and don't respect traffic signals. While there are no laws about drinking and driving, if you're in an accident and have been drinking, you're in serious trouble.

• Don't be surprised if police stop you and want a bribe. If you're delayed for no serious reason, offer some money.

LEGAL MATTERS, SAFETY, AND HEALTH

• Feel free to drink the water and eat fruits and vegetables in Montevideo. Outside the city, observe precautions.

• Women should not go out alone after dark. Take a taxi. Feel free, however, to eat alone in a good restaurant.

• For information about medicine and hygiene products, see "Legal Matters, Safety, and Health" in the Introduction.

VENEZUELA

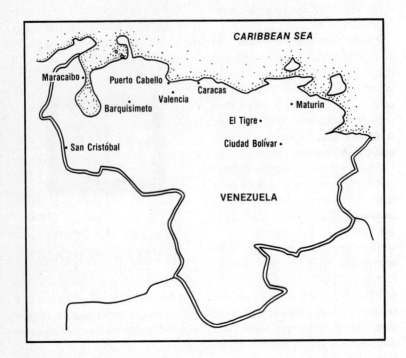

Arriving in Caracas, you may think that there's been a mistake—
that you're actually in a city in the United States. The skyscrapers,
the fast-food chains, even the strong traces of English that have crept into
the language all attest to the country's close kinship to the U.S. No country
in South America exhibits greater North American influence than Venezuela.

Had you arrived at the beginning of the century, you would have found
a country little changed since its discovery in 1498. But in 1914 came the
great miracle—oil. In the span of some eighty years, Venezuela has whizzed
through five centuries of growth.

Besides the wealth brought by oil, you'll also notice the reverence paid
to the hero of South America's liberation, Simón Bolívar, who was born in
Caracas in 1783.

GREETINGS

Language: The official language of Venezuela is Spanish.

• When you first meet someone, shake hands when meeting and leaving. After the first meeting, men touch one another's shoulders, while women kiss one another on the cheek.

• When men know one another well, they shake hands and embrace or pat one another on the right shoulder. Men and women who are good friends often kiss, and women kiss one another.

• Always accept or return whatever greeting is offered.

• Use titles. They are important to Venezuelans. Some common titles: Doctor (for Ph.D. and medical doctor); architect; engineer; lawyer; professor. (See "Key Words and Phrases" at the end of the book for Spanish equivalents.) Use the title with the last name.

• Don't use first names until you are invited to do so.

• At large parties, introduce yourself. At small parties you will be introduced by the host or hostess.

At either type of party, shake hands and say good-bye to each person when you leave.

CONVERSATION

• Be aware that people stand very close to one another when conversing. Don't back away.

• Good subjects for conversation: people's jobs; sights you should see; art and literature.

• Note that Venezuelans are very interested in a visitor's view of their country's economy. Don't initiate a conversation on the subject, but be prepared to answer questions.

• Don't discuss politics—especially Venezuelan politics—or tell political jokes.

• Don't bring up the problem of illegal aliens from Colombia.

• Don't ask whether a person is married, has a family, and so forth. You should know someone fairly well before you ask personal questions.

TELEPHONES

• Look for public telephones in pharmacies, subway stations, and in blue phone booths on the street.

• Long lines of people form, waiting to use public phones that are functioning. Try to find phones in hotel lobbies or shopping centers. Although every Metro station in Caracas has pay phones, they are not so secluded as the lobbies or shopping-center phones. Cellular phones have become extremely popular as a status symbol and as an alternative to broken public phones.

• Note that coins have basically disappeared from the market, so almost all public phones take phone cards (*Tarjeta CANTV*). They come in denominations of 2,000 and 5,000 *bolívares* and can be used for local, long-distance, and international calls. Purchase phone cards at kiosks, stationers, pharmacies, or from street vendors. Make sure the card is in a clear plastic wrapper with an unbroken red seal. For a local call, you have unlimited time. For a long-distance call, look for the timer, which will keep clicking and

will show how much time you have left.

• For long-distance calls, go to the telephone office, called CANTV (kahn-teh-**veh**).

• Realize that calling collect to another country is much less expensive than using Venezuelan phone services.

• Expect people to say "Sí," when answering the phone.

• Note the following emergency phone numbers (if possible, find someone who speaks Spanish to call for you, since the operator may not speak English): Caracas: Police—169; Traffic police—167; Fire—166; Medical emergency—483-7021; Ambulances (central suburbs)—545-4545; (eastern suburbs)—265-0251.

IN PUBLIC

• If you see someone clenching the fist with the thumb between the index finger and middle finger, he is wishing good luck.

• Always say *"Buenos días"* when entering a shop or office before noon. After noon, say *"Buenos tardes."* Usually everyone will respond. When leaving, say *"Hasta luego."*

"Adiós" is used when you don't expect to see a person for a very long time.

• Never show disrespect for Simón Bolívar. For example, don't put your feet on a bench in the Plaza Bolívar.

• For taking pictures, note that Venezuelans are not terribly concerned about privacy and won't mind being photographed.

• Don't take pictures near embassies.

• If you shop at places frequented by tourists, ask if there is a discount for paying cash.

DRESS

• If you've been to Venezuela before, expect to find people dressed less formally than in the past. Men frequently wear Bermuda shorts. Movie theaters and most restaurants do not require men to wear a jacket. Private clubs may require more formal dress, but there will be a sign on the door to that effect. If you're in doubt when you plan to visit a private club, phone to inquire about the dress code.

• For casual dress, women may wear pants or skirts, but they shouldn't wear shorts except at home, at the beach, or while playing tennis.

• Realize a movie theater may refuse to admit you if you're wearing shorts or rubber thongs.

• For business, men should wear a suit, white shirt, and tie. Women may wear a suit, a dress, or a skirt and blouse.

• Venezuelan women rarely wear stockings, but do wear them when you want to make a good impression, e.g., for a business meeting.

• Note that men wear tuxedos only to large balls, such as the ones held for a girl's debut when she has her fifteenth birthday. The invitation will state that tuxedos should be worn. For formal occasions, women should wear cocktail dresses.

MEALS

Hours and Foods

Breakfast: Families with children breakfast early (about 6:00 or 6:30 A.M.), since children must be at school by 7:00 A.M. Families without children usually eat between 7:00 and 8:00 A.M. The usual meal is scrambled eggs, *arepas* (see "Specialties") and butter, and coffee with milk. In other families, the meal is lighter: bread and rolls (which the maid buys fresh each morning) with strong coffee, similar to espresso. With either type of morning meal, there will be fresh fruit juices.

Lunch: Noon to 2:00 P.M. The main meal of the day, lunch features several courses: soup, salad, meat and vegetables, fruit, and desserts (often European pastries such as cream puffs, tortes, and fruit tarts). Beverages might be beer, mineral water, lemonade, or a soda.

Dinner: About 9:00 P.M. Usually a light meal, e.g., soup and a sandwich, or *arepas*, or *empanadas*, or bread and eggs. Beverages would be the same as those at lunch. Because of the large noontime meal, many people don't eat dinner.

Beverages: Before dinner the most common drink is whiskey with ice and water. Also popular are rum, wine, sangria, and beer.

• The favorite alcoholic drink is beer, the major brand being Polar.
• A popular drink is *merengada* (made from fruit pulp, ice, sugar, and milk). Probably, it is best to avoid this drink unless you're sure that the water the ice was made from is safe.
• Note that most women in Ven-

ezuela don't drink beer or strong liquor.
• Expect coffee to be available in a great variety of ways: *guayoyo*, a large cup of mild black coffee; *negro*, a large cup of strong black coffee; *negrito*, a demitasse of strong black coffee; *marrón*, a large cup of strong coffee with a little milk; *marroncito*, a demitasse of strong coffee with a little milk.
• A *plus-cafe* is an after-dinner liqueur.
• Another popular beverage is hot chocolate, which people sometimes drink at breakfast or in the evening.

Table Manners

• Keep in mind that some dinner parties don't begin until 11:00 P.M. and sometimes last until 3:00, 4:00, or 5:00 A.M. Fortify yourself with a snack early in the evening. Even after a dinner that begins earlier, people tend to stay late—till midnight or 1:00 A.M.
• Note that the seats at the head and foot of the table are usually reserved for the mother and father. Wait for your host to seat you. If you're the guest of honor, you will probably sit next to the host or hostess.
• Unless you're at a large dinner, which is often a buffet, expect the maid to serve food onto individual plates.
• Always wait until everyone at the table has been served before beginning to eat.

• Don't feel obliged to finish everything on your plate, and don't worry that people will push you to have second and third helpings. They won't.

• To indicate that you have finished eating, place your utensils at an angle, with tips pointing to 10:00.

Eating Out

• Expect better restaurants in larger cities to stay open until 11:00 P.M. or midnight, but those in small towns close at 9:00 P.M.— or even earlier. Many restaurants close on Sunday.

• Choose where you will sit with care. Every restaurant or drinking establishment adds a 10 percent service charge for dining at a table. To avoid the charge, eat or drink at the bar, if one exists. You'll find the bars in *tascas*, Spanish-style bars/restaurants, pubs, and taverns.

• Look for *cafés*, which serve sandwiches, pizza, pastries, coffee, juices, milk shakes, and beer (the only type of alcohol they offer).

• To purchase bread or rolls, head for a *panadería*.

• For pastries, look for a *pastelería*. In some, you can sit down and have coffee, orange juice, or a soft drink. You'll often find *panaderías* and *pastelerías* combined.

• Note that there are fresh-fruit stands (called *juguerías*) everywhere. Fresh fruits are put in a blender and mixed with ice and water. Don't buy juice from these stands, since the water may not have been boiled.

• When ordering a drink, realize that imported whiskeys are very expensive.

• For meals at better restaurants, be sure to make reservations.

• To summon a waiter, say *"Mesonero"* (meh-soh-**neh**-roh). To call a waitress, say *"Mesonera"* (meh-soh-**neh**-rah).

• If you see *muchacho* (which means "boy") on the menu, realize that it is a cut of beef.

• Note that beef is very good, and portions are large.

• To order beer on tap, ask for *lisa* (**lee**-sah). A bottle of beer is *tercio* (**tehr**-syoh). Ask for beer by brand, either local or imported.

• Remember that the person who suggests the meal pays. There is no such thing as a "Dutch treat." Note that if a man and woman go out, the man *always* pays.

Specialties

• Taste the national dish, *pabellón*. You will be served three separate dishes: black beans with white rice; shredded beef mixed with tomatoes, onions, and green peppers; fried plaintains.

• No Venezuelan party is complete without *tequeños*—small, bite-size pieces of white cheese wrapped in dough and deep fried. They are served as appetizers.

• At Christmastime, try *hallacas*, a kind of *tamal*—ground-corn dough with a filling of a meat and/ or chicken mixture, all wrapped in banana leaves, and then boiled. To eat one, you unwrap it, discard the leaves, and eat the *hallaca*.

• Special soups are *hervido de gallina* and *sancocho*—hearty soups made of chicken, meat, or fish and vegetables.

• Two dishes based on corn: *bollos de maíz*—spiced corn puffs fried in deep fat; *arepas*—flat white corn flour pancakes filled with butter, meat, or cheese; *empanadas*—filled with either meat, cheese, or fish.

• Sample dishes made with plaintain: *tortas de plátano*—cakes of plaintains and cheese, spiced with cinnamon, and served with meat dishes; *tostones* (often served as appetizers)—slices of plaintain which are cooked in oil, pounded, and fried again until they're very crisp.

• Other specialties are *lechón*—a pig carcass stuffed with its own meat, rice, and dried peas, and then baked; *mondongo*—tripe cooked in bouillon with corn, carrots, potatoes, and other vegetables; *cachapa*—a round pancake made of corn, served with cheese or ham.

• Two popular desserts: *quesillo*—a flan which is steamed rather than baked; *bien-me-sabe de coco*—a cake topped with muscatel wine and coconut cream.

HOTELS

• Note that Venezuela can boast of several world-class hotels.

• If you decide to stay at a less than luxury hotel, be sure that the air-conditioning works and that there is hot water before you take the room.

• Note that some of the smaller, budget hotels are used for "trysts"—or for brothels.

• Consider staying at one of the *posadas* or *pensiones*—small, family-run guesthouses, which are inexpensive. Most rooms have a private bathroom (shower and toilet). Check out the room before agreeing to stay, because sometimes the air-conditioning doesn't work. Also check to be sure that the bathroom facilities all work.

• Be aware that some inexpensive hotels have a reception area where guests can watch TV. Be sure that your room is away from this area, because the volume can be very high.

• Note that most of the better hotels accept credit cards, but you may find that there's an additional charge for using one.

TIPPING

• Give porters the equivalent of $1.00 U.S. per piece of luggage. There is a set price for porters at the airport.

• Don't tip taxi drivers unless they have carried luggage or have gone out of their way to do something special.

• Restaurants and hotels add a 10 percent service charge. If service has been very good, leave an extra 5 percent.

• Leave hotel maids at top hotels the equivalent of U.S. $2.00 per day.

• Tip gas station attendants from 2 *bolívares* to *Bs*. 10 to 50. Gas station attendants may try to keep the change. Make it clear that you want the change, and *then* give the tip.

PRIVATE HOMES

• Don't visit or phone people between 1:00 and 3:00 P.M., which is siesta time.

• Expect to be invited to a home only if you're a close friend.

• Realize that if Venezuelans want you to arrive at their house at 8:00 P.M., they will invite you for 6:00 P.M. Never show up until one or two hours after the time of invitation, or people will think you're too eager. You may also embarrass your host and hostess, who will not be ready.

• Try not to decline the offer of coffee when you visit. To offer a small cup of black coffee is a symbol of hospitality.

• Don't expect people to be fanatic about saving energy, as people in other parts of the world are. Venezuelans tend to leave lights and TV sets on, so you needn't be as conscientious about saving electricity as you would in other places.

• Feel free to take a daily shower. Most middle-class homes have constant hot water. Don't, however, stay in the shower for a long time as there can be water shortages.

• Expect your hostess to ask if you need laundry done. She'll take it and give it to the maid (in middle-class homes). If your hostess doesn't inquire, ask where you should wash your clothes.

Gifts: Note that Venezuelans appreciate whiskey, wine, or flowers, if you're invited to dinner.

• Give women orchids (the national flower). Give men items—such as pens—for the office.

• From abroad, bring electrical gadgets, cameras, pocket calculators, fashion magazines, perfume (if you know someone well), bestsellers in English (if you know that the person reads English), or chocolates.

• Note that it's unlucky to give handkerchiefs.

BUSINESS

Hours

Businesses: Monday through Friday, 8:00 A.M. to noon and 2:00 to 6:00 P.M.

Government Offices: Open to the public 8:00 A.M. to noon, Monday through Friday. However, if you need an appointment with an official, make it between 2:00 and 5:00 P.M.

Banks: Monday through Friday, 8:30 to 11:30 A.M., and 2:00 to 4:30 P.M.

Shops: Monday through Saturday, 9:00 A.M. to 6:00 or 7:00 P.M. Many shops close from 1:00 to 3:00 P.M., while others stay open. Shopping hours vary greatly from city to city and shop to shop.

Currency

• Note that the unit of currency is the *bolívar*, abbreviated *Bs.*

• Coins are ½, 2, and 5 *bolívares,* but they have ceased to be used and are practically worthless.

• Notes are 5, 10, 20, 50, 100, 500, 1,000, 2,000, and 5,000 *Bs.*

• Be aware that in the eastern part of Venezuela, most banks will not change travelers' checks. Even in Caracas, some banks will change only one brand of travelers' checks (the brand will differ from bank to bank). You can change the checks in shops, where there is a poor rate of exchange, or at *casas de cambio* (**cah**-sahs deh **cahm**-byoh), money exchange bureaus.

• Realize that there is no black market in currency, and there is no limit on how much local currency one can import or export.

• Expect credit cards such as Visa, MasterCard, and American Express to be honored in many establishments. Cards may also be used for cash advances from banks and ATMs.

Business Practices

• As soon as you know that you'll be going to Venezuela for business, make appointments. It may take a long time to set up appointments, so begin arrangements as far in advance as possible. Make appointments from abroad at least two to three weeks in advance.

• Note that the best time for business in Caracas is January to June and September to November; in Maracaibo, it's March to June. Avoid the two weeks before and after Christmas and Carnival, as well as the three weeks before and after Easter. At Christmastime, many companies close entirely for a few days, and government offices are open for limited hours.

• Use telephone and fax to make arrangements for your trip. They are more reliable than airmail to Venezuela. Major hotels have fax machines, which may be useful for making living arrangements and for communicating with your home office while you're in Venezuela.

• Send faxes from major branches of CANTV offices or from private companies in large cities, which offer fax services. The best hotels will send and receive faxes, but the service is very expensive.

• Don't suggest a business meeting after 4:00 P.M. on a Friday.

• Be prepared to make several trips to accomplish your goals, particularly because Venezuelans may not meet deadlines.

• To make a good impression, stay at the best hotels.

• To ensure success, make initial contacts with the top people in the Venezuelan firm. Decisions are *not* made by teams.

• If you don't have contacts in Venezuela, try to find one through an international bank, the commercial offices of your embassy or consulate in Venezuela, the American Chamber of Commerce in Caracas, or the *Centro Venezolano-Americano* (CVA) in Caracas.

• Should you need to hire an interpreter, check the ads in *The Daily Journal*, the English-language newspaper.

• If you're doing business in Caracas, allow yourself much more time than you think you need to arrive at your destination. The traffic is so terrible that streets become "parking lots" during rush hour.

• As a foreigner, try to be punctual, but don't "work up a sweat" to be on time. The typical excuse for lateness at any time of the day or night is, "I was stuck in traffic."

• Have business cards printed in English on one side and Spanish on the other. If a Venezuelan businessperson doesn't offer you a business card, ask for it.

• Bring any materials and specifications you'll be using in your presentation in Spanish. To really impress people, bring audio-visual material, such as videotapes. If possible, have the audio on the tapes in Spanish.

• Remember that Venezuelans like to do business in person rather than on the telephone.

• If you have a morning appointment, don't make plans for lunch. While a businessperson usually goes home at noon, he or she may invite you to lunch, but may not ask you until you arrive for your appointment. A good strategy is to make an afternoon appointment with one company and then a morning appointment for the next day with another firm.

• Expect to be offered a cup of coffee or tea at a meeting. It's good to accept, even if you just sip a little.

• Remember that even when men have met only a few times, they greet one another with an *abrazo* (bear hug). Be prepared—and don't back off if someone initiates this gesture. Another important gesture that a man will make to show friendship for another man: he will put his arm around you or touch you on the forearm. This gesture indicates that you've been accepted; never flinch.

• Don't anticipate a long period of socializing before business discussions begin. Venezuelans are much less likely to follow this practice than other Latin Americans. However, should negotiating sessions be long, never show impatience by pacing, tapping your pen, or other such gestures.

• Be aware of the rank of the person with whom you are dealing. Show respect for people in high rank and for elders. Let them precede you through doorways, and never interrupt them in a discussion. Always allow senior ranking officials to speak first at a group meeting.

• Anticipate dealing with businessmen who are well educated and sophisticated.

• Expect Venezuelans to be very direct. There will be no subtlety and no beating around the bush. They will say "No" when they mean "No"; they won't say what they think you want to hear. Reciprocate this directness.

• Don't be surprised if Venezuelan businesspeople complain about problems in the country. If you complain, they will join in with you. They are not much offended by any criticism about their country. Venezuelan businesspeople are willing to discuss their country's problems.

• If you want to keep in touch with your home office, arrange for someone there to call you at prearranged times, since phoning out from Venezuela costs much more than a call in from abroad.

• Stay on the right side of the law. If you have a court case against you—whatever the reason—you will not be allowed to leave the country until the case is resolved.

• Note that business lunches are

more common than business dinners. Fewer people observe the custom of going home at noon than in other Latin American countries.

• Don't invite a businessman's wife to a business dinner unless he asks if your wife will be coming—and she will.

• Check with the concierge at your hotel to find a prestigious restaurant at which to entertain.

• Be careful of complimenting a business contact's wife or of giving the impression that you are interested in her. Venezuelans can be very sensitive in this regard.

• Don't expect to be invited to a businessperson's home. Such an invitation is very rare. Most business entertaining is done at a restaurant or club.

• To succeed, a businesswoman should be very proper and businesslike. Dress elegantly; wear jewelry, makeup, heels; never wear anything too revealing.

• Remember that "thank-you" notes are very important. People tend to use them much more than telephone calls. Write such a note if someone has entertained you, if they have picked you up at the airport, or if they have arranged for your wife to be taken sightseeing.

HOLIDAYS AND SPECIAL OCCASIONS

The following are national holidays on which banks, shops, government offices, and many restaurants will be closed. Check with the tourist office to learn if the region you will be visiting has special holidays when offices will be closed in the area.

Holidays: New Year's Day (Jan. 1); Carnival (Monday and Tuesday before Lent); Holy Thursday; Good Friday; Declaration of Independence (April 19); Labor Day (May 1); Battle of Carabobo (June 24); Independence Day (July 5); Bolívar's Birthday (July 24); Columbus Day (Oct. 12); Christmas Eve and Christmas (Dec. 24 and 25).

• Realize that many banks and businesses close on the following religious holidays: Feast of St. Joseph (March 19); Feast of the Ascension (the Thursday which occurs 40 days after Easter); Feast of Corpus Christi (the eighth Thursday after Easter); Feast of All Saints' (Nov. 1);

Feast of the Immaculate Conception (Dec. 8).

• Be aware that many banks and businesses close on December 17, the anniversary of Bolívar's death.

• Note that when a holiday falls on a Tuesday or Thursday, an extra day is often added to the holiday to make a four-day weekend. This is called *hacer puente* ("to bridge").

• If you're in Venezuela during Carnival (before Lent), expect water fights, parades, and dancing in the streets. Statues of Simón Bolívar will be hung with wreaths and flowers.

TRANSPORTATION

Public Transportation

• Be sure to get specific information about your destination. First give the name of the neighborhood, then the name or number of the street (many streets don't have names), then the name of the building or the house. Every private house has a name.

• Take the subway (*Metro*) in Caracas. It's efficient, air-conditioned, and relatively quiet, as the cars are on rubber wheels. It runs from 6:00 A.M. to 11:00 P.M., Monday to Saturday, and 9:00 A.M. to 9:00 P.M. on Sunday. The fare is based on the length of the trip. Deposit money in a machine, and take your ticket. Keep the ticket because you will need it to leave the subway.

• If you take one of the large city buses, pay on the bus. There is one fare, no matter what the distance. Buses are uncomfortable and crowded.

• Look for small vans, called *carritos por puesto*. They are shared taxis, which stop on main streets. Pay either when you get on or when you get off. When you want to get off, tell the driver, "Donde se pueda" (**dohn**-deh seh **pweh**-dah), which means "Stop wherever you can let me off." Drivers of the small vans may be reluctant to take luggage. If you are the first to get on, wait for the van to fill up, or you will be expected to pay for the entire vehicle. For longer trips, the vans cost twice as much as buses, but they are much faster.

• Consider taking taxis. They are reasonable, but drivers never use their meters. All good hotels have their own taxi service, with well-maintained and reliable taxis. If you have to take a taxi on the street, check its condition. With all taxis, negotiate the fare before you get in. At the airport, use the taxi stand, where you pay first and receive a receipt. Don't go with drivers who approach you independently.

• For a long-distance trip, take buses, which are fast and comfortable. (There are no railways of importance in the country.) All the country's main roads are surfaced, so travel is smooth. Book ahead for one of the frequent buses between major cities. Be at the station 30 minutes before departure. Seats are not numbered, so prepare to grab a seat as soon as possible. People with tickets for a later bus will try to squeeze on an earlier bus.

• Consider flying. The cost is very reasonable.

Driving

• To rent a car, bring your driver's license and a major credit card. You must be at least 18 years old.

• If you are seated in the front seat, be sure to wear your seat belt.

• Note that traffic coming from the right has the right of way, but usually the larger vehicle takes priority.

• When driving in large cities, keep doors locked and windows closed to avoid having handbags or jewelry snatched at red lights or in traffic jams.

• Be wary about driving in Venezuela. People don't respect traffic laws. They pass on the right, exceed the speed limit constantly—and usually get away with it. Driving is a contest about who has the best reflexes.

• If you are stopped for a traffic violation, say "I don't speak Spanish" and hope that the policeman is nice. If a Venezuelan is stopped, he usually says, "Let's arrange it ourselves" and gives the officer $10 to $20. Paying a ticket involves long waits in line and dealing with the bureaucracy.

• If you're renting a car, first find out what your needs will be. In some areas of the country, you may need four-wheel drive.

LEGAL MATTERS, SAFETY, AND HEALTH

• When driving to the interior, expect to meet police roadblocks, designed to stop drug traffic. If you've bought a large amount of merchandise and/or expensive merchandise, be sure to keep the receipts, because the police will want to see them. If you've purchased only a few small items, you don't need the receipts.

• Because of recent socioeconomic decline, crime has risen. Check with your hotel to learn if an area is safe if you intend to go out after dark. Neither men nor women should wear gold or flashy jewelry. On the Metro, guard against pickpockets. Leather jackets and skirts and sneakers may be stolen at gunpoint. Avoid wearing anything unusually striking. Women should also be sure not to wear tight or revealing clothing. Such attire would provoke unwanted attention from flirtatious men.

• Women should pay close attention to their surroundings and avoid solitary beaches, bars, and sports matches (which are considered male territory).

• If you're walking, be careful. In their haste, motorcyclists often drive on the sidewalks.

• Some motorcyclists try to snatch purses or jewelry.

• Don't walk at night. Always take taxis.

• Women should not wear jewelry. People pull chains off women's necks.

• Note that water in all main towns has a large amount of chlorine added, so it's safe to drink. Nevertheless, many people drink bottled water. If you have any doubt about the safety of the water, stick to bottled water.

• For maximum safety, use a money belt. Women should consider carrying a purse with a strap that can be slung over one shoulder with the strap crossing the chest. Then hold your purse firmly between your arm and your body—always on the side away from the street.

• Be sure to leave your car in a guarded car park when possible. Never leave valuables in the car.

• For information about medicine and hygiene products, see "Legal Matters, Safety, and Health" in the Introduction.

KEY WORDS AND PHRASES:
Spanish

Following are some words and phrases we hope you'll find useful in Spanish-speaking Latin America. Remember that in Spanish, accents vary from country to country as widely as they do in English in the various places where it is spoken. If you're having trouble being understood or understanding another person, point to the word in the list of phrases. That, and possibly a little body language, should help.

Spanish is actually an easy language to pronounce; the spelling is fairly phonetic. Remember that *o* in Spanish does *not* carry the *w* sound with it, as it does in English (*grow, go, now*). The *e* in Spanish is pronounced similarly to the *e* of the English word *met*.

In the pronunciation section, note that *h* at the beginning of a syllable represents a hard *h* sound, similar to that of the English *hip*; when the *h* appears within a syllable or at the end, it represents only a slight aspiration (except of course for the case of *ch*, which is pronounced just as you might expect). The *r* in Spanish is always pronounced with some trill. In the pronunciation section, a single *r* represents a single trill (as in *throw*), and a double *r* represents a double trill. Note that the syllable stressed in a word is set in boldface.

Hi	*Hola*	o-lah
Good morning	Buenos días	**bweh**-nohs **dee**-ahs
Good afternoon	Buenas tardes	**bweh**-nahs **tahr**-dehs
Good evening/night	Buenas noches	**bweh**-nas **noh**-chehs
Today	Hoy	oy
Tomorrow	Mañana	mah-**nyah**-nah
Good-bye	Adiós	ah-**dyohs**
How much is it?	¿Cuánto cuesta?	**kwahn**-toh **kwehs**-tah

It's too much.	Es demasiado.	ehs deh-mah-**syah**-doh
Where is ___ ?	¿Dónde está ___ ?	**dohn**-deh ehs-**tah**
Where is ___ ?	¿Dónde están ___ ?	**dohn**-deh ehs-**tahn**
Is/Are there?	¿Hay?	ay(rhymes with *my*)
a bathroom	un baño	oon **bah**-nyoh
a restaurant	un restaurante	oon rehs-tow-**rahn**-teh
a hotel	un hotel	oon oh-**tehl**
the post office	el correo	el ko-**rreh**-oh
the bus station	la estación de autobuses	lah ehs-tah-**syon** deh au-toh-**boo**-sehs
A bus to ___	un autobús a ___	oon au-toh-**boos** ah
the train station	la estación de ferrocarril	lah ehs-tah-**syon** deh feh-rroh-kah-**rreel**
the market	el mercado	el mehr-**kah**-doh
a hospital	un hospital	oon os-pee-**tahl**
a doctor	un médico	oon **meh**-dee-koh
a bank	un banco	oon **bahn**-koh
a taxi	un taxi	oon **tah**-ksee
a telephone	un teléfono	oon teh-**leh**-foh-noh
the police station	la estación de policía	lah ehs-tah-**syon** deh poh-lee-**see**-yah
the embassy	la embajada	lah ehm-bah-**hah**-dah
a bakery	una panadería	**oo**-nah pah-nah-deh-**ree**-ah
the gas station	la estación de gasolina	lah ehs-tah-**syon** deh gah-so-**lee**-nah
a garage	un taller de reparación de carros	oon tah-**yehr** deh reh-pah-rah-**syon** deh **kah**-rros
the pharmacy	la farmacia	lah fahr-**mah**-syah
the church	la iglesia	lah ee-**gleh**-syah
the museum	el museo	el moo-**seh**-oh
the ruins	las ruinas	lahs **rruee**-nahs
the airport	el aeropuerto	el ae-roh-**pwehr**-toh
in front of	en frente de	en **frehn**-teh deh
near	cerca	**sehr**-kah
far	lejos	**leh**-hos
to the left	a la izquierda	ah lah ees-**kyehr**-dah

to the right	a la derecha	ah lah deh-**reh**-chah
straight ahead	directo	dee-**rek**-toh
At what time is ___ ?	¿A qué hora es ___ ?	ah keh **oh**-rah ehs
What time is it?	¿Qué hora es?	keh **oh**-rah ehs
At what time does it open?	¿A qué hora abre?	ah keh **oh**-rah **ah**-breh
At what time does it close?	¿A qué hora cierra?	ah keh **oh**-rah **syeh**-rrah
Glad to meet you.	Mucho gusto.	**moo**-cho **goos**-toh
How are you?	¿Cómo está usted?	**koh**-moh ehs-**tah** oos-**tehd**
I'm fine.	Estoy bien.	ehs-**toy** byehn
What is your name?	¿Cómo se llama usted?	**ko**-mo seh **yah**-mah oo-**stehd**
My name is ___ .	Me llamo ___ .	meh **yah**-moh
Yes	Sí	see
No	No	noh
Please	Por favor	pohr fah-**vorr**
Thank you	Gracias	**grah**-syas
You're welcome	De nada	deh **nah**-dah
I'm sorry.	Lo siento.	lo **syehn**-toh
Excuse me.	Perdóneme.	pehr-**doh**-neh-meh
Speak more slowly.	Hable más lentamente.	**ah**-bleh mahs lehn-tah-**mehn**-teh
I don't understand.	No entiendo.	no ehn-**tyen**-doh
I don't speak Spanish.	No hablo español.	no **ah**-bloh ehs-pah-**nyol**
Do you speak English?	¿Habla usted inglés?	**ah**-blah oo-**stehd** een-**glehs**
I would like	yo quisiera	yoh kee-**syeh**-rah
I have to	yo tengo que	yoh **tehn**-go keh
I need	yo necesito	yoh neh-seh-**see**-toh
I don't like (it)	no me gusta	noh meh **goos**-tah
Help! Police!	¡Socorro!¡Policía!	soh-**koh**-rroh poh-lee-**see**-yah
Leave me alone.	¡Déjeme en paz!	**Day**-hay-may en **pahss**

Don't bother me.	¡No me moleste!	Noh may moh-**less**-tay
a man	un hombre	oon **ohm**-breh
a woman	una mujer	ooh-nah moo-**hehr**
a child (*m.*)	un niño	oon **nee**-nyoh
a child (*f.*)	una niña	oo-nah **nee**-nyah
cold	frío	**free**-oh
hot	caliente	kah-**lyen**-teh
iced	helado	eh-**lah**-doh
Mr.	Señor	seh-**nyohr**
Mrs.	Señora	seh-**nyoh**-rah
Miss	Señorita	seh-nyoh-**ree**-tah
Doctor	Doctor, Doctora	dok-**tohr**, dok-**toh**-rah
Engineer	Ingeniero(a)*	een-heh-**nyeh**-roh (-rah)
Architect	Arquitecto(a)*	ahr-kee-**tek**-toh (-tah)
Attorney	Abogado(a)*	ah-boh-**gah**-doh (-dah)
Professor	Profesor(a)*	proh-feh-**sohr** (-**soh**-rah)
to eat	comer	koh-**mehr**
to drink	beber	beh-**behr**
to go	ir	eer
to see	ver	behr
to be	estar	ehs-**tahr**
I am sick.	Estoy enfermo(a).*	ehs-**toy** ehn-**fehr**-moh (-mah)
I am tired.	Estoy cansado(a).*	ehs-**toy** kahn-**sah**-doh (-dah)
I am thirsty.	Tengo sed.	**ten**-goh sed
I am hungry.	Tengo hambre.	**ten**-goh **ahm**-breh
I am lost.	Estoy perdido(a).*	ehs-**toy** pehr-**dee**-doh (-dah)

*Change the *o* to *a* to make it feminine.

AT THE HOTEL

one bed	una cama	oo-nah **kah**-mah
a double bed	una cama doble	oo-nah **kah**-mah **doh**-bleh
hot water	agua caliente	**ah**-gwah cah-**lyehn**-teh
a shower	una ducha	oo-nah **doo**-chah
a room	un cuarto	oon **kwahr**-toh
a (private) bathroom	un baño (privado)	oon **bah**-nyoh (pree-**vah**-doh)
air-conditioning	aire acondicionado	**ay**-reh ah-cohn-dee-syoh-**nah**-doh
a television	un televisor	oon teh-leh-vee-**sohr**

TELEPHONING

collect call	cobro revertido	**koh**-broh reh-vehr-**tee**-doh
"Hello" (on the phone)	aló *or* ¿quién habla?	ah-**loh**, kyehn ah-blah
credit card call	llamada con tarjeta de crédito	yah-**mah**-dah con tahr-**heh**-tah deh **creh**-dee-toh

AT THE PHARMACY

deodorant	desodorante	deh-soh-doh-**rahn**-teh
toothpaste	pasta dentífrica	**pahs**-tah den-**tee**-free-kah
sanitary napkins	toallas sanitarias	**twah**-yahs sah-nee-**tah**-ryahs
antacid	pastillas antiácidas	pahs-**tee**-ahs ahn-tee-**ah**-see-dahs
laxative	laxante	lah-**ksahn**-teh
anti-diarrheal medication	medicina para la diarrea	meh-dee-**see**-nah **pah**-rah lah dee-ah-**reh**-ah

RESTAURANT

the menu	el menú	el meh-**noo**
the check	la cuenta	lah **kwehn**-tah
the tip	la propina	lah proh-**pee**-nah
cover charge	el cubierto	el kooh-**byehr**-toh
large	grande	**grahn**-deh
small	pequeño	peh-**keh**-nyoh
a little	un poco	oon **poh**-koh
a lot	mucho	**mooh**-choh
a fork	un tenedor	oon teh-neh-**dohr**
a knife	un cuchillo	oon kooh-**chee**-yoh
a spoon	una cuchara	oo-nah kooh-**chah**-rah
a glass	un vaso	oon **bah**-soh
a bottle	una botella	oo-nah boh-**teh**-yah
a cup	una taza	oo-nah **tah**-sah
a plate	un plato	oon **plah**-toh
fried	frito	**free**-toh
boiled	hervido	ehr-**vee**-doh
broiled or roasted	asado	ah-**sah**-doh
baked	al horno	ahl **or**-noh
scrambled	revuelto	reh-**vwehl**-toh
well-done	bien cocido	byen koh-**see**-doh
medium	un poquito crudo	oon poh-**kee**-toh croo-doh
rare	crudo	croo-doh

MEATS AND FISH

steak	filete	fee-**leh**-teh
chicken	pollo	**poh**-yoh
fish	pescado	pehs-**kah**-doh
pork	cerdo	**sehr**-doh
ham	jamón	ha-**mon**
bacon	tocino	toh-**see**-noh
chops	chuletas	choo-**leh**-tahs
shrimp	camarones	kah-mah-**roh**-nehs

lobster	langosta	lahn-**goh**-stah
clams	almejas	ahl-**meh**-has
white bass	corvina	kor-**vee**-nah
squid	calamares	kah-lah-**mah**-rehs

VEGETABLES

corn	maíz	mah-**ees**
spinach	espinaca	ehs-pee-**nah**-kah
beans	frijoles	free-**hoh**-lehs
tomato	tomate	toh-**mah**-teh
avocado	aguacate, palta	ah-gwah-**kah**-teh, **pahl**-tah
potatoes	papas	**pah**-pahs
mushrooms	champiñones	chahm-pee-**nyoh**-nehs
plantains	plátanos	**plah**-tah-nohs

FRUITS

pineapple	piña	**pee**-nyah
mango	mango	**mahn**-goh
banana	banana	bah-**nah**-nah
melon	melón	meh-**lon**

OTHER FOODS

rice	arroz	ah-**rrohs**
bread	pan	pahn
butter	mantequilla	mahn-teh-**kee**-yah
sugar	azúcar	ah-**soo**-kahr
eggs	huevos	**weh**-bohs
a sandwich	un sandwich	oon **sahn**-dweech
soup	sopa, caldo	**soh**-pah, **kahl**-doh

BEVERAGES

beer	cerveza	sehr-**veh**-sah
wine	vino	**bee**-noh
red	rojo	**roh**-hoh
white	blanco	**blahn**-koh
mineral water	agua mineral	**ah**-gwah mee-neh-**rahl**
tea	té	teh
coffee	café	kah-**feh**
with milk	con leche	kon **leh**-cheh
orange juice	jugo de naranja	**hoo**-goh deh nah-**rahn**-hah
pineapple juice	jugo de piña	**hoo**-goh deh **pee**-nyah

DAYS OF THE WEEK

Sunday	domingo	doh-**meen**-goh
Monday	lunes	**loo**-nehs
Tuesday	martes	**mahr**-tehs
Wednesday	miércoles	**myehr**-ko-lehs
Thursday	jueves	**hweh**-vehs
Friday	viernes	**byehr**-nehs
Saturday	sábado	**sah**-bah-doh

TIME

at 1:00	a la una	ah lah oo-nah
at 2:00	a las dos	ah lahs **dohs**
at 3:00	a las tres	ah lahs **trehs**
at 4:00	a las cuatro	ah lahs **kwah**-tro
at noon	al mediodía	ahl meh-dyoh-**dee**-yah
at midnight	a media noche	ah meh-dyah **noh**-cheh
at 2:15	a las dos y cuarto	ah lahs dohs ee **kwahr**-toh
at 2:30	a las dos y media	ah lahs dohs ee **meh**-dyah

at 2:45	a las tres menos cuarto	ah lahs trehs **meh**-nos **kwahr**-toh
a day	un día	oon **dee**-yah
a week	una semana	oo-nah seh-**mah**-nah
a month	un mes	oon mehs
a year	un año	oon **ah**-nyoh

NUMBERS

one	uno	**oo**-noh
two	dos	dohs
three	tres	trehs
four	cuatro	**kwah**-troh
five	cinco	**seen**-koh
six	seis	seis
seven	siete	**syeh**-teh
eight	ocho	**oh**-choh
nine	nueve	**nweh**-veh
ten	diez	dyehs
eleven	once	**ohn**-seh
twelve	doce	**doh**-seh
thirteen	trece	**treh**-seh
fourteen	catorce	kah-**tor**-seh
fifteen	quince	**keen**-seh
sixteen	dieciséis	dyeh-see-**seis**
seventeen	diecisiete	dyehs-ee-**syeh**-teh
eighteen	dieciocho	dyehs-ee-**oh**-choh
nineteen	diecinueve	dyehs-ee-**nweh**-veh
twenty	veinte	**bein**-teh
thirty	treinta	**trein**-tah
forty	cuarenta	kwah-**rehn**-tah
fifty	cincuenta	seen-**kwehn**-tah
sixty	sesenta	seh-**sehn**-tah
seventy	setenta	seh-**tehn**-tah
eighty	ochenta	oh-**chehn**-tah
ninety	noventa	noh-**vehn**-tah
one hundred	cien	syehn
two hundred	doscientos	dohs-**syehn**-tohs
one thousand	mil	meel

NATIONALITIES

English	inglés(a)*	een-**glehs** (ah)
Welsh	galés(a)*	gah-**lehs** (ah)
Scottish	escocés(a)*	ehs-kon-**sehs** (ah)
Irish	irlandés(a)*	eer-lahn-**dehs** (ah)
North American	norteamericano(a)†	nohr-teh-ah-meh-ree-**kah**-no (ah)
from the United States	de los Estados Unidos	deh lohs ehs-**tah**-doh soo-**nee**-dohs
Canadian (male or female)	canadiense	kah-nah-**dyehn**-seh

*Add an *a* to the end to make it feminine.
†Change the *o* to *a* to make it feminine.

KEY WORDS AND PHRASES:
Portuguese

Following are some words and phrases you should find useful in Brazil. Of course, Brazilian usage is given, which is not always the same as in Portugal.

There are nasal sounds in Portuguese that are made by passing the breath through the mouth and the nose at the same time. A line above letters in the pronunciation section indicates that there is a nasal sound, e.g., $\overline{oo}$ as in *soon*, nasalized; $\overline{au}$ as in *town*, nasalized; $\overline{ee}$ as in *seen*, nasalized; $\overline{oh}$ as in *own*, nasalized. Note also that the syllable stressed in a word is set in boldface.

Hi	Oi	o-ee
Good morning	Bom dia	bo͞h **dee**-ah
Good afternoon	Boa tarde	boh-ah **tahr**-dih
Good evening/night	Boa noite	boh-ah **noy**-tih
Today	Hoje	oh-zhih
Tomorrow	Amanhã	ah-mah-**nyah**
Good-bye	Adeus	ah-**deh**-oss
Yes	Sim	$\overline{see}$
No	Não	$\overline{nau}$
Please	Faça o favor	**fah**-zih oh fah-**vohr**
Thank you	Obrigado	oh-bree-**gah**-doh
You're welcome	De nada	dih **nah**-dah
I'm sorry.	Desculpe.	dih-**skool**-peh
Excuse me.	Com licença.	ko͞h lee-**sen**-sah
Speak more slowly.	Fale devagar.	**fah**-leh dih-vah-**gahr**
I don't understand.	Não compreendo.	$\overline{nau}$ kohm-**prein**-doh
I don't speak Portuguese.	Eu nõ falo portugâs.	eh-oo $\overline{nau}$ fah-loo por-too-**geish**

Do you speak English?	Fala inglês?	**fah**-lah een-**gleish**
Glad to meet you.	Muito prazer.	**mooy**-toh prah-**zehr**
How are you?	Como vai?	**koh**-moh vie
I'm fine.	Muito bem.	**mooy**-toh bay
What is your name?	Come é o seu nome?	**koh**-moh eh oh **seh**-oo **noh**-mih
My name is _____ .	Meu nome é _____ .	**meh**-oo **noh**-mih eh
How much is it?	Quanto é?	**kwahn**-toh-eh?
It's too much.	Isso é muito.	ee-soh eh **mooy**-toh
Where is _____ ?	Onde está _____ ?	**ohn**-dih es-**tah**
Where are _____ ?	Onde estão _____ ?	**ohn**-dih es-**tau**
Is/Are there?	Há?	ah
the bathroom	o toalete	oh twah-**leh**-tih
a restaurant	um restaurante	oo res-tow-**rahn**-tih
a hotel	um hotel	oo oh-**tehl**
the post office	o correio	oh koh-**rray**-yoh
the bus station	a estação de ônibus	ah ihs-tah-**sau** dih oh-nee-**booj**
a bus to _____	um ônibus a _____	oo oh-nee-**booj** ah
the train station	a estação de trens	ah ihs-tah-**sau** deh trays
the market	o mercado	oh mehr-**kah**-doh
a hospital	o hospital	oh aws-pee-**tahl**
a doctor	um médico	oo **meh**-dee-koh
a bank	um banco	oo **bahn**-koh
a taxi	um táxi	oo **tahk**-see
a telephone	um telefone	oo teh-**lay**-fo-nih
the police station	a delegacia de polícia	ah deh-leh-gah-**see**-ah dih poh-**lee**-syah
the embassy	a embaixada	ah ehm-bay-**zhah**-dah
a bakery	uma padaria	oo-mah pah-dah-**ree**-ah
a gas station	um posto de gasolina	oo **pohs**-toh dih gah-zoh-**lee**-nah
a garage	uma garagem	oo-mah gah-**rah**-zhay
a pharmacy	uma drogaria	oo-mah droh-gah-**ree**-ah

the church	a igreja	ah ee-**greh**-zhah
the museum	o muséu	oh moo-**zeh**-oo
the ruins	as ruínas	ahs roo-**ee**-nahs
the airport	o aeroporto	oh ay-roh-**pohr**-ton

in front of	em frente de	$\overline{ay}$ **fren**-tih dih
near	perto	**pehr**-toh
far	longe	**lohn**-zhih
to the left	à esquerda	ah ihs-**kehr**-dah
to the right	à direita	ah dih-**ray**-tah
straight ahead	diretamente em frente	dee-reh-tah-**men**-tih $\overline{ay}$ **fren**-tih

At what time is ____ ?	A que hora é ____ ?	ah kih **oh**-rah ih
What time is it?	Que horas são?	kih **oh**-rahs $\overline{sau}$
At what time does it open?	A que hora abre?	ah kih **oh**-rah **ah**-brih
At what time does it close?	A que hora fecha?	ah kih **oh**-rah **feh**-shah

I would like	gostaria de	gohs-tah-**ree**-ah dih
I have to	tenho de	**teh**-nyo dih
I need	preciso	prih-**see**-zo
I don't like (it)	não gosto	$\overline{nau}$ **goh**-stoh
Help!	Socorro!	soh-**koh**-rroh
Leave me alone.	Deixe-me em paz.	**Day**-zha mee en pas.
Don't bother me.	Não me chateie.	$\overline{Nau}$ mee sha-**tay**-eh!

a man	um homem	$\overline{oo}$ **oh**-mehm
a woman	uma mulher	oo-mah moo- **lehr**
a child	uma criança	oo-mah cree-**ahn**-sah
cold	frio	**free**-oh
hot	quente	**ken**-tih
iced	gelado	jeh-**lah**-doh

to eat	comer	koo-**mehr**
to drink	beber	bah-**behr**
to go	ir	eehr
to see	ver	vehr
to be	estar	ihs-**tahr**

I am sick.	Estou doente.	ihs-**toh** doh-en-tih
I am tired.	Estou cansado.	ihs-**toh** kahn-**sah**-doh
I am thirsty.	Estou com sede.	ihs-**toh** k$\overline{oh}$ say-dih
I am hungry.	Estou com fome.	ihs-**toh** k$\overline{oh}$ foh-mih
I am lost.	Estou perdido.	ihs-**toh** pehr-**dee**-doh

AT THE HOTEL

one bed	uma cama	oo-mah **kah**-mah
a double bed	uma cama de casal	oo-mah **kah**-mah dih **kah**-zahl
hot water	água quente	**ah**-gwah **ken**-tih
with a shower	com chuveiro	k$\overline{oh}$ shoo-**vay**-roh
a room	um quarto	$\overline{oo}$ **kwahr**-toh
with a bathroom	com banheiro	koh bah-**nyay**-roh
air-conditioning	ar condicionado	ahr kno-dee-syo-**nah**-doh
a television	um televisor	$\overline{oo}$ teh-leh-vee-**zohr**

TELEPHONING

collect call	uma chamada a cobrar	oo-mah shah-**mah**-dah ah koh-**brahr**
"Hello" (on the phone)	alô	ah-**loh**
credit card call	chamada com cartão de crédito	chah-**mah**-dah k$\overline{oh}$ car-t$\overline{au}$ dih **creh**-dee-toh

AT THE PHARMACY

deodorant	um desodorante	$\overline{oo}$ dih-zoh-doh-**rahn**-tih
toothpaste	pasta de dentes	**pahs**-tan dih **den**-tihs
sanitary napkins	toalhas higiênicas	toh-**ah**-lyahs ee-zhee-**eh**-nee-kahs
antacid	anti-ácido	ahn-tee-**ah**-see-doh
laxative	um laxante	$\overline{oo}$ lah-**shahn**-tih

anti-diarrheal medication	medicamento contra diarréia	meh-dee-kah-men-toh-kon-tra dee-ah-rray-ah

AT THE RESTAURANT

the menu	o menú	oh meh-**noo**
the check	a conta	ah **kohn**-tah
the tip	a gorjeta	ah gohr-**zheh**-tah
cover charge	couvert	coo-**ver**
large	grande	**grahn**-dih
small	pequeno	pih-**keh**-noh
a little	um pouco	o̅o̅ **poh**-koh
a lot	muito	mo̅o̅y-toh
a fork	um garfo	o̅o̅ **gahr**-foh
a knife	uma faca	oo-mah **fah**-kah
a spoon	uma colher	oo-mah **koh**-lehr
a glass	um copo	o̅o̅ **kaw**-poh
a bottle	uma garrafa	oo-mah gah-**rrah**-fah
a cup	um copo	o̅o̅ **kaw**-poh
a plate	um prato	o̅o̅ **prah**-toh
fried	frito	**free**-toh
boiled	cozido	koh-**zee**-doh
broiled or roasted	assado	ah-**sah**-doh
well-done	bem passado	ba̅y pah-**sah**-doh
medium	medio	**meh**-dioh
rare	sangrento	sahn-**gren**

MEATS AND FISH

steak	bife	**bee**-fih
chicken	galinha	gah-**lee**-nyah
fish	peixe	**pay**-shih
pork chop	costeleta de porco	koh-steh-**leh**-tah dih pohr-koh
ham	presunto	prih zoon-toh
bacon	bacon	bay-ko̅h

shrimp	camarão	kah-mah-**rau**
lobster	lagosta	lah-**gohs**-tah
codfish	bacalhau	bah-kah-**lyau**

VEGETABLES

corn	milho	**mee**-lyoh
spinach	espinafre	es-pee-**nah**-frih
beans	feijão	fay-zhau
tomato	tomate	toh-**mah**-tih
potatoes	batatas	bah-**tah**-tahs
mushrooms	cogumelos	koh-goo-**meh**-los

FRUITS

pineapple	abacaxi	ah-bah-kah-**shee**
mango	manga	**mahn**-gah
banana	banana	bah-**nah**-nah
guava	goiaba	go-**yah**-bah

OTHER FOODS

rice	arrôs	ah-**rrohs**
bread	o pão	oh pau
butter	a manteiga	ah mahn-**tay**-gah
sugar	o açúcar	oh ah-**soo**-kahr
eggs	ovos	**aw**-vohs
a sandwich	um sanduíche	oo sahn-**dwee**-shih
soup	sôpa	**soh**-pah
ice cream	sorvete	sohr-**veh**-tih

BEVERAGES

beer	cerveja	sehr-**veh**-zhah
wine	vinho	**vee**-nyoh
red	tinto	**teen**-toh
white	branco	**brahn**-koh
mineral water	água mineral	ah-gwah mee-neh-**rahl**

milk	leite	lay-tih
tea	chá	shah
coffee	café	kah-feh
coffee with milk	uma média	oo-mah meh-dyah
small cup of black coffee	cafézinho	kah-feh-zee-nyoh
orange juice	suco de laranja	soo-koh dih lah-rahn-zha
pineapple juice	suco de abacaxi	soo-koh dih ah-bah-kah-shee

DAYS OF THE WEEK

Sunday	domingo	doh-meen-goh
Monday	segunda feira	sih-goon-dah fay-rah
Tuesday	terça feira	tehr-sah fay-rah
Wednesday	quarta feira	kwahr-tah fay-rah
Thursday	quinta feira	keen-tah-fay-rah
Friday	sexta feira	sehs-tah fay-rah
Saturday	sábado	sah-bah-doh

TIME

at 1:00	à uma hora	ah oo-mah aw-rah
at 2:00	às duas horas	ahs doo-ahs aw-rahs
at 3:00	às três horas	ahs trehs aw-rahs
at 4:00	às quatro horas	ahs cua-tro aw-rahs
at noon	ao meio-dia	au meh-yoh-dee-ah
at midnight	à meia-noite	ah meh-yah-noy-tih
at 2:15	às duas e quinze	ahs doo-ahs ih keen-sih
at 2:30	às duas e trinta	ahs doo-ahs ih treen-tah
at 2:45	às duas e quarenta	ahs doo-ahs ih cuah-rehn-tah ih seen-koh
a day	um dia	oo dee-ah
a week	uma semana	oo-mah seh-mah-nah
a month	um mês	oo meis
a year	um ano	oo ah-no

NUMBERS

one	um	o͞o
two	dois	doys
three	três	trehs
four	quatro	**kwah**-troh
five	cinco	**seen**-koh
six	seis	says
seven	sete	**seh**-tih
eight	oito	**oy**-toh
nine	nove	**naw**-vih
ten	dez	dehsh
eleven	onze	**ohn**-zih
twelve	doze	**do**-zih
thirteen	treze	**treh**-zih
fourteen	catorze	ka-**tor**-zih
fifteen	quinze	**keen**-zih
sixteen	dezesseis	dih-zeh-**says**
seventeen	dezessete	dih-zeh-**seh**-tih
eighteen	dezoìto	dih-**zoy**-toh
nineteen	dezenove	dih-zeh-**naw**-vih
twenty	vinte	**veen**-tih
thirty	trinta	**treen**-tah
forty	quarenta	kwa-**ren**-tah
fifty	cinqüenta	seen-**kwen**-tah
sixty	sessenta	se-**sen**-tah
seventy	setenta	sc-**ten**-tah
eighty	oitenta	oy-**ten**-tah
ninety	noventa	no-**ven**-tah
one hundred	cem	sãy
two hundred	duzentos	doo-**zen**-tohs
one thousand	mil	meel

ABOUT THE AUTHORS

✴ We have written four other books in the "customs and manners" series: *European Customs and Manners, The Travelers' Guide to Asian Customs and Manners, The Travelers' Guide to Middle Eastern and North African Customs and Manners,* and *The Travelers' Guide to African Customs and Manners.* Despite delayed and canceled flights, uncomfortable trains, and roads filled with potholes, we've retained our love of travel and our curiosity about the lives of people in other countries. (Note: Nancy is by far the more intrepid and adventurous.—E.D.)

ELIZABETH DEVINE, a professor at Salem State College in Massachusetts, has written books and articles and has edited reference books, including *The International Dictionary of University Histories.* NANCY L. BRAGANTI has taught foreign languages in the U.S., Europe, and the Middle East.

Researching the book involved not only travel but also countless hours of interviews and reading. We've interviewed dozens of people from the countries covered, as well as a great number of North Americans who have lived in and done business in those countries.

ELIZABETH DEVINE
NANCY L. BRAGANTI